Rome

20th March, 2017

In the Shadow of the Church

By Colin Short

In the Shadow of the Church

First published in 2024

ISBN: 978-1-7385588-0-3

TAUK Publishing

DEDICATION

For Fiona.

ONE

The ghosts of Rwanda were all around me again, jostling for my attention, as if they too had come to hear the words of apology before they could finally rest in peace. They had dominated my thoughts ever since the invitation arrived. Even in the crisp, clear spring morning as I stood in front of St Peter's, if I closed my eyes, I could see again their mutilation, their faces stretched wide in agony. I must have wrestled with my demons for a long time because the shadow of the great Basilica had closed around me while I stood rooted in the past. It was time to go, and I felt relief when I stepped back into the sun, unsure if the memories or the chilly air made me shiver.

The magnificence of the Vatican was in such contrast to the ramshackle brick and wood churches I remembered from the weeks of criss-crossing Rwanda, and it was hard to imagine that they were all part of the same body. I was so anxious to see Liliane again that the splendour of the room where the Pope was to address us went unnoticed.

I saw her straightaway, of course, when I was ushered

through the crowd of journalists and camera crews waiting outside. It wasn't just the vivid coloured dress among the dark suits of her countrymen. I had forgotten how tall she was, even for a Tutsi. She turned from her conversation as if she could feel my gaze on her or hear the emotions churning inside me. Before I could smile or wave, an attendant in gold and red ushered Liliane to her seat, and the moment was gone. I felt a guiding hand on my shoulder and moved inside the room. I was suddenly nervous, yet Liliane, for whom this was such a defining moment in her life, betrayed no emotion.

Pope Francis, his face sombre, entered with President Kagame and his wife from a side door and took his place at the lectern. His presence stilled the small group who had been allowed to hear him speak, and I realised I was holding my breath as he began reading out the apology.

"I implore anew God's forgiveness for the sins and failings of the Church and its members, among them priests and religious men and women who succumbed to hatred and violence, betraying their own evangelical mission."

I didn't hear the further expressions of regret. That one sentence was enough for me. I was back in the hills and forests of Rwanda with my memories of the genocide that swept through the country like a plague. I have witnessed and written about many atrocities since, but it is always Rwanda that wakes me in the early hours. I had walked this road for so long, waiting for the day when the Church, like many other world leaders and organisations before it, would finally apologise.

I sat apart from the delegation of ministers who were with Kagame, although I knew most of them. They crowded around their president after the event was over, and I saw their relief that the Church was finally confessing to its part in the massacre of the Tutsi race. I left them to enjoy the moment and stood on the steps outside to let the fresh, spring breeze clear my head of the memories of those dreadful days. I was about to leave when a secretary to the delegation caught and reminded me that I was meeting the health minister for dinner that night. I needed no reminding. It was the other reason I was there.

***

We met in a restaurant that I sometimes used. It had a few small booths at the back, which encouraged private conversation. I was early and felt like a teenager on a first date as I stared at the menu without reading it and sipped my drink without tasting it, looking up at the door every time it opened. When Liliane did arrive, I don't think there was a head that didn't turn when she walked across the room to my table. Maybe it was the lime-green dress that shimmered as she moved or her jet-black skin that seemed to gleam under the lights. Or perhaps it was the scar on her head, no longer hidden. She wore it now as a badge of honour, a symbol of her own suffering. It gave her the right to sit in government and tell her people she knew what they had been through.

She was so much more confident than I remembered, which was the politics and responsibility, I supposed, whereas I felt tongue-tied. The waiter hovered around, flattering Liliane and suggesting drinks for her to try. It was only when we were alone that I relaxed. Soon, we were swapping stories of people we knew and catching up on each other's lives until our conversation turned, as we knew it would, to the Papal apology. For Liliane, it had been a personal crusade, and as she talked, I could see how much it meant to her.

The apology had given her closure, and after we had ordered our meal, she said, "I want you to tell my story—all of it. Especially the things I've never told anyone. People need to know. They need to understand why today had to happen, for Rwanda." She paused, and I could see it was a big decision for her. "And for me."

I was shocked at first, and the silence between us lengthened as I absorbed the implications of what she had just said.

"Of course, Liliane. I'd be happy to, although I'm not sure I'd know where to start." It seemed inadequate in the circumstances, but it was the best I could manage.

Her hands sought mine and pulled them towards her. There was an intense, unsettling look in her large, oval eyes, as if she was already reliving that time.

"It started when the UN came to Kitabuye."

Kitabuye, Rwanda

1994

TWO

It appeared in the night. Paint, daubed in ugly red slashes, bleeding down the whitewashed wall around the yard. Just the one word.

Inyenzi.

It was the sign of a Tutsi house. The Hutus would be back with more than paint next time when the Interahamwe arrived, which would surely be soon. This is how it starts, Liliane realised, sending their people out at night to mark the Tutsi homes to make sure they wouldn't miss any.

Father had scared her that morning when he stood in the doorway, his shoulders slumped and told them what was on their wall. Despite his insistence that the madness would pass by Kitabuye, the hope drained from him in his faltering words and in the following silence he seemed to age. When he finally roused himself, he sent Liliane to get whitewash. It was a futile gesture to reassure Mother, whose simple faith in his certainty aroused only contempt in Liliane.

She continued to stare at the wall despite the large spots of rain that blurred her vision. Inyenzi. It was what the Tutsis were: cockroaches who crawled out of the ground and threatened the country's security. The radio said so, every hour of every day until even the Hutus in Kitabuye began to believe it. None of the other houses at the end of the lane bore the mark. It was deserted, but Liliane felt as if she was being watched. Unnerved by the silence, she turned and ran as fast as the mud and uneven ground would allow.

Uncle OK's store was on the main street, where the trouble was the night before. The blackened and twisted shell of a car was still in front of it. She edged past it, her head turned away and jumped onto the sidewalk under the shelter of the tin roof. Only when she bent over to shake her wet hair did she catch a glimpse inside the car. The bodies were gone, and as she looked up the street to the hospital, she wondered if that was where they now were.

There was a look and feel of desolation about Kitabuye that morning, drab and ugly under the clouds that tumbled down from the mountain tops. The recent storms had carved deep ruts in the road and the damp, decaying buildings looked like rotten teeth with gaps where some of the wooden shacks had collapsed. None of the shops were open and it was too early for the bars. The only sound was the hammering on the roof above her.

She rattled the door and peered through the glass, looking

for Uncle OK. Behind her, she heard feet splash through the pools of water and turned to see Alice running up the other side of the street. She seemed to be heading for the hospital, but when she saw Liliane, she waved and ran over to join her, pausing to cross herself as she passed the car. Even now, with everything that was happening, she still believed.

They held each other tight for a long time, both of them frightened by the suddenness and ferocity of the violence in the night. Alice stepped back to wipe her legs with the hem of her dress, her hair plastered against her head, her skin shiny under a sheen of water, her breasts hugged by the damp cotton. You're too beautiful, Liliane thought, fighting back tears as she watched her, knowing how desired she was by the Hutu men.

With a nervous glance at the car, Alice whispered, "Did you?"

Liliane nodded. The smell reminded her of the fire pit behind Alphonse's cabaret when she walked past in the mornings on her way to the plantation. She was with Patrick in the field behind the church when it all started, and by the time they were dressed, the car was already ablaze. It lit the frenzied faces of the Hutus as they beat the doors shut, trapping the Tutsi family inside. The French doctor ran from the hospital and pushed the mob away, but it was too late; the heat was too intense. While he raged at the Hutus, they just turned away and melted into the shadows, back to the bars. When she woke that morning, Liliane could still hear the screams of the children.

Lightning sheeted across the valley, and Alice flinched. "It'll be worse next time, won't it?" Although they all tried to pretend that the violence was something that only happened elsewhere, the killings were spreading like a virus to the nearby villages, and now it was among them.

"Doctor Le Paih will stop anything happening until the UN get here." But even as she said them, Liliane's words sounded hollow to her.

"Those people escaped from Nyarube." Alice looked at the car again. "The UN never got there, did they?" Liliane remained silent. Alice pointed to where Liliane was staring. "They're saying we should go there when the Interahamwe come. To the church." Fear had been a way of life for so long now that Liliane almost wished they would come. "You'll be all right though, won't you?" She looked into Alice's eyes and could tell that she had always known. Alice seemed to realise this wasn't the time and added, "Patrick, Lili. He's promised, hasn't he?"

"They've stopped him seeing me. I'm a Tutsi whore. That's why we meet in the field." Just one conversation with the priest, Father Malabanda, had been enough to frighten Patrick's parents, but Alice seemed not to have heard.

"I'm afraid, Lili." Liliane bent closer to hear. "I'm scared of what the Hutu men will do to me."

It was what all the Tutsi women feared, having to watch their husbands, fathers and sons butchered before being taken by the Hutu men. Yet it was Patrick that Liliane was afraid for and the choice he would have to make. She didn't know if he would be strong enough when the time came, and he had to fulfil his promises to her. It was too painful to think about, and she turned away.

Though the floods were gone, large pools of red water still filled the hollows at the bottom of the street where it curved away, past the administration building where Father worked, and out of town into the hills, now barely visible through the clouds. She thought she heard a different sound in the stillness, but there was nothing to see.

The door behind them jarred, the wood swollen after the days of rain, and she heard Uncle OK curse as he struggled to push it open. "It'll stop soon," he said as he peered past them to the mountains that rose beyond the lake. She strained to hear his words and wasn't sure if he was reassuring himself or them.

Liliane loved the old man. He wasn't a relative, and he seemed to have no family. He was just Uncle OK to everyone, even the Tutsis. No one knew his real name, and few could remember a time when his store wasn't there, but today, the sparkle was gone from his eyes, and the lines on his face, so often creased with laughter, were furrowed in concern.

"You look tired." She touched his arm, and he acknowledged her affection with a weak smile.

"The cabarets were noisy." He nodded at the car.

"I thought they were going to come last night." She kept her voice low, her head turned away from Alice. "They've marked our wall. Inyenzi."

"It's everywhere now. They know where you all live."

"I know. Alice saw a list in the Burgomaster's office."

"They're organised this time." He drew her to him. "The radio's telling them what to do, Lili. You hear what they say."

He was right. The division between Hutu and Tutsi had always been apparent and manipulated for political reasons. However, it was usually worse in the cities and big towns and discrimination against the Tutsis was deeply ingrained everywhere. Here in Kitabuye, life was hard for everyone, and a Tutsi back would be as stiff after a day in the fields as that of a Hutu. In recent months, though, the voices on the radio had stirred up trouble and created hatred and mistrust where it had never before existed. The Hutus in Kitabuye no longer ignored the outside world. They, too, listened to the radio.

"Listen, listen. Coming down the hill." Alice pulled at them, frantic. Although the clouds were lifting, the nearby hill was still shrouded in a grey mist. Liliane could hear it as well: the rumble of engines. "It's them. I know it is." Alice ran to the edge of the sidewalk as if she could escape, but Kitabuye was remote, surrounded by mountains and lakes, and there was nowhere to run to. The Hutus knew, as well as the Tutsis, what would happen when the Interahamwe militia arrived in their lorries, bringing the spears and machetes. The thin ties of humanity that bound them together would erode when they swept into town as surely as the mountain storms would wash away the roads and fields.

The roar of engines came first, and then a surge of water as the vehicles rounded the corner. Spray shimmered in their headlights, and she could make out the shapes of two jeeps and a lorry, its canvas body bucking as its wheels hit the ruts. Alice sank to her knees, her hands clasped in front of her. They were closer now, and as they sped past, mud sprayed out from under the wheels and spattered their faces. Liliane closed her eyes, readying herself to run, to find Patrick, to be with him. The moment they had dreaded was upon them.

"They're white. They're white," Alice shouted. Liliane looked round at Uncle OK, uncomprehending. "UN vehicles are white, Lili. They've come," Alice continued.

Liliane leaned back against him, her legs slack. Hutus and Tutsis alike rushed out of the lanes and alleys and lined the street, as on the previous night, drawn by fear and curiosity and watched as the vehicles braked and skidded outside the hospital. The white canvassed sides of the lorry were streaked with red dirt, but their presence in the shabby town was imposing and reassuring, and the residents of Kitabuye seemed overawed by their sudden arrival. The soldiers in the jeeps jumped out first, all wearing blue helmets except one in a beret, who Liliane assumed must be their leader. They unfastened the tailgate of the lorry, swept the canvas aside, and more soldiers piled out and formed a circle around the vehicles, their rifles pointed outwards as if they expected resistance. The soldier in the beret ran up the steps to the hospital, followed by two others.

Liliane pulled away from Uncle OK, her hands tight on the rail on the edge of the sidewalk and fought the urge to vomit. A few cheers and shouts rippled through the crowd when the vehicles arrived, but as the minutes passed and nothing more happened, they became anxious, and their faces turned towards the top of the town. Liliane found the silence as oppressive as the heat that had built over the town, and doubt began to eat away at the exhilaration she had felt a few minutes earlier. A loud shout came from inside the hospital, and Alice cried out when the soldier in the beret kicked one of the doors open and scanned the street, his revolver held out in front of him. The crowd was uneasy, and many looked across the road to Uncle OK, who ignored them and kept watching, his eyes narrowed. At a command from the soldier, the Belgian nurse stepped tentatively onto the top step, then hurried past him and ran to the lorry, where a soldier reached out and pulled her into the back.

"Uncle?" Alice turned, seeking reassurance just as Anna,

the English schoolteacher, stumbled backwards through the doors, followed by two soldiers. As she fell, she grabbed hold of the stair rail and kicked wildly at them as they tried to restrain her.

"I won't go. I won't leave them," Anna cried.

Her hysteria spread to the crowd, and some of the Tutsi women began to wail. The soldiers wrenched Anna down the steps, her face contorted with anger. The closeness of the lorry seemed to renew her frenzy, but with a shout from the officer, a soldier ran forward and swung the butt of his gun into her stomach. Her legs sagged; she slumped forward and was bundled into the vehicle.

Doctor Le Paih's angry shouts echoed down the street, but his words were too quick and urgent for Liliane to understand. The soldier ignored him and watched as the last of his men guided Sister Maria, the elderly French nun, down the steps. Her progress was slow, a little battered case in one hand, her other clasped tight on the soldier's arm, her head bowed. As she picked her way through the mud, there was a commotion from the hospital, and the three nurses pushed past the soldier and kneeled in front of her. Their cries echoed along the street.

"Sister Maria. Sister Maria." One of them reached out, and her fingers made jagged, red streaks down the white robes. The nun pulled the woman closer and bent her head as if to speak words of comfort until a soldier pulled the nurse away and shoved her to the ground. Le Paih protested, but when the officer pointed his gun at him, he raised his hands in resignation and then turned to help Sister Maria into the truck. The nurses knelt in the mud, their arms outstretched.

"The babies. Take the babies," one of them cried.

A soldier slammed the tailgate shut and bolted it with a finality that silenced the whimpers from the crowd. The lorry's engine roared, its wheels span and churned the ground as they tried to gain traction while the nurses, their faces and tunics sprayed with blotches of mud, continued to cry out, and their distress spread to the crowd. The jeeps sped past, the lorry between them, the canvas pulled tight over the back.

Alice turned away, her face streaked with mud and tears. "They've gone." She stared at the bottom of the road as if expecting them to come back. "They just came for the whites. What about us, Lili?"

"We'll be safe at the church. God will help us even if the UN won't."

Uncle OK stirred behind them. "God just left in that truck, Lili. There are no witnesses left. No one will ever know." He stepped back into his shop and pushed the door behind him.

Liliane looked up the street towards the church. The priest stood in front of the building; he had been watching.

THREE

The crowd watched the lorry grind up the steep road out of the valley. The tyre tracks in the mud were the only evidence that the UN had been in Kitabuye. Stunned and frightened, the crowd turned towards the hospital where the nurses beat their heads with their fists and rocked on their knees, their unrestrained grief the only sound to disturb the stillness that had fallen over the town. Liliane remembered seeing such a sight before at funerals, and it struck her that the nurses were grieving for the Tutsis already. Further up the street, Uncle OK stepped off the sidewalk and joined them in the mud, and soon their wailing ceased. In the unbearable silence that followed, the Tutsis were the first to leave, back down the lanes and alleys to the homes that were marked. There was no hiding place left for them.

Even just a year ago, it had all been so different when the whole town gathered at the football pitch to cheer their team on. Hutus and Tutsis passed to and tackled each other while their families and friends cheered from the sidelines. The only rivalry was between them and the supporters from Arusha, further up the valley. Then the news programmes began on the radio, spreading their toxic messages and blaming the Tutsis even for the previous year's drought and crop failures. Gatsinzi, the Burgomaster, then closed the Tutsi shops, accusing them of profiteering from the Hutus. That was when Liliane first felt fear in her belly as she watched the Hutus loot the little cabins and shacks until they were empty.

Alice still clung to Liliane: her fingers entwined so tight around the fabric of her dress that Liliane thought it would tear. She pulled Alice closer, the girl's sobs hot against her skin, and felt rage well up within her. The whites had infected the country with their presence when they arrived all those years ago, and now they had left and condemned the Tutsis to hide and cower like hunted animals.

The last of the Tutsis crept away, heads down as if that would make them invisible. Even the Hutus seemed ashamed of the divide that was opening between friends and neighbours, and they began to slink away, silent and sullen, into their own alleys. They knew the Interahamwe would find them as well and hold them to account.

This is what our country does, Liliana thought. It's what happens. It's part of life, like the rains, the harvest.

"Do you think they'll wait for the Interahamwe?" Alice asked. She had turned seventeen a few days earlier yet seemed like a child again, craving some shred of comfort where there was none to give. The Interahamwe would know what had happened. They would come soon.

"They'll wait. And then there'll be no choice. For anyone." Liliane hadn't meant to say what she was thinking, but it was too late now and anyway, she didn't think it would be long before they came.

Kill or be killed. The Hutus knew the rules. Kitabuye's remoteness made life hard, yet the Hutus and Tutsis had always lived together, survived together, but now the town's location was a death sentence. There was nowhere to run to after Kitabuye, nowhere to hide.

"There's no hope, is there?" Alice's voice cracked as the reality of her friend's words sank in.

"There is if we fight. All of us. Together."

"But the Interahamwe have got guns and grenades." Alice's face crumpled at the thought. "I don't want to die. Not like how they say they do it." Her words soaked into the coarse, brown cloth of Liliane's dress. They both knew she was right. It would be brutal and painful, and now Liliane's cheeks were hot with fear and moist with the tears she could no longer restrain. They stood for a long time tight in each other's arms, neither comforting nor comforted.

"Mother will need me. The little ones." The ordinariness of the thought seemed to galvanise Alice. She pushed herself away and wiped a hand across her blank, empty eyes, the hope now gone from them. "I've always loved you, Lili, since the first day you came. You know that." Her tears were uncontrollable, and before Liliane could stop her, she turned and ran across the road and down one of the alleys. A desperate sense of isolation settled on Liliane as if she was the last Tutsi left in Kitabuye, waiting alone to face the coming madness.

She stared at the spot where Alice had disappeared and willed her to return, thinking of all the things she wanted to tell her, but the lane remained empty except for a few hens pecking in the dirt. Reluctantly, she looked away, back up the street, past the school and hospital to where the dark and ugly church looked down on the town. The white people had built it for their god with his magic spells, for their version of the world. Now they had gone, hidden in the back of a lorry with the canvas pulled tight so they couldn't see what they were leaving behind while the old ways of living together in peace had been lost forever in the decades of mistrust and bloodshed.

Uncle OK was right; the town's conscience had been taken away. Doctor le Paih's quiet authority had restrained the Hutus in the last few weeks while the rest of the country went mad. But it was the effect on Father Malabanda that Liliane feared most now that the calm influence of Sister Maria was gone. Liliane knew the evil that was in him; she felt it in his touch and saw it in his eyes. She suspected that Sister Maria had known this as well and had stayed in Kitabuye for so long because of it, despite her health.

When she saw Malabanda leave the church, Liliane stepped back into the shadow of Uncle OK's verandah and watched the priest hurry down the street to the town hall. Malabanda and Gatsinzi. Despite the heat, she shivered at the thought of them working together as they listened to the reports of savagery from across the country, waiting for their chance to unleash it on Kitabuye, far from disapproving eyes, free to act as they wished.

Alphonse's bar was already open, and laughter and raucous cheers drifted up the street from a group of men gathered in the concrete yard. Rusty, metal poles held up a tattered, green canvas awning that sagged in places where the rain pooled. Little flags, symbols of countries Liliane had never heard of, were strung between them and fluttered in the breeze. Alphonse had put them up years before for a football tournament, and they were still there now, ragged and dirty. The men joined in with an old tribal war chant that the radio was playing over a speaker slung with rope on one of the poles. They jumped in time to the drum beat, arms linked to form a circle. The boys used to do that when the team scored, but the men weren't playing a game. It was life and death now for the Tutsis.

"Stamp on the cockroaches. Send them back to Hell," they sang next.

It was what Father Malabanda had preached the previous Sunday, and Liliane noticed how the Hutus' backs straightened and their heads lifted as he spoke as if he was proclaiming the love of Jesus in their lives. Behind the heavy, black-framed glasses, his eyes were alive, and his hands gripped the wooden rail in front of him so hard that his knuckles turned pink.

"He didn't mean all of us, Liliane. He was talking about the troublemakers among us. Not all Tutsis are angels, you know," Mother said after the service as Liliane raged and cursed Malabanda.

"That's what we are. Cockroaches. Even you. He hates us. Can't you see it?"

"Hold your tongue, Liliane. He's a man of God."

Father refused to believe the killings would come to Kitabuye. He still believed that Gatsinzi would maintain peace in his little empire. "He has too much to lose," he would always say, yet they both knew Malabanda controlled the family's fate. When the killing did come, Father had faith that Malabanda would honour their bargain.

"You'll only believe me when the knife's at your throat," Liliane shouted while Bernard bundled her into her room before Father got his belt off.

She kicked the post in front of her, her fury stoked by the memory.

"Not too hard, Lili. You'll have the roof down." Uncle OK stood in front of the car, his trousers now stiff with mud. He looked exhausted, and Liliane heard the defeat in his voice. "You should be at home. Joseph will be worried."

"He sent me to get whitewash."

He shook his head. "You'll need more than that."

The clouds were now beyond the hills, the sky a deep blue, and the washed, polished freshness of the light hurt her eyes. She looked around the town as if it might be for the last time. The earth walls of the buildings were all different shades of red and pink as they dried, and the metal roofs shimmered as the heat began to build over the town. Smoke drifted from the deserted alleys and was carried away on the light airs that came down from the hills.

She glanced again at Uncle OK, his eyes fixed on the track out of town and wondered if he was expecting the Interahamwe so soon. He was the one she ran to after she fought with Father; he was easier to love as well. No one knew where he came from nor how long ago. His emporium had always been there, selling everything to everyone. She didn't even know his real name, she realised. He was the only man who truly respected her for who she was, not for her looks or the size of her breasts or for how subservient she was.

"Can't you do anything, Uncle? They would listen to you."

"They only listen to the radio these days. And Malabanda. He makes it hard for them to resist." He stared up the street to the church.

"I hate him." Her vehemence surprised him, and he searched her face so intently she felt sure he must be looking inside her to the secrets buried deep within. She had never told him anything about Malabanda, but she was sure he knew. He knew everything that happened in Kitabuye.

"Tutsis killed his family. He was a child. The nuns took him in." He held his hand up to silence her. "Our history has harvested much hatred and bitterness on both sides."

"So you think that made him what he is? Maybe he was just born bad." She had suffered too much already to be placated by any excuse for the Malabanda she knew. "Sister Maria knew him for what he is, and now she's gone, and there's no one to restrain him." She needed Uncle OK to talk to her, to reassure her, but his face was grim.

"Yes, there's only us left now. They mean to finish it this time. You know that, don't you?"

She felt the last shreds of hope evaporate like the dark strands of smoke above the straw roofs, and in that one moment, she felt them vanish in the breeze. She stared at the ground, and a few tears rolled off her cheeks and made a dark stain in the earth.

"I'm scared for Patrick," she said, and Uncle OK nodded.

Patrick, where all her hopes and fears converged. Always the biggest and strongest, the one the boys looked up to and the girls desired, the leader of the gang. Yet he wasn't a leader, Liliane knew. Easily influenced, like so many townsfolk, he would be lost without the authority of the whites and be easy prey for the likes of Malabanda and Gatsinzi. Despite his bravado and his promises to fight for her, Liliane sensed his fear for the choice he would have to make. He didn't want to kill, but he didn't want to die, and his fear was fertile ground for Malabanda.

"You've made a heavy burden for him, Liliane. I hope he is strong enough to carry it."

She had wanted him to tell her that Patrick would stand firm and protect her.

"I don't know, Uncle," she whispered, the emotion finally overwhelming her. He moved closer and laid a hand on her shoulder until she was calmer. From his touch, she knew it was consolation, not reassurance.

"You're Hutu, Uncle. You can stop it." Her faith in him was steadfast. He was different. He never took sides.

"I've been through this long ago before you were born. It's always the same. People are too scared. You Tutsis have done it too. It's in our souls. We can't escape it."

"Don't." She was frightened of what more he would say, of what she might learn.

"They make it impossible not to join in, Lili," he continued, his voice unrecognisable from the Uncle she knew. "They play on your fears. I've been there." He looked at her. "I know how hard it is," he paused and swallowed, "when there's a gun at your head." There was distress in his eyes, regret in the creases of his face.

"And this time?"

"I'm old and tired. I've had enough of all this." He turned away as if he feared she would see the memories reflected in his eyes, and she watched his diminished figure disappear into the shadows of the packing cases and boxes. She could never imagine Uncle OK as a young man, running with the pack. He seemed to be a timeless example of better days before the whites came and ruined their country. If even Uncle OK could have been infected by the madness, what chance did Patrick have?

FOUR

The chanting grew louder, the laughter more raucous at Alphonse's and the crowd, emboldened by the departure of Doctor Le Paih and the others, swelled and spilled out into the road. It was only mid-morning and already the last vestiges of order seemed to have been cast off by the Hutus. Ever since the Europeans who ran the plantation left a few months ago, just after the president's plane was shot down, a rootlessness had pervaded the town, and every day, the bars were busier for longer. The Hutus were waiting for the Interahamwe to arrive and impose their own perverted sense of order, a regime in which there was no place for Tutsis.

Liliane turned away and stared at the steps where Anna had fought so hard. She would never see her again and never had the chance to say goodbye. Anna would know what to do now. She always seemed able to think Liliane's thoughts before she did. She had taught Liliane so much besides English: about being with a boy, her body and her changing emotions. Now, she was gone as well.

Overwhelmed by the impending catastrophe, Liliane looked to the far end of the road where the Burgomaster's offices stood on the bend, his jeep just visible in the yard behind the red and green gates. Despite everything, Father would be in his office by now, poring over his ledgers and counting the taxes that he delivered for Gatsinzi.

"He'll look after us, Joanna," Father would say in response to Mother's ever more hysterical outbursts as the madness swept across the land. Each day, more Tutsis, mute with shock, many badly injured, began to arrive in Kitabuye looking for sanctuary. They brought with them images of the horror that was coming, unhinging the fragile equilibrium of Kitabuye. He would stand at the head of the table and proclaim that he spoke with Gatsinzi every day about the situation across Rwanda as if between them, they were in control of matters. The Burgomaster was focused on keeping Kitabuye safe from the madness, he insisted, his hands tight on the back of the chair, beads of sweat on his brow.

He had been so different when she was young, when they used to walk the hills. In those days, she would catch glimpses of the man he was before they fled from Kigali. Now Liliane could see his protestations about Gatsinzi were shallow and for Mother's benefit. Gatsinzi was just a corrupt, small-town administrator, a Hutu extremist who would do his duty when the time came. Deep down, Father knew this. It was why he had ultimately sold his soul to Malabanda. It was why she needed to talk to him and force him to tell her what was expected of her when the time came.

With a last look back at Uncle OK's and a sense of a final farewell for the second time that morning, she stepped off the boards and crouched low in the shadow of the car. The buckled metal was rough and sticky, and the stench of death lingered around it. As she paused, uncertain, the commotion outside Alphonse's grew louder with the arrival of a big, plastic vat of urwagwa. The foaming, grey brew slopped over the sides when it was set down on a wooden trestle, and the men cheered and jostled around to dip their mugs in and drink like it was already late evening. Liliane used the distraction to run down the street and press herself against the crudely nailed-up wooden shutters of Mr Naranga's fabric shop. The boardwalk at the end of his building was a mess of sodden, rotted planks, and she jumped over the pool of mud and water onto the harder, uneven earth beyond. Once out of the shade of the tattered, striped awning, the sun exposed her and created a jerky shadow that flitted and bent itself across the corrugated sheets that hid the derelict Tutsi shops down that side of the street. The iron leaned outwards in places, forcing her closer to the bar. A few men turned to stare at her as they drank, but it was too late to go back, so she quickened her steps and aimed for the safety of a shaded alley further down the street.

"Inyenzi bitch."

A woman's cry pierced the murmur of the drinkers. Distracted by the shout, Liliane slipped on a patch of damp earth and fell against the hoarding, which shifted inwards under her weight. The rusty edges screeched as they grated against each other, and the noise from the bar quietened. A shadow straddled Liliane as she scrabbled in the mud, and the same voice, more menacing for its quietness, whispered close to her.

"Thought you'd won, didn't you, cockroach whore, when you stole him from me?"

Liliane's head dropped. This was where Delphine Nirere worked. The girl came closer. The rank stink of sweat, smoke and goat fat was heavy on her. "Thought you'd sneak past, did you?" Liliane's breath exploded in a loud grunt as the girl's boot thudded into her stomach, and a ragged cheer rippled across the road from the bar. "Did you kiss him goodbye last night?" She shouted this so the men would hear. "You should have done. He's mine now. I'll comfort him when you're dead." The crowd was silent now, intent on watching the confrontation. Aware of their attention, Delphine stepped back so they could see her rival, splayed on her back in the mud, helpless and vulnerable. Liliane scrabbled to get up, but a number of men surrounded her in a ragged circle. Some of them were fathers of boys she had gone to school with, and they were now glassy-eyed with drink. Delphine pushed Liliane back down in the mud, grabbed the hem of her dress and yanked it above her waist. "Who's first?"

Liliane tried to roll over and push herself away, but one of the men planted his boot on her chest while another knelt behind her head. He then pinned her arms under his knees while he struggled to undo his trousers. She felt hot breath on her thighs as her knickers were pulled down to her knees, but when she tried to scream, a hand went to her mouth and smothered it.

"Go on, Haby, do her," Delphine urged one of the men who had kneeled between her legs and was unbuckling his belt.

Liliane's muffled cries leaked through the fingers over her lips, and she writhed to shake herself free as her legs were ripped apart and fingers clawed at her.

"I wouldn't if I was you, boys. Malabanda won't be happy." It was Alphonse, standing on the steps of his bar. "Wait till tomorrow. There'll be plenty of pretty little Tutsi girls to go round." The men grumbled and cursed at Alphonse, but the pressure on her chest eased, and her hands were released. Even as befuddled by drink as they were, the Hutus wouldn't risk crossing Malabanda, not now, with the Interahamwe due soon.

Alphonse's warning had cooled the men's desire, and they straggled back to the bar. Delphine turned her rage on Liliane, who rolled away just as the girl's foot sliced past her ear. Liliane braced herself for another blow, but before Delphine could get closer, Alphonse called to her to get back to the fire; the men wanted more food. At the gate into the yard, she paused and turned to Liliane. "You haven't won, Liliane Iwo. I can wait another day."

The men were no longer interested in the fight between the girls, and a new song rose from the far side of the yard. Liliane scrambled up and ran down to the wall of the Burgomaster's offices, where she rested her head against the bars of the gate and retched. Her stomach had been empty for days, and only a few drops of bile trickled down her chin. When the dizziness had passed, and her breathing was steadier, she lifted her head and saw that the compound, normally bustling on a weekday with queues of men waiting to pay their dues to the Burgomaster, was empty save for the battered pick-up. His new Mercedes, another symbol of his power in the town, was not in its normal prominent position. She shielded her eyes from the glare off the white walls as she looked for signs of life in the building.

One of the large doors, garish in its new red, green and black stripes, was slightly ajar, but no sound or movement came from within. Where usually the Burgomaster's booming voice, issuing his instructions or hurling abuse at some unfortunate resident, filled the building and spilled out of the windows into the yard, there was only an ominous silence.

Liliane imagined Father bent over his desk, writing figures in his columns, the scratch of his pen pleasing to his ear in the unusual quietness. The days when he was an important official in the Finance Ministry in Kigali were long gone, and he had to be content with his accounts and collecting the petty taxes that mostly went into Gatsinzi's pocket.

She pushed on the gates, which swung open on freshly oiled hinges and stepped into the yard, ridged with rotting vegetation and debris left by the flooding. There was no movement behind the windows in the shadows of the corridor that stretched either side of the lobby. When she pressed her ear to the gap between the doors and listened, she could hear no sounds from Gatsinzi's office. Father's room was at the far end of the opposite corridor, which was also silent and empty.

The high-ceilinged lobby was in shade now, and the new green paint on the walls gave it a sombre feel that seemed to match the mood in the town. A smell of polish hung in the air. Liliane remembered how she and Alice had recently spent a whole day with Kenzi, polishing the floorboards and then polishing them all over again until the Burgomaster approved. "He just wanted us on our knees with our bums in the air and our tits hanging out," Alice complained afterwards. When Gatsinzi took Kenzi to one of the empty plantation houses afterwards, Alice sneaked into his office. That was when she saw the list—pages of it. "It's got the name of every Tutsi in the town on it, Lili," she whispered, breathless, "even yours." The marks began to appear on the walls soon after.

Hurrying past the doors on her left, she reached Father's office. It was empty, and she leaned her head against the door frame, disappointed and angry with him for not being there. The air was still heavy with his cigarettes, the French ones he ordered from Kigali, and his desk, just in front of the window, was unusually untidy with files and loose sheets of paper scattered across it. A drawer jutted out of the grey filing cabinet, the one he always kept locked to safeguard the secrets he cherished. A folder lay open on top of it.

Liliane looked behind her. She was sure he must be near and that he would come bustling down the corridor, but no one came. It was so unlike him to leave his papers lying around. A sudden dread seized her that they had already come for him and, if she looked through the window, she would see his body, hacked and mutilated, in the scrub at the back of the building. She closed her eyes and tried to imagine him sitting at his desk, but the image wouldn't come. When she looked again, the chair was still empty. It was then she felt sure he would never sit in it again. Anna told her once that the whites believed they would see their whole past life just before they died. For a moment, she saw herself as a little girl back in Kigali, walking on the hilltops on a Sunday morning, just her and Father, while he taught her the history of their country and how close to paradise it was before the Europeans came. But soon after that, he had taken her own paradise of innocence away, and in a moment of clarity, she suddenly understood that he knew this day would come. Even then, he was preparing her for what he would later force her to do. And as she tried to make sense of it all, she didn't hear the creak of the floorboards behind her.

"I hope you haven't been spying on us, Liliane."

It was Malabanda.

FIVE

His breath was warm on the back of her neck, and Liliane's throat tightened with the sour odour of his sweat. There was menace in his voice, so different to the soothing tones he spoke in when she visited him, and it sent a chill through her despite the heat. His fingers brushed against her neck and she flinched.

"Nervous, Liliane?" His hand cupped her chin and tightened its hold on her. "You're not frightened of me, are you?"

Behind them, Gatsinzi sniggered, but Malabanda ignored him and pinned her so tight against the doorframe that she felt the tremor of his suppressed anger in his grip. A burning pain shot up her neck as he twisted her head until she had to look into his eyes, magnified and misshapen by the thick lenses of his glasses. His fingers tightened and the nails dug deeper into her cheek.

"There's only one punishment for spies at a time like this, even for you, Liliane."

Gatsinzi's face appeared over the priest's shoulder, the

folds of fat creased in a grin. Malabanda loosened his hold, and Liliane stumbled into the office. She backed away until she felt the edge of Father's desk against her legs. He motioned with a curt nod towards the lobby, and as she hurried past, he grabbed her arm.

"Remember what is expected of you, Liliane. Do as your father tells you."

Gatsinzi's bulk filled the corridor in front of her, and he rubbed himself against her as she tried to pass. Big moons of sweat stretched across his khaki shirt, and she felt the sticky dampness through the thin fabric of her dress. She squeezed past as his booming laugh taunted her while she ran down the corridor and into the yard. From the gate she watched the two men move back along the corridor. Despite his smaller frame, Malabanda was the real power in the town these day- him and Gatsinzi. How quickly Mother and Father had become charmed by them and even now were blinded to the evil that Liliane was sure these two men were about to unleash on Kitabuye.

When the two men didn't appear in the opposite corridor, she realised they must be talking in the lobby and that the priest would be crossing the yard soon. She slipped through the gate, ran along the front wall and down an alley where she pressed herself into the side of a straw hut and turned just in time to see Malabanda hurry up the street towards the church. The racket from Alphonse's bar subsided, and she imagined the men shrinking back into the shadows, trying not to catch his eye, but soon, the laughter filtered down the narrow alleys again, and she knew he must have carried on to the church.

She was in a Hutu area. Even in Kitabuye, each side was drawn to its own. Piles of rubbish and old beer crates littered the alley, and rubble from a collapsed house blocked the drainage channel down the middle. Most of the huts were made of dried mud, their straw roofs blackened by smoke from the fires inside. Father said that it was in the nature of Hutus to be lazy and that if they worked harder, they could live better. Yet when she asked him what jobs they should do when there weren't any, he would just mutter about the Tutsi birthright. Blood ties and history, like the seasons and the harvest, seemed to regulate their lives.

The roars of the men echoed down the alleys and bounced off the walls around her. "Death to Inyenzi," over and over. Even with her hands clamped against her ears, the sound reverberated in her head and made her dizzy. With a sense of foreboding, she knew her only option for getting home was by working her way through the maze of Hutu lanes. She felt vulnerable without Patrick, although there were few people around and those that were seemed preoccupied with their own problems.

The only route she knew led to his house, so she set off,

keeping into the shadows of walls where she could. Hens pecked in the dirt at the top of his alley while a goat, tethered to an iron ring in the wall, stared at her before it returned to grazing on a tuft of grass. She glanced absently at Father's money, still screwed tight in her hand. There would be an argument about the paint, but if Patrick was with her when she went home, Father might restrain his temper.

The Hutus turned their backs on her or lowered their eyes as she passed as if she was now tainted. Smoke seeped from the straw roof of Patrick's house. His parents always resented the Iwo's corrugated iron. His father would grumble it was the Tutsi way to steal the Hutu roofs. "Now the bitch is stealing my son," he muttered the last time she went to see Patrick.

"If he didn't drink his money away, he could afford a good roof," Father said when she told him.

A rock thudded into her chest and she doubled over, the breath knocked out of her.

"Tutsi scum!"

An old woman scrabbled in the debris of the gutter a few feet away, and as she straightened, her fingers bent around a piece of broken concrete, Liliane realised it was Mrs Bamini from church. She had sat at the woman's feet so often when she was younger on a Sunday morning while Mrs Bamini told the children stories from the Bible, often handing out little boiled sweets at the end. Liliane remembered her as a timid soul, softly spoken, yet now she was cursing Liliane, and her shrill cries brought more Hutus into the lane. It was a poor area, and most of the people wore filthy, tattered clothes and seemed as frightened of Liliane as she was of them. They all knew the punishment for being seen with a Tutsi. She pressed her back against the wall like a wild animal snared and cornered, her eyes darting across the shuffling crowd to see where the next blow might be from.

"Leave her." It was Patrick. His broad, round face betrayed his confusion at what was happening until he saw Liliane through the crowd and pushed his way between them. He had grown stronger and taller in the last year since working in the fields around Kitabuye. He jostled the other Hutus aside, grabbed the old woman's arm and prised the rock from her hand.

"Patrick, don't." His mother pushed through the crowd, her words strident and brittle above the muted curses, her features a mix of rage and fear. A Tutsi whore was sleeping with her boy, and she would infect the whole family. "Patrick, come," her voice softer as she approached, her cajoling that of a forgiving mother for an errant child. Liliane pushed herself upright and watched the conflict within him. The boy who hated to upset anyone was now a man with choices to make. She saw how heavy the burden was as he looked from her to his mother and back again, his eyes unfocused. Then, in a rush, he grabbed Liliane and pulled her up the lane while his mother's cries chased after them. Only when they reached the church did Patrick pause and hold Liliane until her breath returned and she stopped shaking.

Patrick was with her. It was what she wanted. She would feel no fear while he was close. Safe in his presence, she let him guide her around the wall surrounding the church until they reached the dip in the gently rising grass slope. It was their place, where they came to sit and talk. It was where they made love. She slumped down and ran her hand over the flattened grass as if she could still feel the warmth of their bodies from the previous night.

"You shouldn't have come." He stood apart from her, irresolute.

"Mrs Bamini…" Each word was painful. "From Sunday school."

He kneeled beside her, his face close. "Malabanda's been to see us again. Just before you came. He warned them. And me." His shoulders were slumped, and she could see how her love was crushing him. She straightened up and looked at him, but he avoided her eyes.

"What are you going to do?"

"I'm here," he said, but she knew his mind was far away, his unseeing eyes turned towards the mountains. When she ran her fingers over his face the skin was damp and he jerked his head away.

"I…I ask too much of you." She searched his eyes for some hope of his denial. "That's what Uncle OK said." Still he was silent. He was always the biggest and strongest in the class; nothing ever seemed to scare him, but there was something different in him now. It was what she had seen in his mother's face. The priest had frightened them.

A movement down the hill distracted her, and she turned to see the door open at the back of the church.

"Malabanda. Get down."

He grabbed her dress and dragged her flat, but Liliane raised her head just as the priest looked up the slope, and she saw his body stiffen when he saw them. Patrick's grip was rough, and the suddenness of his violence frightened her more than the thought of Malabanda seeing them together. He had never hurt her before. His heart pounded beneath his shirt, and sweat ran off him onto her face as if fear was seeping out of him. The burden on him was heavier than ever.

"He mustn't see me," he whispered. It was no longer us. They were winning, and Liliane could feel Patrick slipping away from her. They lay still, their breathing shallow, until she could take it no longer.

"You're hurting me." She felt him raise his head and twist to look down at the church. "Please. Patrick." His weight eased off her and she rubbed her shoulders as she sat up.

"Did he see?"

"No." She had never lied to him before. "I don't care. Anyway, it's too late now."

Patrick pushed himself away from her as if she was contaminating him. "Not for my family it isn't." He sounded resentful. "You weren't there. You didn't hear. He threatened us." His eyes were red, his face laced with dirt and tears. She had never seen him cry before. He was always so confident in his protestations, so dismissive of danger, but he could no longer ignore Malabanda's opposition to their relationship, and she watched him disintegrate in front of her. She knew how they frightened the Hutus. The radio had been doing it for months. "He said they'd all be killed, unless…"

"Unless what?" Liliane grabbed his shirt and pulled him to her. He flinched as her fingers clawed at his face and pulled him closer. "Unless what?" she hissed through gritted teeth, her lips curled. She wanted to hear him say it. Droplets of blood bubbled where she had scratched him. As the silence lengthened, the years of hatred and loathing against the priest boiled over within her. He had stolen her childhood and now he was taking Patrick from her. "I hate him. I'm going to kill him."

"Lili, don't. They'd kill you first."

She stared at his broad, innocent face, his eyes blank and

uncomprehending. "Patrick, they're going to kill me anyway. Tonight. Tomorrow. Whenever. I'm on the list. I'm dead already."

He shook his head, bewildered. Like the other Hutus, he still hoped the Interahamwe wouldn't make it to Kitabuye. The night before they had watched silently and scared as the mob, friends and neighbours among them, burned the car. His body was tense and unyielding against hers as she buried her face in his shirt. She remembered there had been no comfort in his embrace, only resignation in his eyes. She realised now that was the moment the Hutus accepted the role that history was laying on them again, and she knew Patrick sensed his own part in it.

"I want to be with you when they come. You know that." Still, he wouldn't look at her. "You've always known that." Her voice was louder, insistent, as she tried to bring him back to her.

"Mum and Dad—"

"We promised each other! You said you'd protect me, Patrick." She grabbed his head and pulled him to her, searching his eyes and face, desperate for him to slough off his fear and be the warrior she imagined he would be. But his brow was peppered with beads of sweat and she felt the tremors from deep within him. "Promise me. Again." She shook him and drops of sweat and blood flicked onto her face. He forced his arms apart and broke her grip, then pushed her to the ground.

"I didn't realise. They'll kill them if I…." His voice was flat. "You have to go. Your parents…"

"I don't care about them. I want to be with you."

"Well I care about mine."

"More than me?" She clambered out of the little grassy hollow, 'their spot' she always called it. The place where they met, talked, made plans for a future that would never happen. He stood away from her, his breathing erratic as if exhausted by the argument, the distance between them defined by bloodlines and decades of bloodletting. Patrick hated arguments, and his body was tense with the conflict within him, the veins in his neck throbbing as if they would burst.

Liliane knew he wanted to go, to be home before Malabanda told his parents, but it was already too late. She saw movement at the bottom of the slope by the wall around the church and her shoulders slumped in defeat. It was his father and brothers. They knew where he went to escape them, to be with her, even if Malabanda hadn't told them. Now they were close, spurred on by their hatred and fear. Patrick tensed, his fists clenched, and swore words she had never heard him use. As she reached out to him, his brothers pushed Patrick aside and fell on Liliane, kicked her, screamed at her until she was on the ground, knees to her chest, hands over her head. She felt Patrick's hands on her, his nails deep in her skin as he pulled her out of their reach and placed himself between them.

His brothers drew away and gathered around their father like a pack of hyena cubs.

"What the fuck, Patrick? You want us all dead?" Fear seemed to seep from their skin and cling to their clothes. "They'll kill us. Your mother…" His blood tied him closer to them than her love ever could.

"Go with them." Her voice sounded stronger than she felt. "Just go." She pushed him away across the grass towards his father, then sank to her knees. He turned and stood over her, the sun behind him, his face in shadow, and she was glad. She didn't want to see the pain in his eyes nor remember the anguish on his face.

"What do you want from him, Liliane Iwo?" His father stepped forward and pulled him closer. "To die with you?" He took his son's arm. "Come."

His brothers slapped his back and clasped his arms. He was theirs, not hers, a prisoner of their past. It was always the same in the end, just like Uncle OK said.

His face was still in shadow when he turned to look at her sprawled on the grass. They pulled him away. He never looked back as they hurried down the hill in a tight little group. The Hutus had won again. Today was their day. And tomorrow would be.

Her fingers tore at the grass where they would lie, the spot where he made his promises and declarations of love, his strong arms around her, telling her they would never be parted, that nothing could ever harm her while he was with her. But he wasn't. She was alone, and even in the heat of the day, she shivered and clutched her arms around herself. Whatever it was she imagined, Patrick holding back the machetes, the strength of his love overwhelming everything, was just a schoolgirl daydream that vanished like the morning mist in the valley.

She knew deep down it was a fantasy she had created since the day she had fought Delphine for his affections, scrabbling and scratching in the dirt playground at school. And she had often wondered if Patrick chose her because Bernard was his best friend, and he enjoyed coming around to kick the ball with him in their yard. Mother had said more than once that the boys were more like twins and just as inseparable. They were the same height and build, had the same springy, curly hair and, above all, shared a placid nature and desire to be liked. Whereas Liliane had a fiery temper and spoke her mind when silence would have been better.

She lay for a long time with these thoughts and watched the shadow of the church lengthen until the tall grass at the top of the slope whispered as the evening breeze rose off the lake.

"I don't care about them." The shame of her denial pricked at her skin. She must go home now and be with them tomorrow when it happened. It was where she belonged. It was where she was expected to be. It was part of the arrangement.

SIX

A warm draught played over Liliane's face in the dark room. She stared at the ceiling and tried to remember the happy times here, playing with her doll with Alice and Kenzi or talking into the night with Bernard, her twin, her soul mate. It was no use. All that would come to her was the thought that someone else would be lying there tomorrow morning, that a Hutu family would have claimed the house as their own.

She had made Patrick feel ashamed of his fear. Yet her own now pinned her to the bed with a dread of what would come with the new day. She imagined the Hutu girls, always so jealous of her looks, slashing her face; the Hutu boys, the ones she scorned so often, fighting over her like a pack of dogs, taking their turns with her, then when she was no more use, cutting her until her blood stained the ground. Even when she shut her eyes, she could see them taunting and abusing her as she lay naked in the dust.

Bernard was waiting, as she knew he would be, when she returned from the field. She had let him embrace her, accepted his chiding and heard his warning. She then pushed past him and slipped through the grey metal gates. Father was at the door, as she knew he would be, his face strained, the burden heavy on him as well.

"We heard there was trouble at Patrick's. You could have been killed." His voice faltered, and for a moment, she saw a flash of the intense love he used to show her when she was younger. In return, she felt an upsurge of pity for him. Once so confident and respected in his work, he was now a shell of the man he had been, a coward so scared of the blade that he had sold himself to Gatsinzi and Malabanda. Their eyes met, and she knew that the anger which these days was only ever a scratch below the surface would soon erupt and consume all his other emotions.

"Lili. Lili." Mother had appeared behind him, her face smaller, as if her tears had drained the life out of her. Her frame seemed shrunken by fear for her daughter's life and the wild imaginings that were still evident in her features. As Liliane took in her mother's appearance, the memory of her own denial of her family swept through her anew, more keenly felt now by their presence. They were all gripped by the reality of the sense of loss they had been adjusting themselves to.

"Lock the gate, Bernard," Father ordered, then turned away to comfort Mother while his bunched fists and the pulsing veins in his neck betrayed the rage that was boiling within. Behind her she heard Bernard ram the bolt. The yard was their prison now, disturbed only by the noise of the Hutus: the drunken laughter, the chants that ebbed and flowed between the different bars and, always, the drums beating the primeval rhythms that once called their ancestors to war. Once they were all inside, Father's announcement that Malabanda had told the Tutsis to gather at the church for safety the next morning sparked another row between father and daughter.

"Thank God," Mother sighed and fell to her knees, her eyes glassy with tears, hands clasped to her chest, but Liliane, unhinged by the stress of the day, lost the last traces of her self-control.

"It's a trap. Can't you see it?" she shouted and grabbed Father's shirt with a strength that seemed to surprise him even though she was so much taller than him. "Since when did Malabanda have such concern for us Tutsis? You've heard him. I've seen them today. Him and Gatsinzi. Planning it all. That's why Gatsinzi got rid of you when Malabanda arrived, isn't it?" Father recoiled as if his daughter had slapped him, but Liliane carried on, twisting her accusations deeper into him. "I saw your office, your precious papers all over the place. They got rid of you so they could arrange everything for tomorrow. You're not as important as you think, are you?"

Bernard moved closer but Father's speed and strength surprised them both as he manhandled her into the bedroom, kicked the door shut and pinned her against the wall.

"Church is for everyone else," he hissed so his voice wouldn't carry through the flimsy wood door. "We stay here. All of us. Together. He will come for us. For you. Our lives depend on your obedience. For once in your life, Liliane, do as you're told." He withdrew to the door and pulled his sleeve across his mouth. His spittle dripped down her chin but she didn't move, fearful of provoking his violence again. "You know what's expected, what he wants from you. It's for all of us."

She felt the walls close in as he watched her with narrowed eyes from the doorway. No further words were needed. Shame and fear in equal share were written into the lines on his face. The responsibility for her family's survival was the burden laid on her many years ago.

Bernard came to her when it was safe, and she told him about Patrick and his family. "I've lost him, Bernard. We've lost him." She cried as she recognised the same anguish in her brother that already possessed her.

"I'll go to him," he said after a long silence. "They won't mind me. He'll listen." She loved her twin so much. She knew her pain was eating into Bernard, joining with his own to debilitate him at the prospect of Patrick turning against them, and yet she felt a flicker of hope that the boys would come up with a way of saving them. The two of them were always planning and scheming about their future, how they would play for one of the big city football clubs together or maybe run a plantation and become rich. Liliane envied the bond they shared, which had somehow weakened her own with her brother. Surely Patrick's love for both of them was stronger than that which tied him to his family. But when Bernard tried to sneak away to see Patrick, Father had already anticipated his children's scheming and was waiting at the gate. It was unusual for Bernard to argue with Father, and Liliane stood by her open window behind the curtain and listened. She cursed when Bernard's innate sense of obedience held him back from forcing his way out and cried when she heard their steps come back across the yard and the front door slam shut.

Eventually, she lay on the bed and listened to the singing from the bars that continued to roll down the lane late into the night, an incessant drumming that pounded in her head long after it stopped. Her stomach was cramped by dread of what the next day would bring. When she did fall into a fitful sleep, she dreamed of the Hutus coming through the window and slashing at her with their blades.

She woke with a start and felt a cooler breeze on her skin through the curtains. As a faint grey glow grew around her, she pushed her covers back and dressed quickly. It was the time of year when the dark rain clouds lingered past dawn and masked the first rays of the sun. Emboldened by the stillness, she went out into the yard. The breeze was laden with the scent of hibiscus, and she stood for a while and wondered at the tranquillity around her after the previous night's commotion.

There was no water left to wash with, so she grabbed the jerry cans, hoping for some small redemption by fetching the water early. The bolt on the gate grated in the silence and she paused, held her breath, but no one stirred in the house. She padded down the soft earth track but as the light grew, a sense of unease gripped and grew within her.

At the lake, she hoisted her skirt around her thighs and crouched barefoot in the water. She was first to disturb it that morning and it was still clear. As she filled the second jerry can, she inhaled the fetid odour of the marshes that were laced with the sweeter fragrance of the white water lilies and sensed something strange in the air. The sighing and shifting of the marshes and the rustle of the trees didn't seem normal. There was the usual racket of the ibis further out on the lake and the short, explosive whistles of the long-tailed talapoin monkeys away in the distance. But around her the woods and the hills were silent. There was no rustling of the antelopes, no grumpy grunting of the foraging pigs. The big, green, white-crested turacos, usually early risers in the fig trees, were not uttering their piercing, punctual dawn calls. The silence was unnatural, as if nature was holding its breath and dawn was reluctant to appear. Unnerved, she settled one of the jerry cans on her head and, crouching, lifted the other and climbed the hill through tangles of brush and wild vines, her sense of dread now as heavy on her as the water.

At the top, where the path forked, she stopped and set the heavy load down, her laboured breathing the only noise to disturb the stillness. The left-hand path led home. The sun's rays now brushed the tops of the tallest trees and she knew she should hurry, but it was down the other path that she looked. If she left the cans here, she could be at his house in a few minutes if she ran. He was always up early and might be out in the yard. She could say all the things that she had rehearsed in the night. Maybe, even after everything that had been said, she could persuade him to come with her.

She looked again at the path home, half wishing Bernard would appear and relieve her of this choice, but it was deserted. The longer she hesitated, the more the silence seduced her, drawing her to Patrick. It'll only take a few minutes, she told herself. If I don't see him, I'll come straight back. What harm could it do?

With a last look to the left, she ran off down the opposite path, the cans tucked into the scrub until she returned. In the darkest hours of the morning, she had forgiven Patrick for his weakness and heaped the blame on herself instead for expecting too much of him. Her own demons chastised her for being selfish. If she could just explain it all to him, tell him it was her fault, now that the time was nearly upon them, and confess to the choice she faced, a choice worse than his, he would understand, would want to protect her from it. But soon the doubts crowded around her again and she stopped, anxious and uncertain.

A murmur disturbed the silence. Maybe it was the plantation workers gathering, yet it was too early even for them. Ignoring a turning that would take her to Patrick's, she carried on up the path that came out behind Alphonse's bar, curious to know yet fearful of what it might mean. As she strained to hear, the low thrumming noise became voices, excited, too loud for the hour, and she wondered if the Hutus had been drinking all night.

The shouts and laughter were still muffled by the wild hedge of overgrown rose trees that bordered Alphonse's. Thorns scratched at her arms and face as she parted the branches and peered through. Men gathered in the yard, jostling closer together as it became more crowded, clinking bottles, laughing and talking as if it was sunset not sunrise. A speaker on a metal post spewed out more dire warnings about the Tutsis and some of the men listened. Adalbert, Ignace and Pancrace were there, kicking their heels against the low wall while they watched the older men talk and drink. They were men themselves now, yet not men at all. Delphine was grilling goat meat and making brochettes with her mother at the fire pit behind the bar. Alphonse brought more jugs of urwagwa and the men cheered.

Someone turned up the volume on the speaker and the bar was silent. Although it was the usual message of hate, they all seemed to pay more attention today as the vitriol seeped out of the radio like a poisonous cloud, infecting everyone present.

"Kill every cockroach. Send them back to hell."

The voice was seductive, reasonable, as if exhorting the Hutus to wipe out a plague of locusts that was threatening their crops. The same voice had preached the insidious message since the plane crash a month ago; the Tutsis killed the president, it said, and the rest of the world no longer cared about Rwanda. Today, they listened because yesterday they had seen the UN abandon them, so the voice must be speaking the truth; the Tutsis were a threat that must be dealt with, even in Kitabuye. Some of the men started to chant and soon the whole bar joined in. It was not a song to Liliane but an outpouring of hatred, and she collapsed against a eucalyptus tree while the last shreds of hope withered inside her.

Through the fog of fear that clouded her mind, she thought again of the boys on the wall. They were always together, yet he wasn't there. Straightening, she knew she had to hurry now, a fresh resolve within her to find him, to keep Patrick away from the madness that was enveloping the town. A loud cheer drew her back to the hedge and she watched Alphonse bring more crates of Primus from his store and dole them out to eager hands. The faces of the men glistened with sweat, even at that early hour, greedy for beer.

She was about to leave when she saw him. Her legs crumbled and, as she staggered back, the branches of the hedge whipped at her and pricked blood on her face. His father and brothers were behind, keeping him close, their prisoner, and she knew there would be no chance to reach him. He grabbed a bottle and then joined Pancrace and the others on the wall, slapping palms with each in turn. They looked like the boys she remembered, sitting on the wall surrounding the school field, laughing, joking, eyeing up the girls. He turned as Delphine came over and handed him a brochette. She ran her fingers down his arm and squeezed his muscles. He said something in response and the others laughed.

A wave of hatred overwhelmed Liliane. It incensed her with a fury that made her pull at the branches in front of her, heedless of the thorns that ripped at her fingers. She had to get to him. This is life after I'm gone, she thought. Patrick with Delphine. It was unbearable.

The mob was suddenly still, the silence more menacing than the boisterous clamour. Liliane froze, her attempt to wrestle her way through the thorns and scrub abandoned. The Burgomaster was there, his head just visible to Liliane, too far away to hear his words, but his message was clear, and it whipped the Hutus into a frenzy.

"Death to Inyenzi," they echoed.

The banging of fists on tables and the chanting rose to a crescendo that echoed across the valley like the claps of thunder that presaged the arrival of a storm. Alphonse leaped on a table. "To the football ground," he shouted. Months of suspicion and jealousy of the Tutsis, stoked by the voices from the radio, fed by the authority of Malabanda and Gatsinzi and now fuelled by alcohol, had become hatred. The mob was in charge now. Metal chairs scraped on the concrete floor, and the crowded bar emptied as the men barged against each other in their enthusiasm. Patrick and his friends jumped off the wall and, with arms linked around each other's shoulders, followed as if going off to play a match on a Saturday afternoon. Liliane watched them go, desperate for Patrick to turn, to feel the pull of her love, but he was already caught up in the excitement. His father followed close behind, the younger brothers at his heels, just to make sure he didn't waver.

A roar rose from across town, the guttural, primitive cry of men going to war and was answered from further away. He was in the mob, on his way to the football ground. Nothing else mattered, neither her family nor her own safety. She lifted her dress above her knees and hurtled along the tracks that circled the town. She had run them all her life, often trying to find Patrick and Bernard, but that morning, the tree roots seemed higher, the ruts deeper, and she fell often as she hurtled towards the pitch. She must reach him before it started, get him home, away from the men and Delphine.

A row of acacia trees ran down two sides of the football ground, and she hurled herself into the grass behind them and peered through the branches. What she saw appalled her, and her fingers pulled at her hair, distressed by the sight. It couldn't be possible. There seemed to be thousands of men herded onto the pitch, so many more than lived in Kitabuye, and the eucalyptus trunks used as goalposts swayed as the men pushed up against them. They were arriving on foot or in battered buses and vans, men who now had a taste for bloodshed and weren't yet sated by the carnage in their own villages. Chants rose up, then died down. The men were restless, waiting for something to happen.

Liliane kneeled forward, head to the ground, disoriented by the raucous clamour in front of her after the quiet of dawn. Her impulse had been futile; how could she even see him in such a mass of faces, let alone reach him? Patrick was lost to her. He would be sucked into the fervour that radiated across the field. She suddenly wanted to be home, to face what was coming with her family. Bernard would never deny her, and Mother would give her own life to save her children. And Father? He had sacrificed her innocence and happiness, not, as he had assured her, to protect the family, but because she now knew he feared death as much as Patrick.

She rose and steadied herself against a tree, unsure if her legs would carry her. A gunshot silenced the commotion. The crowd parted, and two lorries and some jeeps, olive green, not white, bumped across the pitch to the middle where men in khaki uniforms jumped out. It was the Interahamwe, and the men of Kitabuye seemed overwhelmed by their presence. This was the hour of reckoning. It was time to show their loyalty.

Gatsinzi's voice boomed through a megaphone as he ordered them into groups while the militia jumped from the vehicles and strode among the crowd. They herded the Hutu men to the trucks, where others doled out the machetes and knives that were stacked in the back of the lorries. Eager hands reached up, anxious to show their enthusiasm for the day's work. She caught a glimpse of Pancrace in the melee, an incredulous look on his face as he stared at the blade in his hand. A militia soldier screamed at the man next to him and forced a machete into his hand—Patrick. His friends gathered around him but none of them spoke. It was no longer a game. Liliane could see in the slump of their shoulders and the strained looks they exchanged that the reality of what they were about to do had hit them.

"Today, we rid this land of Tutsi scum. Leave none alive." Stood in the back of his pick-up, Gatsinzi's voice echoed across the field, but Liliane didn't hear. She stared at Patrick, willed him to turn, to break away from the pack and come to her. His head was down but still he grasped his metal. Pancrace slapped him on the back, pushing him further into the throng. He hesitated and looked over his shoulder as if he knew she was there, then turned, the machete swinging by his side, and the crowd swallowed him. Liliane turned and fled.

Under the thick canopy of trees, the path ahead was dark. Her feet slipped on the wet earth, pitching her headfirst into a eucalyptus tree. Her vision blurred, she dug her fingers into the soft ground as the world tilted around her. A drumbeat started in the field and its rhythmic, hypnotic pounding vibrated inside her head. It seemed to be getting closer as if the Hutus were marching towards her, but when she opened her eyes the track behind her was empty. The trees seemed to shake as the chorus of one of the old tribal songs reached a crescendo that rolled down the track and over her prostrate body. The beat of the drum quickened, metal banged on metal, and the engines of the vehicles roared. They were on the move.

Liliane's stomach knotted in panic. She clawed herself upright against the tree, desperate to get home before the killing started. She had to be there. Her family's lives depended on her. She had denied them once, wished them out of her life in return for Patrick. She couldn't deny them the chance to live. Her blood froze at the thought that she was too late, that

Malabanda was already there, raging at Father then ordering them to be taken outside.

Another roar surged through the trees and galvanised her anew. The quickest route was the path to the church, even though it meant braving the Main Street. It would be full of Tutsis by now, making their way to the promised sanctuary, so she should be able to lose herself in the crowd. The path was firmer, flatter and soon the red bricks of the church showed through the branches. The side wall was still in shadow and she pressed herself against the rough stone and tried to catch her breath. The town was in uproar, the air filled with shrill, high-pitched cries. She edged forward and peered round to the front of the church. Hutu women were lined up on each side of the street, their shouts unrestrained, their hatred directed at the Tutsis drawn to the church in the hope of safety. Malabanda was at the gate in the low wall, speaking words of encouragement to some, shouting at others as they shuffled forward, distressed and bleeding, children clinging to their legs and clothes. To Liliane, they seemed like animals being herded for slaughter. It was a scene of utter horror, and yet Liliane felt an absurd sense of relief that Malabanda was still at the church, directing operations. He knew she had nowhere to run, nowhere to hide.

She loathed the man, a revulsion that grew each evening she went to his house, and yet her eyes kept getting drawn back to him and the power of life and death he exerted over her and her family. He seemed to be concerned for the Tutsis yet made no effort to stop the violence or temper the fury of the Hutu women. The church was already full as the crowd spilled into the grounds around it, unaware that the mob of men, drunk and high on the khat that the Interahamwe had been doling out, would be there soon. Time was running out. She had to get down the main street before they arrived.

Taking a deep breath, she pushed herself away from the church, across the uneven grass and over the low wall, keeping behind the line of Hutu women, their faces turned to the street, the still air heavy with their hatred. She had reached the top of a wide alley when a shout stopped her.

"Liliane." The voice was familiar, but as she turned a rock thudded against her cheek, and she fell to the ground, stunned by the suddenness of the attack. She looked up and saw that it was Mrs Narinda, a neighbour, a close friend of Mother's, who had hurled the stone at her. Blood trickled from the corner of her mouth, and she rubbed at it angrily, but before she could struggle to her feet, another blow landed on her head from behind. Liliane turned to where the strike had come from, at first blinded by the sun.

"Dirty, stinking, cockroach bitch." She didn't need to see. It was Delphine. She stood over Liliane and howled in triumph. Felice came up behind her, and together, they fell on Liliane, their fingers grasping and pulling at her. "Where's Patrick now to save you?" With each word, Delphine slammed Liliane's head on the ground, then, when she was out of breath, pulled it close to her own. "I'll be in his bed tonight while you're rotting in the field." She reached inside her dress and pulled out a thin blade, her eyes wild, her face contorted with hate, but before she could strike, a hand, a man's, slapped Liliane's face, and her head whipped back onto some bricks embedded in the earth. She peered into the white glare. Uncle OK.

"Go back to the street. I'll finish her." He had hold of Delphine's wrist.

"Leave me. She's mine." Years of jealousy and hatred had strengthened Delphine, and she writhed and twisted until she broke his grip, her hand scrabbling in the dust for the knife.

"Go back. This is man's work." Uncle OK grabbed the girl again and pushed her up the lane towards the mob of women. "That's where you should be, to welcome the Interahamwe."

"Come on, Delphine," Felice urged her as Uncle OK grabbed Liliane's hair, pulled her head back and pressed a knife against her exposed throat until she felt the skin break. She clawed at his face, and her feet scrabbled in the dirt, but he was too strong for her.

SEVEN

Liliane's neck and shoulder felt damp when she came to, and through the slit of a half-opened eye saw a dark stain on the ground beneath her head. This is how it ends, she thought, alone, face down in the dirt, killed by a man she loved like a father. Her family, disowned and betrayed by her, would die needlessly because of her folly. Her fingernails scraped the earth in desperation; it wasn't meant to be like this. She flinched as a stone hit the back of her leg, and she heard steps picking their way through the rubble in the lane. She tensed, fought against the tremors she could feel in her limbs and tried to fake the death that would surely come soon.

"Get up. Hurry." Hands grabbed her arms and pulled her to her knees. It was Uncle OK. He dragged her over the stones and left her slumped against the brick wall behind his store while he shoved the door open. "Liliane. Move."

The effort and emotion had weakened him, and he could only watch as Liliane pulled herself up and staggered over to him. Together, they helped each other into his storeroom and collapsed against the packing cases. She felt her neck, but the line of blood was already hardening in the heat of the day.

"I had to. She's still suspicious." His words came in short bursts between his laboured attempts to suck breath into his lungs. "It's only the skin. You'll live."

"Only for them to kill me."

She should already be dead and knew she should be grateful to Uncle OK, but her words were laced with bitterness and resentment. Death, even at the hands of Delphine, seemed preferable now to the fate that had been arranged for her.

"What were you doing?" His hoarse voice struggled to get the words out, and she saw his weariness. Her recklessness had laid a burden on Uncle OK now. "You're meant to be at home," he said, and she wondered again how much he knew.

She glared at him. "I was trying to get home." Her frustration boiled over as she felt the minutes slip away from her. "I must get home. I have to be there." She ran to the front door, but Uncle OK had already barred the way, her hands held vice-like in his.

"You can't leave. You're dead. I killed you, remember." She stared at him as the reality of what had just happened struck her. Delphine would already have told the crowd around her, and Liliane could imagine her complaining loudly that Uncle OK had ruined her chance of revenge on the Tutsi whore who had seduced a decent Hutu boy. Uncle would die if she was seen in the street. Her family would die if she stayed here. "You won't make it now anyway. The Interahamwe are in town." His grip on her eased, but he watched her like he would a cornered wildcat.

"I saw them at the football ground." She felt guilty admitting it.

"What were you doing?" he asked again, wide-eyed. She could see he was incredulous that she would be where the Hutu men were gathering.

"I went to get water—early, before dawn. Then I thought I would see if I could find Patrick. We argued yesterday." She waited for a reaction, but the old man's face was impassive. "His father took him away from me. They're all frightened. Malabanda threatened them." She paused again. "Because of me."

"And did you?" Uncle OK asked her. "Go to his home? See Patrick?" The anger in his voice rose with each question.

"I heard the crowd at Alphonse's; I stopped to watch. He came there." The memory was too hard to recount, even to Uncle OK. "Then they all went off to the field. Now they're headed this way."

"So, he was with them then." He shrugged his shoulders in resignation.

"He was frightened," she repeated, knowing it was only for her own benefit. "He didn't want to be there. I know him."

Uncle OK watched her in silence as she tried to explain, to apologise for him. "They hit him, forced a machete into his hand. I don't know what he'll do." The old man let her go and turned away rather than answer her, and they stood in silence for a while, each with their own thoughts and fears. "They won't be safe at the church, will they? They must know they can't trust him."

"It's hope, not trust. Like your father." His eyes narrowed as he said this, and she felt uncomfortable under his scrutiny as the sadness in his eyes and the shake of his head told her he knew after all. Liliane laid her head on his chest and sobbed as she felt the guilt and shame drain out of her. There was no need for words with Uncle OK. But the emptiness left behind was replaced by dread as the change in tempo in the noise outside told them the Interahamwe had arrived. It was too late. She turned to the window and, with her face pressed against the glass, could see the bend in the road where the lorries and jeeps from the football ground were edging into sight. Men in khaki hung off the side of the trucks, guns or machetes held high. The women clapped and cheered as the vehicles moved slowly up the street. It was only a day since the UN had driven that way.

Liliane beat her fists against the glass, trapped like an angry insect, haunted by the anguish that she had inflicted on her family.

"It's no good, Lili," Uncle OK said as he watched her eyes turn towards the church.

He was right. The windows rattled as the lorries rumbled past, and the ground seemed to shake, the rabble army of Hutu men close behind, their machetes swirling in the air while Interahamwe walked among them to enforce their enthusiasm. Now that the last of the Tutsis were squeezed into the church grounds, the street erupted in a frenzy of Hutu hatred. It reminded Liliane of when Ojo had hidden in the teachers' room, hoping he would be safe, while the Hutu boys howled and beat on the door until the planks cracked open and he was dragged into the field and beaten.

Someone pounded on the back door, and Liliane wondered if those planks would break so easily. She felt Uncle OK tense as shouts echoed in the back alley. Liliane looked at him and mouthed 'Delphine', and when the back door burst open, he thrust himself in front of her, arms wide, one hand reaching for a knife on the counter as boots stomped through the shadows of the storeroom.

"Uncle OK. Uncle OK." A voice, hoarse with fear, crept through the gaps between the packing cases.

Uncle OK let the blade fall to his side as a man, about Father's age, appeared from behind the stack of crates. It was Mr Musaveni, one of the plantation managers. His face was covered in a sheen of sweat, and the clothes stuck to his body as terror leached out of him. Musaveni made straight for Uncle OK and clenched his shirt front in his fists. "Help me, Uncle."

Uncle OK shook his head. "Look out there, man, for God's sake. What can I do?" he said as he pulled his shirt out of the man's grasp.

"The church. It's not safe. You know that. Hide them. Please." Fear rendered him almost incoherent. "The children. The baby. Please." His voice cracked and he sank to his knees. "They're outside. I can't take them to the church. I won't." His arms encircled Uncle OK's legs, and his tear-filled eyes in his upturned face pleaded with Uncle OK.

"They'll search everywhere. You know that."

The man rubbed his face in anguish. "They won't come here. You're Hutu, Uncle. I have to stay with Femi. She won't leave the house." He stood and took hold of Uncle OK's shirt again, the strength in his desperation enough to unbalance the old man. "Your shed in the hills then." His head was on Uncle's chest, his arms around his neck, laying another heavy burden on the sagging shoulders. Uncle never turned anyone away and never said no; it was why everyone loved him.

"How many of you?" His voice betrayed the hopelessness of what was being asked. "I've had enough of all this," he had told her the day before, and Liliane wondered if he had the strength left to help.

"All of them—seven. The older ones will help." He looked

at Liliane as if seeing her for the first time. "She can help. Please. Before it's too late." He embraced Uncle OK and then ran back through the shop. At the storeroom door he stopped to urge them on.

"Liliane, help me."

"Let me go home, Uncle. Please." Liliane now grasped his shirt as if shaking him would make him relent, but the blank stare and the stiffness of his neck told her that he was unshaken by her pleas.

"You stay with me." He pulled her closer, and she was surprised at the strength still in him.

"I promised them." She was crying again, adding to his burden. "They'll die if I don't."

"They may be dead already." His voice was harsh, its tone alien to her. "You should have thought about all this earlier on." He was right. Gangs of Hutus led by Interahamwe were darting into the side streets to look for the houses with the mark. "Come." He led her through the storeroom and into the back lane, where the children were huddled together, silent and wide-eyed. One of the girls held a baby. Liliane waited for Uncle OK to decide, hoping her tears would make him favour her claim on him more than that of Musaveni, but he shook his head and muttered to himself. Musaveni clasped him close, but Uncle pushed him away.

"Go to your wife," he said, and Musaveni ran back down

the alley as if afraid the old man would change his mind. Uncle OK turned to Liliane. "Take the baby and walk at the back of the group."

"Uncle, please." She now sank to her knees in front of him, but he drew her back to her feet.

"It's maybe better this way. Malabanda can't be trusted. Joseph is a fool to think he could. Death is better than the life arranged for you." He pulled her head up and she saw tears in his eyes. "Come."

"Where can we go?"

"The shed. It's the only place." His voice was flat, his words barely audible, and she could see that he knew it was hopeless.

"But we'll be trapped up there."

"What do you suggest?" He walked over to the children and turned. "I owe him," he said, as if that explained everything, even though Musaveni would be dead soon and the debt forgotten. Liliane watched in despair as he took a child's hand in his and walked along the alley. With a glance through the door into the storeroom, she lifted the baby and shepherded the rest of the children after Uncle OK. At the end of the alley, he stopped and peered around the corner, but the women were turned towards the street where the Interahamwe convoy was almost at the church, and they were able to turn down the next alley towards the woods and the track that led to the top of the hill.

The baby was a deadweight, and Liliane felt a sudden urge to run, but when Uncle OK stopped at the edge of the trees to check she was with him, she nodded, submissive, then turned her back on the town and her family.

The track curved upwards, and as they got higher, she stopped to shift the baby to her other hip and peered through the branches, down onto the clearing in front of the church. A few Tutsi men stood at the gate in the wall, armed with machetes and sticks and to their side was Malabanda, his face turned to the street. The Hutu mob had stopped short of the wall, and the lorries were drawn up outside the hospital. Apart from a few sporadic shouts and the low sobbing of women and children, the town fell silent.

The men from Kitabuye seemed intimidated by the church, and a few backed away, but their resolve was soon strengthened by the guns of the Interahamwe. Further behind them, Gatsinzi stood in the back of his pickup and observed the scene in front of him like a general commanding his army.

Liliane turned to Uncle OK, who was bent against a tree. His breathing was loud and erratic, and she feared he wouldn't make it to the top. The children pulled at her for attention, their whimpers the only sound in the silence. She ignored them, her gaze on Malabanda. He crossed himself and then raised an arm as if he was about to bless them. There was a gleam of metal in his hand. The sun's rays caught on the knife, and glints of light reflected up to the trees where Liliane stood, her breath held, her free hand over her mouth. It was as if he was signalling to her. His hand arced down, and the blade flashed and plunged into the chest of the nearest Tutsi. A crimson stain spread over his shirt, and even as his legs collapsed, his eyes were on Malabanda, wide and disbelieving.

"It is time to do God's work." Malabanda's words carried up the slope, but it was not a voice she recognised. It was cruel, heavy with the hatred stored up within him. "It is time to rid this land of Inyenzi. God is with you today. Leave none alive."

A roar like a crack of thunder erupted from the Hutus and seemed to force the Tutsis further back into the enclosure and pin them against the walls of the church. The ground trembled as the attackers stamped their feet and threw themselves high in the air in a frenzy. The children and women cried out, their voices shrill and pitiful against the deep-throated roars that rolled up the hills and across the valley.

Uncle OK turned and pulled at the children, but Liliane was paralysed by the scene below and stared as the Hutus surged forward, machetes raised high, urged on by Gatsinzi. A few Tutsis swung their own metal, and for a moment, she thought they would prevail until the Interahamwe pushed the rabble aside and fired into them. Women screamed as their men fell. A grenade landed amongst them, and the crowd parted where it lay on the ground. The noise of the bedlam subsided momentarily; the Tutsis frozen as if in a picture. The flash came first, blinding even against the midday sun, then the explosion cracked up the hill and reverberated across the valley. The Hutu mob surged forward. Liliane turned away as the blades rose and fell.

"You can't help them now," the old man said. The words rasped in his throat, and his breath rattled in his chest. "But you can help me."

The children straggled up the path ahead of them, urged on by the old man. The small ones sobbed; the older ones had been shocked into silence. Liliane looked at him and knew he had seen this before; it was why he seemed able to function. The trees shaded them from the worst of the sun but not from the continuous wall of noise and mayhem below them. The heat was oppressive, and sweat mingled with tears streaked the dirt and blood on her face. With each step, the baby got heavier, and she tripped frequently as the smaller ones crowded around her legs. Each time she stopped to hoist the baby up her hip, she turned to check on Uncle OK. The life seemed to have drained from him, and he stumbled up the path, his back bent, head down. A larger explosion rocked the town, and a hot blast of air swept past them, followed by more screams. The children wailed and fled up the track, as if each scream was a blade stabbing at their backs as they ran.

Liliane stumbled over the brow of the hill into the clearing where the children had gathered in a huddle, mute with fear. Behind them was Uncle OK's hut, but it no longer held the anticipation of excitement she used to have as a child when he allowed her and Bernard and Patrick to scramble among the packing cases. The big, wooden slatted sides with bars on the windows made it look more like a prison now. She knew they would be trapped up here. There would be no escape off the hill.

EIGHT

Liliane laid the baby in the shade, too shocked and drained of emotion to tend to it and walked to where the children were gathered at the far edge of the clearing. A rough road, just wide enough for a vehicle, fell away to her left, down to the plantation buildings hidden behind the trees. From there, it wound its way back into Kitabuye one way and to the plantation itself the other. The plantation vehicles had long ago stopped coming up the road, and it was only trucks bringing deliveries for Uncle OK these days, but even these were infrequent now, and the track was becoming overgrown. The Interahamwe would come that way when their work down the hill was finished, she was sure.

The neat rows of tea bushes stretched away below Liliane across the undulating, tranquil valley, undisturbed by the madness nearby. In the distance, the land rose in terraces of greenery layered between red slashes of earth. Uncle OK hobbled to her side and put a hand on her shoulder. Sweat pooled in his wrinkled face, and his grim features spoke of the pain that gripped him. There was nothing more to be said, and they stared across the valley to the mountains beyond in shocked silence while the children crowded around.

"Malabanda started it." Liliane kept her gaze on the bushes below, but Uncle OK said nothing. "They wouldn't listen." She looked at Uncle OK. "I tried."

"It was all they had. Don't blame yourself."

But she did. Her family would die like the rest now. It wasn't supposed to be like this. She was meant to be there, and then they would be safe. She was the price agreed. Now it was too late. Her stupidity had condemned them, and she would die a lonely death, up here on the hill, as her punishment. It was too much to bear now that she had time to think, and the implications of her actions became a grim reality.

She felt her dress being tugged, and when she looked, she saw one of the older girls point down the hill to the plantation. At first, there was no difference in the view, just the orderly rows, serene and peaceful, but the girl pushed at Liliane more urgently. Closer to the edge now, she saw the Tutsis appear and run along the rows of bushes. They filled the channels that stretched across the valley and spread out like a ripple across the lake when the afternoon breeze came.

Liliane grabbed Uncle OK, but he pushed her away, and when she looked at him, he was shaking his head in resignation. "Come away, Liliane. Don't let them see."

Flashes of steel flickered on the fringes of the plantation, and soon the Hutus were on the Tutsis with their weapons. The screams were more distinct, more piercing without the barrier of the trees and for the first time, the children could see what was happening. Uncle OK shepherded the children, rigid with shock, to the shed, where he heaved one of the double doors open. The sun was overhead, and the corrugated roof had sucked heat into the building.

Liliane only tore herself away from the carnage below when the ruddy blades were lifted high in celebration. She walked to the shed, numbed by the ferocity that had been unleashed. A blast of heat tumbled out of the shed as she got near it.

"They'll die in there. Even before they find us."

"I don't know what to do then, Lili. Help me." Uncle OK had always been the town fixer, the man people went to with their problems, but now he was old and defeated.

Still unhinged by the images of the bloody slaughter, Liliane struggled to focus on the implications of what he had said. She knew the children were too young to hide in the trees. There were the marshes around the edge of the lake that would offer a hiding place in the reeds, but they wouldn't get that far without being seen. She looked around the clearing for inspiration, then back to the shed and watched two of the children run inside and clamber over the packing cases. It seemed a lifetime ago, a different age when Liliane would come up with Uncle OK to sort his deliveries. She would pull out brightly coloured dresses and shirts from the wooden cases or marvel at the tools and machinery that gleamed and smelled of oil and brown paper.

One of the girls stood at the top of the old road and stared down the slope. She shouted and pointed. Liliane could hear the noise now; the grind of an old engine, maybe two, was labouring up the hill. She looked at Uncle OK, slumped against the shed wall, his chin on his chest, eyes on the ground. He looked broken and defeated. The terror of the slaughter had sapped his strength, and she reached behind to steady herself against the shed. She had been lucky to survive so far, but this time, she knew it was different. There would be no Patrick to pull her to safety and throw his strong arms around her. There was no hiding place left for a Tutsi in Kitabuye.

The children jostled around her and buried their faces in the fabric of her dress, all of them too shocked to cry. The first vehicle, a battered jeep, strained over the lip of the hill, and three Interahamwe soldiers jumped out. They grabbed guns from the vehicle, but each of them had a blade strapped over their shoulders, and the khaki cloth was damp and stained where the metal touched it. Liliane closed her eyes and groaned when she saw the fourth person in the back of the jeep.

Uncle OK reached across and pulled her to him, his face grim. "I'm sorry. I couldn't fool her."

"Don't." Liliane reached up and held a finger to his lips. "It's my fault. I brought this on you." She looked into his eyes. "I love you, Uncle. Please forgive me." Uncle OK nodded, and a faint smile flickered at the edges of his mouth before the roar of an engine and the stink of diesel swept across the clearing, and the moment was broken. A lorry, one she had seen at the football ground, was now behind the jeep, and the Hutus jumped out even before it stopped. Their laughter and high spirits were incongruous with the terror in the town below. It had been so quick, too easy, the way they had turned against their friends and neighbours. Liliane could see it wasn't just the threats from the Interahamwe; they were unrestrained, lawless, without consequences. Uncle OK had been right; there were no witnesses left. They were doing what they wanted, with the blessing of Malabanda.

Most of them were drunk, and a few leaned against the vehicle for support. They all clutched bottles, an untidy rabble, their clothes stiff and matted with blood, their machetes stained crimson. Even when the Interahamwe leader cursed them and pointed his revolver at them, they continued to joke among themselves. They didn't yet seem to realise why they had been brought to the hilltop clearing until Delphine stood up in the jeep, and her voice silenced the Hutus.

"That's her!" She was exultant. "I told you she wasn't dead." She leaned out to touch the leader, and Liliane could see how desperately she wanted his approval. "Whore!" Her finger jabbed in the air. "I knew he would never kill you." A sly grin crept across her face. "Patrick's down there, killing." Her words hammered into Liliane like nails. She had betrayed her parents, and now Patrick had betrayed her. It was her punishment.

In the silence that followed Delphine's outburst, the children began to wail. It seemed to dawn on the men why they had been brought up the hill and tried to climb back in the lorry only to be clubbed and pushed back to the clearing by the Interahamwe. In the commotion, Liliane edged towards the doors of the hut and pulled the children with her. She looked for Uncle OK and saw that he had walked out to the centre of the clearing to face the soldiers.

"Kill him." The leader pointed at Uncle OK, but his gun ranged over the sullen faces of the Hutus. No longer the broken man who had stumbled into the clearing, Uncle OK stood defiant, straight-backed in front of them. His silence and unrelenting stare seemed to unnerve the soldiers as well as the rabble bunched behind them. Liliane pulled the older children to her and turned their faces into her body, their fingernails biting into her skin. The younger ones sobbed, but there was no point in stilling them now; she just wanted to protect them from watching.

"Our Father in Heaven, hallowed be your name." Uncle OK's voice, strong and confident, rang across the clearing. The Hutu men stared at him, and one of them began to cry. "May your kingdom come; may your will be done." His words grew louder. "On Earth as it is in Heaven." Some of the men joined Uncle OK, and one of them knelt down, and now the prayer resounded in the clearing. "Give us today our daily bread."

A gunshot shattered the spell that the prayer seemed to be casting over the clearing, and Liliane felt the children's grip tighten.

"Enough!" the leader shouted, his face flecked with spittle. "Kill him!"

Two Interahamwe soldiers stepped forward, their rifles trained not on Uncle OK but on the Hutus. It was another test of their loyalty, their commitment to the cause.

"Forgive us our sins, as we forgive those who sin against us." A solitary voice now, Uncle OK continued to taunt the soldiers with his prayer. "And lead us not into temptation."

Liliane pulled at the children. "Close your eyes and hold me tight." The small knot of children huddled closer to her. She watched some of the men take pulls from their bottles. Most of them were sweating, their eyes wide.

One of the Hutus strode forward, and an empty bottle

slipped to the ground as both his hands reached for his blade, then raised it above his head. Two others followed, so drunk now that they staggered across the clearing. Liliane's last sight of Uncle OK was of the proud man she knew, unyielding, his head high as the blades felled him. Each of the dull thuds felt as if they were hammering into her own body. One blow. A second. Then a frenzy as the men rushed to impress the Interahamwe who would not hesitate to kill them if they flinched from their duty.

Liliane slumped against the wall, too distressed to comfort the hysterical children. The men stepped away from the body, their heads bowed. One of them rubbed his clothes and skin as if trying to rid himself of Uncle OK's blood. Another vomited while the rest, silent and subdued, bent over in the grass and wiped their blades.

The older children fled into the store, pulling the smaller ones behind them. When Liliane tried to follow, she felt strong hands round her throat and waist. It was the leader. He grunted with exertion as he wrestled Liliane to the side of the jeep, where he dumped her in the dirt, his foot on her chest.

"Kill the rest," he shouted over his shoulder.

"No. Not them. Have me. Kill me. Not them." Years of fear, guilt and repression seemed to rupture inside her. She punched and scratched at the man while her legs thrashed, creating a cloud of dust that choked her mouth. Her screams panicked the children, and the men faltered until the other soldiers fired their guns into the ground around them, and they shuffled forward again.

Liliane's strength was drained, and the soldier pulled her up, their foreheads almost touching, the stink of beer on his breath and the stench of death on his skin.

"Watch them die, Tutsi bitch, and be thankful it's not you."

His free hand pawed at her breasts and then rubbed her between her legs. He pinned her against the jeep, her head gripped tight so there was nowhere else to look. The rabble moved forward in a ragged line, the children now in a tight bundle in the doorway. An older girl cried out a name, and one of the men paused, but a shove in his back from a rifle butt pushed him closer. Liliane's legs crumpled and darkness descended over her eyes.

NINE

Liliane was sprawled on a hard floor when she came to. Even though her eyes were gummed tight with blood and grime, she knew where she was and recognised the smell, thick and cloying in her nostrils. As she breathed it in, like a poison entering her body, she wished they had killed her up on the hilltop. She knew the pattern on the rug onto which she had been flung, where the furniture stood, what pictures were on the walls and what was on the shelf. This, in the end, was her worst fear, and now it numbed her limbs and kept her pinned to the floor. She had been here alone so often, but this would be different. He would want more this time. It was part of the deal; it had to be honoured, even if her family were already dead.

Outside, in the heat of the afternoon, the killings continued around the town. An occasional cry of terror, high-pitched and shrill, penetrated the walls and shuttered windows. Inside, the room was cool and dark, but in the silence, the clock was loud. A door slammed somewhere in the house, and her stomach turned as she thought of him coming to her. She had been resigned to death for so long, had been so close to it throughout the day, but now, as she lay there waiting, she knew that she would have welcomed death above this.

When the throbbing in her head lessened, she rubbed the mess from her eyes and let them flicker open. The room was always the same. His chair was opposite the sofa, where he would sit while she knelt in front of him, his hand on her head as if blessing her. The piano was against the far wall and the big, silver cross was on the centre of the shelf under the pictures of Jesus and Mary. Incense hung in the air. As did his presence.

She was sure the door would be locked, even if she was able to crawl that far, and the windows were barred. There was no escape. He would come. There were voices outside in the yard and then movement in the hallway beyond the door. She tried to think of how she could fight him, make him kill her but knew how strong he was, how futile it would be to resist.

The door opened noiselessly, and a draught of warm air wafted over Liliane, who saw someone silhouetted in the doorway. The boards behind the sofa creaked, and then she felt his presence over her. She was alone with Malabanda.

There was a rustle of material as he bent closer, and Liliane flinched as his hand stroked her bare arm.

"Don't be anxious, Liliane." He touched her cheek. "Have

some water." He stood again, and she heard the clink of glass by the table. "Here." His hand held her head as he put the drink to her lips, but they were too swollen, and most of it slopped down her chin onto her neck. He pulled her further forward, and she winced as pain shot through her back and neck. "Let me help you." He hooked his hands under her arms, his thumbs on her breasts, and pulled her upright so she could lean against a chair. Her chest hurt with every breath, and she was conscious of his gaze on her.

"Look at me," he said, taking hold of her chin.

There was a faint smell of soap on him, and she realised he must have washed the blood of her people off his skin. He forced her head further up until she could no longer avoid looking at him. His collar gleamed white above the gloom of his black suit and his face was close to hers.

She was disconcerted by his stare, disorientated by the kindness being shown to her. "You weren't at home where you should have been." There was a hint of reproach in his words, but he reached to the table behind him for some cloth and wiped the cuts and bruises on her face. His breathing became faster, his actions deliberate and unhurried. The cool material was soft and smelled of mint, and as tiredness swept through her limbs, she thought she might faint again.

"It had to happen. You know that, don't you?" He held her head in his hands, his voice soft, insistent in its concern for her.

"We had to protect the country." He continued to dab at her wounds. "And the church. That is why I had to be involved." He moved his hands to her shoulders, and she felt a gentle squeeze of reassurance. "The church, our church, was in danger, Liliane, from the rebels. But of course you wouldn't know that. It has been a constant worry for us. They are Communists. They would have torn the church down and killed all us believers." He shook his head to show her how great the burden had been on him. One of his hands moved to her back and pulled her closer. She wanted to push against him but was too dazed and exhausted, and her lack of protest seemed to encourage him. The heavy frames of his glasses almost touched her nose, and his eyes, large behind the thick lenses, mesmerised her.

"Everything is ready for you. You will keep house for me. Mrs Mutsinzi will be gone, Liliane. You will have a better life." He paused. "And your family, of course." His face was turned away. "Once all this is over, we shall rebuild our country and make it fit to live in once and for all. You can be part of it." His voice was soft, almost a whisper. He moved his other hand behind her and pulled her towards him, but she bowed her head and felt his mouth brush her forehead. A murmur of disappointment escaped from his lips, and he tightened his grip on her hair, pulling her head up again. "I want you to look after me, to take care of my needs." His hand was on one of her breasts, his fingers searching until they found her nipple and squeezed it through the fabric of her dress. "This is your chance to have a good life at last, Liliane. Along with your family, of course. It's what your father wanted. What we agreed." He paused to concentrate on her buttons. The reminder of those evenings repulsed her, and she shuddered at the thought of how much more he would want now, but the mention of her family, of their safety, kept her from resisting. He pulled her closer and she felt his hardness. "You will see, Liliane. It will be better than you imagine." She had faced death, had expected it, but now he was offering her life. "You would have status in the town. There will be more and better things in the shops when we rebuild. You will have the best of everything. No one will ever threaten you again."

Liliane had a sudden image of Delphine, jealous of her again, and her hesitation seemed to give Malabanda encouragement. He bent to kiss her exposed nipples while his hands eased the dress off her. She wanted to pull away, but his hold on her was firm. As his tongue flicked over her skin, she shivered. It was only when his hand moved between her legs that she found the strength to resist.

"Don't struggle, Liliane. I won't hurt you." His words were faint as if he was out of breath.

He put his mouth on hers, and she could feel him tugging at his belt, his movements rushed and clumsy. She was frightened. It was always going to come to this, but the more she struggled, the more she seemed to goad him. His hand was over her mouth and she couldn't breathe. He was out of his trousers now and between her legs. She pulled her face away and tried to pummel his back with her fists, but he was too strong. He lifted her off the floor and slammed her against the wall next to the shelf. The force knocked the breath out of her and she fainted. When she came to, his mouth was on hers, his grunts louder, his movements more violent, the rough bricks scraping against her skin.

Eventually, Malabanda pulled away from her. He had claimed her at last. She tried to think of her parents and Bernard, but the image wouldn't come. All she could see were his eyes behind the thick lenses in the heavy, black frames. The image burned into her soul.

She leaned her head against the wall and closed her eyes, overwhelmed by shame and revulsion. One of her arms was spread up against the wall for support. Her fingers felt the cold metal of the cross and closed around it. She looked down at him. "Father Malabanda." He raised his face from her breasts, and she brought the heavy cross down on him—a hard blow, strengthened by years of fear and hate and abuse. It caught him on the temple and carried on down the side of his face, the sharp edge of the cross slicing through the skin on his cheek. Blood burst from the ruptured flesh, and he roared, his eyes wide with pain and shock. Then his anger erupted, and Liliane saw the real Malabanda, the one she knew had always been there, the malevolence that always lay just below the surface exposed. There would be no forgiveness. Nor did she want it. He was going to kill her. She wanted him to. He slammed a fist into her face, and her head hit the wall with a force that made the paintings jump on their hooks. His blood dripped onto her naked body as she fell at his feet while he kicked at her. He then turned away to buckle his trousers.

"Father Malabanda. Father Malabanda." Someone hammered on the door.

When he turned back to her, there was a knife in his hand, the one she had seen him use that morning. "Stupid bitch. You've just killed your family." She tried to shield herself with her hands as the knife fell on her, bounced off her knuckles and sliced into her neck. The pain spread all the way down to her breast, and warm blood flowed through her fingers. Malabanda grunted with exertion as he raised the knife again, but this time, his aim was more controlled, and her head bounced off the floor with the force of the blow as it cut into her skull. There was a loud bang as the door slammed open, and she became aware of others in the room.

Malabanda, his knife raised for another blow, turned and, when he saw the two men, lowered it. "Kill her. Now. Then dump her with the rest," he shouted. He turned away and hurried from the room, his hands holding a cloth to his face to staunch the blood.

Liliane was barely conscious as the men grabbed hold of her. Through the film of blood in her eyes, she recognised one of them.

"Pancrace." Her word was barely a whisper, but he heard it.

"Liliane?" He wiped the blood off her face. "Liliane." He looked behind him to the open door, but the priest had gone. His hand moved to the wound on her head and she saw him flinch.

"Pancrace. Come on." The other's voice was urgent. "She's going to die. Don't get us into trouble for a dead Tutsi."

"We can't kill her, Seth. She's Patrick's girl." Pancrace spoke in a whisper as he turned to the door again. "She'll be dead by the time we get her there anyway."

"Looks like Malabanda fucked her," Seth said as he stared at Liliane.

"Quiet, man," Pancrace hissed while he looked over his shoulder and listened, then bent down and wiped the blood out of her eyes. "Liliane, I'm sorry." He seemed embarrassed by her nakedness. She managed a small nod to show she had heard.

Beside him, Seth fretted. "Come on, Pancrace. If he finds she's still here, he'll kill us."

Liliane felt them grab her arms and legs and could tell they were trying to be gentle with her even as they staggered out of the room and into the yard in front of the priest's house. The brilliance of the afternoon after the shaded room hurt her eyes even though they were shut, and every step shuddered through her body. She heard Seth complain, and they laid her on the ground for a while. Pancrace dropped to his knees by her head. "Nearly there, Liliane." She opened her eyes, looked at him to acknowledge his concern and saw they were at the church.

The wall in front of it had disappeared under the bodies that stretched up the hill like a shadow across the land. Hutus staggered around, bottles clutched in their hands, blades cast aside, their skin and clothes stained crimson. A few men watched as Pancrace and Seth picked Liliane up and continued their journey to the field, traversing the piles of bodies that spread up the slope, twisted in unnatural shapes, three or four deep. Her throat tightened with the smell, and she had to clench her teeth to stifle a cough. They should have killed her at Malabanda's, and she wished Pancrace hadn't taken this risk for her. The pain in her head was relentless. She was getting weaker when Seth stopped without warning, and she bit her lip as her head jolted against his legs. She recognised the voice of the man who had challenged them as one of Gatsinzi's cronies. Not daring to open her eyes, she concentrated on relaxing her body into a deadweight and felt Pancrace tighten his grip on her feet and pull her higher.

"What you guys doing? You're missing all the fun in town," Pancrace shouted to them.

"Checking they're all dead. Burgomaster's orders." The man poked Liliane. "Still warm. She dead?"

"Just now," Pancrace replied. "Malabanda did this one. We were waiting in his yard." The mention of the priest silenced them while Pancrace and Seth carried on.

"If he's finished with her, I don't mind having a go." A different man had decided to walk with them.

"Like doing it to corpses, do you?" Pancrace said.

The man laughed, and Liliane felt his hands on her breasts. "Maybe not," he decided and spat on her face. "Take her over there, as far as you can. It stinks bad already. And give her another cut, just to be sure."

She heard Pancrace breathe out as the man wandered away, coughing and retching. She opened her eyes again when they stopped and saw it was the dip where she and Patrick had hidden from Malabanda the day before.

"Liliane. Liliane." Pancrace's voice was urgent, his face close to hers. "Liliane, we have to go."

"Patrick." The word was barely audible, but Pancrace knew.

"Sorry, Liliane." She couldn't tell whether he hadn't seen Patrick or was sorry for what he had seen him do, and she was too weak now to ask. He stood and unslung the machete from over his shoulder, and his tears splashed onto her face. They had all been so happy together once, a big group of friends where blood ties didn't matter, playing in the school field, swimming in the lake, learning to fall in and out of love. How had they let all this happen?

She had wanted Patrick to give his life for her, but instead, Uncle OK had died because of her; she didn't want Seth and Pancrace to lose their lives for sparing hers. "Kill me," she mouthed at him as he raised his blade high above his head. Anyone watching to make sure he finished her would be sure to see it. None would be left alive. His metal tore into flesh and bone while blood spattered across her face and skin, and she heard Pancrace grunt as he struggled to pull the blade from the body next to hers. A ragged cheer drifted up the slope from the church. They had been watching. Liliane pleaded with Pancrace with her eyes, but he gave a slight shake of his head and walked away. Seth lingered, his machete unslung, and from the way he fingered it, she could see he didn't want to be complicit in sparing her, but Pancrace called out, and he turned and jogged after him.

Pancrace's kindness was cruel to Liliane. He had condemned her to a slow, painful death. Her wounds had torn further apart when the boys threw her down, and she felt the flow of blood on her face and neck again. This surely meant the end. She was reconciled to it now, to freedom from pain and humiliation, from guilt for her family and Uncle OK, from the shame of all those times with Malabanda. And most of all, death meant she no longer had to think about Patrick and his betrayal of their vows or of how he had slipped into the pack and the sort of person he had become. Delphine could claim him now. She no longer needed to care, just wait for her life to ebb away.

But just as on hot, humid nights when sleep eluded her, her mind filled with thoughts of the day, and death refused to take her. Instead, the intensity of the pain seemed to stimulate her mind. This was their place, hers and Patrick's, where they used to sit and talk about their future, about being together, about the family they would have. It was where he had first made love to her on her sixteenth birthday. He had folded her new dress, laid it carefully on the grass and stared at her as if she was too precious, too delicate to touch.

She felt a brief flicker of hope inside her that he had turned away at the last moment, had taken a stand like Uncle OK and maybe, even now, he was lying somewhere close by, and she would join him soon. Then she remembered him again, that last time, walking away from her into the crowd, his blade in his hand. It was hopeless. She had seen the defeat in his eyes and his fear of being killed. He wouldn't, he couldn't choose death.

She mourned for the boy she loved, the burden she had been to him, and the choice she had forced him to make. He was alive, she knew it, somewhere down the slope by the church or in the town or wading in the marshes, scouring them for any who had escaped. In that moment of certainty, she knew she didn't want to die, whatever pain it meant she had to endure. There was really only one thing she had wanted to ask him that morning when she left the jerry cans under the bush. It was all that had filled her mind last night, and now it burned within her anew. It didn't matter who he had killed or what he did with Delphine. It was the only thing she wanted to know. One day, she would find him and demand the answer from him. She knew he couldn't lie to her. She would know the truth. Then she would be free. The desire to live pulsed through her like a wave surging through her veins. It lifted her spirits, gave her reason to fight, to survive.

With it came hatred, a jolt so strong she thought the Hutus would see her moving. She saw Malabanda's face close to hers, his eyes large behind the lenses, gloating at his triumph over her people. And over her. She could still feel him inside her, polluting her, eating away at her, but she would not let him win. She would get her revenge, a reason itself to keep fighting for her life.

The dull thud of metal on bone sounded close by and

Liliane tensed. The Hutus were back, checking again for survivors.

"Hack them. Then hack them again. Make no mistakes."

That had been Gatsinzi's instructions, but it was hard to believe anyone else in the field still lived. They were only a few feet away now, and one of them bent close, the stale smell of urwagwa in her nostrils, his rough hands on her breasts.

"Pity the priest did her. I always fancied this one." His hands were still on her chest, and she was sure he would feel the thump of her heart or her flesh prickling under his touch.

The other laughed. "They've kept a lot of the Tutsi girls alive for us to play with. Come on, we don't want to miss out." She heard them among the bodies and the occasional, inevitable thud, but soon they were gone, and it was silent and still again on the hillside.

The hot afternoon air burned her throat when she breathed, flies buzzed on her skin and fed on her wounds, and a great stench settled over the field as the bodies roasted in the heat. Tiredness swept through Liliane. She felt her grip on life weaken and wondered if she was already in Hell, in the place that Malabanda had told them was reserved for Tutsi Inyenzi. That was where she belonged after what she had done, for condemning her family to death. Sister Maria had taught them that the only way to Heaven was through redemption of their sins. That meant she had to live to have that chance to redeem herself for what she had done. Malabanda had caused all this, and she wanted to make him pay. First, she had to win the fight against the slow death clawing at her. She had to move from this place if she was to survive.

She moved a hand to her face, inch-by-inch, waiting for the shout, for someone to come running, for a blade to be raised. Blood had pooled and thickened over her face, baked hard under the sun, and she had to rub and pick at it until she could feel the strength of the sun once more on her eyelids. The light was too strong at first, but when she looked, it was as if she was already in Hell. Bodies, twisted and tangled, heaped across each other, spread across the slope all the way to the town. As the sun slipped behind the far hills, the shadow of the church lengthened and enveloped the Tutsis. Even in death, they could not escape the church's reach.

She heard the savannah grass at the edge of the trees rustle and felt the evening breeze from the lake lift the heavy blanket of heat. It carried laughter and music up the hill from the town, the sounds of Hutus celebrating. The bars would be full, and Liliane imagined them telling stories of their bravery. They had boasted that everything would be theirs once the Tutsis had gone, and tears pricked her eyes as she thought of a Hutu family in her home, of a girl choosing her room, picking through her possessions.

As the day's heat faded with the strengthening breeze, flies flitted around her head and throat. Hesitant at first, Liliane moved her hand to the side of her head; she had to know, to feel the damage Malabanda had done to her. With her breath held and eyes screwed tight, she braced herself for what she would find, but as her fingers traced the line of ruptured flesh from below her ear to where her nipple should have been, she moaned in shock and then anguish, heedless of whether she would be heard. She let her hand fall beside her, too distressed and frightened to explore the wound on her head, too fearful to know lest it sap her morale further and weaken her resolve to fight.

Her grip on life was getting weaker, and the enormity of her challenge, not just to live but also to escape, pressed down on her. The Hutus would be everywhere, with the Interahamwe determined to eradicate every last Tutsi from the land. It seemed hopeless as the last of the sun slipped behind the hill and darkness crept into the field. Noises from town grew louder, gunshots and cheers, the sounds of raucous drinking. Every so often, a scream, frantic, demented, would pierce through the commotion. Somewhere, a building was on fire, and ragged flames licked at the night sky.

Even though it was cooler, Liliane felt like the sun still scorched her bare skin. While she drifted in and out of consciousness, her mind raced uncontrollably over the images of the day. Deep into the night, when even a chill breeze was unable to check the raging heat inside her, she felt sure that someone was watching her. She turned her head towards the slope where the Tutsis lay. He was standing as she had last seen him, stiff-backed, dignified. Uncle OK had come to be with her, to see her through the night. He came closer, and in his presence, she felt the intensity of the heat inside her lessen. He bent over, his face close to hers. "Stay alive, Liliane. Bring us justice," she thought she heard him say, but his voice was so low and soft that it might have been the whisper of the breeze in the grass. Then he was gone. For a long time, she stared at where she had thought he stood and willed him to come back, but nothing moved except the rats and some foraging pigs rooting amongst the bodies. A desperate loneliness settled on her.

Time no longer mattered. The sounds from the town ebbed and flowed, and then even they faded to leave the dead in silence at last. Her body shook with fever, and she clung on to life. She wanted Uncle OK to come back and tell her what he meant, how she was supposed to fulfil his demand, but he was just a shade in another place now, like the thousands who lay around her. She was still alive, and the night hadn't yet taken her. Even if the whites weren't there to witness the slaughter, she had seen it, and every image would be burned into her soul forever.

By the time dawn began to lighten the sky over the

mountains, slowly, inexorably drawing in the new day, Liliane's body had cooled and her head felt clearer. She had to move, or they would find her. She clenched her jaws and with slow, painful movements, twisted onto her side, then onto her front and pushed herself into a kneeling position. Blood seeped down her neck from the wound, and she rested, afraid that it would drain the last of the life out of her.

The long stalks of savannah grass grew at the top of the slope in front of the woods. From there, it wasn't far to the rough track that led through the trees and down past the lake to the far side of the valley. For now, though, just the small distance to reach the grass felt too far for her ravaged body. She tried to move, to crawl, but her vision exploded in a shower of sparks, and she fell forward, unconscious. Her breathing was shallow and painful when she came to, but she forced herself to crouch and shuffle her body forward until the blinding light returned, and she slumped down again.

The last vestiges of the night seemed to reach inside her and take the pain away. Her muscles relaxed, and her determination ebbed away. It was all too much. The temptation to sleep overwhelmed her until an animal scampered over her body, and the shock sent the pain crashing through her head and neck again. This was her last chance to reach a hiding place before the protection of darkness disappeared or she gave up and yielded to death. It was her fear of being found, of being abused again, which also spurred her on, and as pain gnawed at her wounds and the sun's first rays started to lighten the scene behind her, she dragged herself deep enough into the grass that she could not be seen. The first of the Hutus appeared down by the church, scavenging among the bodies, as she pulled the long grass around her.

TEN

The sun was high when Liliane came to. The tall, thick grass prevented her from being seen from the church grounds but offered no protection against the sun. Her naked body burned, her tongue had swollen, and her lips were cracked and desiccated. Shouts drifted up the hill. She parted the nearest stalks and saw women and children walk among the dead. With wicker baskets slung over their shoulders, they picked away at the bodies, flinging what they took into them as if harvesting leaves from the bushes in the valley. Even in death, they continued to defile the Tutsis. The men's task was more brutal, to look for any sign of life in the mass of bodies. She watched as they kicked at the dead and hacked at them. There were more still alive than she had imagined, and the machetes rose and fell all morning. Down by the church, the men from the Interahamwe stood and watched.

"Leave none alive," the Burgomaster had told them. It had only been yesterday.

She let the grass fall back and lowered her face to the

ground, shattered by the ferocity of the devastation laid bare in front of her. The church was a small island within a black sea whose waves lapped at its doors. How had the people of Kitabuye let it come to this?

She grieved anew for her parents and Bernard, not knowing whether they were lying close by her or had fallen in their home. Her rage at Malabanda and her revulsion at what Father had forced on her had erupted so suddenly, so uncontrollably, when her fingers found the cross on the shelf. Her unrestrained fury had also condemned her family to death. Just as her tears soaked into the earth, Liliane's resolve to live, to bring justice and vengeance, also ebbed away.

The heat from the sun was now at its worst, and there was nowhere to hide from it. She felt she would be dust herself if she spent another day in its unremitting glare. The prospect filled her with dread, but she knew she had to move. She just didn't know where to go or even if she could walk.

"Life is just one step after the other, Liliane," Uncle OK had once said to her. He had always been there for her. Now he was gone and loneliness enveloped her. She felt like the last Tutsi alive.

Stones and roots tore at her skin as she crawled further into the woods, but when the trees were close enough together, and she knew she wouldn't be seen from the field, she decided to stand and clawed herself upright against the rough trunk of an old cedar. The toxic stench from the field hadn't penetrated so far into the woods, and she sucked the clean air in gulps until she was dizzy. When her head was clear, she focused on the next tree and pushed herself towards it until she could clasp her arms around it, desperate to move further away from the shouts that carried in the still, hot air.

The gash in her neck had torn again as she crawled. She hoped the Hutus were too busy or still too drunk to notice the blood now smeared up the sides of the trees like the trail of a wounded animal. But with each tree she reached, her confidence grew, her breathing became easier, and strength returned to her legs. Yet, despite her relief at getting further away from the shadow that lay around the church, each step made her more aware of her nakedness, and she felt ashamed and vulnerable.

She lost count of the number of trees that she passed, but when at last all she could hear was the birds above her, she stopped to get her bearings. There was a track to the right that would lead to the far end of the lake, and although the Hutus would be searching the marshes, she knew she had to drink soon or die. It would take her a few hours at this pace to reach the water. After that, her choices were limited. In one direction were the mountains and forests, but straight ahead, past the lake, were the savannah plains and then more valleys of terraced hills. There would be danger everywhere, but she had no choice; she knew she was too weak for the mountains. At least she might find food and shelter if she walked past the lake and into the plains.

Her body had benefited from the rest, and she forced herself to walk without stumbling from tree to tree until, wading through a denser patch of ferns, she tripped over a hard object on the ground, fell against a tree and collapsed onto the damp earth. Her body protested at the shock of the fall, and blood coursed down her head and neck once more.

She lay still for a while, angry with herself, then stood and parted the grass around her. The verdant foliage hid the body of a young woman, the violence of her death captured in her features. Liliane knelt down beside her, and a cloud of flies rose up from the girl's wounds as she pushed at the body. She saw the girl was a similar age and size as she heaved her onto her back and, after a pause, began to undo the buttons down the front of the dress. It was brown with white flowers, but down one side, these had now turned a deep crimson. The effort of wrestling the dress off the girl tired Liliane, and she continued to kneel while buttoning it on herself. She placed her hand on the naked girl. "I'm sorry," she whispered. "Forgive me." She nearly said a prayer for the girl but remembered Uncle OK's words the day before. It would be a long time before God would come back to their country.

Just beyond the ferns lay the track, and in the shadow of a

mahogany tree she watched and listened until she was sure it was safe. Shaded by the canopy of the trees overhead, the wet ground was soft under her bare feet, and her progress became quicker. Birds whistled and shrieked, and in the peace and tranquillity of the woods, it was impossible to believe that the country was in the grip of madness and evil. She passed through a grove of avocado plants heavy with ripe fruit. There was no one left to pick them anymore, and birds fluttered in and out of the branches, feasting until they could barely fly. The path, usually busy with travellers and fruit pickers, was desolate and eerie. Frequently, Liliane would hear rustling in the trees or in the tangled vegetation that was now beginning to grow across the path, but each time she stopped to listen no one ever appeared, and she would carry on with her journey.

As the sun reached its full height, the humidity rose, her steps slowed and her doubts multiplied. She couldn't remember how far it still was to the lake, and the further she went, the less sure she became of what to do next. Her spirits had reached their lowest when she glimpsed a flash of water through the trees. At the edge of the tree line she parted some branches. The dirt track that ran along the edge of the lake had grown narrower as grass encroached over it. A rumble rolled along the lakeshore, and Liliane shrank back into the undergrowth as a line of lorries came closer, trailing a cloud of dust that spread across the water's edge. They passed in a flash of olive-green canvas, men braced in the open end of each one, guns cradled in their arms. More Interahamwe, she thought, and the hope that had given strength to her legs at the arrival at the lake ebbed away, and her limbs felt heavy again. They were chasing down every last Tutsi, emptying the land of her kind. They would surely find her soon.

The dust settled and silence returned to the lakeshore. Whatever her future might be, she needed to drink. She parted the branches again and stepped through onto the track. There were many signs of death but no life. Bodies lay in the dust in each direction, some still holding bundles of clothing or clutching a small child. The vegetation had flourished with the rains, and strands of it were already clutching at the bodies. The water was calm and peaceful, the antithesis of the storm of violence that had passed through the surrounding villages. There was too much death, too little life left. The earth track was hard and rutted after the springy floor of the forest, and Liliane stumbled across and down the slope until she was able to sink onto her knees at the edge of the still water. In a spot where no reeds grew, she bent low and drank greedily, but the cool draught was too much too fast, and she had to kneel back on her haunches, wracked by a coughing fit which seemed to hurt every part of her.

Black shapes bobbed in the water. When one came closer, borne by the current, she realised they were bodies, bloated and distended. Moving further up the shore to avoid them, Liliane unbuttoned her dress and lowered herself into the water. The shock of the cold made her wince, but for a while the sting of it masked the pain while she bathed her cuts and bruises. The scar that ran down her neck to her chest was an ugly, congealed scab, but after so much bleeding, she was gladdened by the sight of it and kept it well out of the water. She heard more vehicles in the distance when she stood and waded to the shore. The cloud of dust was smaller this time, and from the safety of a bank of reeds, she saw three jeeps flash by.

When it was quiet again, she lay in the short grass and let the sun and the breeze off the lake dry her until the shadows shifted and lengthened. She eased the dress over her stiffening limbs and started the long trek on the track away from Kitabuye. At the end of the lake, in the protection of some trees, she found a clump of banana plants and gorged on the ripe fruit. Ahead stretched a flat expanse of grass and fields, and on either side, the hills with their familiar terraces of red and green rose above. Closer to her, a ribbon of metalled road cut between the fields.

The food had revived her strength if not her spirits, and she set off across the empty landscape. No smoke drifted from the deserted cabins and straw huts that she passed, and the livestock had all gone, looted by the Hutus. Nothing stirred except the breeze that rustled and flattened the long grass and butterflies that hovered above the meadow flowers. She had no destination, nothing to aim for and as her desire to survive ebbed again Uncle OK's words seemed now to be just what they were: a dream. It was becoming too hard to live. She could have coped with death if she had her family or Patrick with her, but out here, in the emptiness and isolation of a land that had been drained of life, death would be lonely.

As she got closer to the road, she saw a roadblock, thin tree trunks balanced on plastic beer crates and manned by a group of men who lounged in the road or on the grass. Empty bottles were scattered around them. They seemed bored and listless. A lone Tutsi woman would be a gift to them. Her skin crawled at the thought. She stopped near some abandoned huts and scanned the horizon for a route past them. With no alternative in sight other than to retrace her steps, she walked on and crouched low in some longer stalks of grass to wait for nightfall.

A jeep arrived at the roadblock and a soldier jumped out. The men, dressed in ragged shorts and tee shirts, stood and picked up their machetes and clubs. They were a rabble but still dangerous and eager to please an Interahamwe with a gun, which was pointed towards where she was hiding. The men fanned out from the road and, in a desultory fashion, slashed at the long grass with their weapons, all the time coming closer to her. Her hiding place was exposed but the nearest huts were too far away, and she would be visible trying to reach them. Her foot kicked against a log hidden under the grass. The underneath had rotted and created a hollow, and she tore at the edges to make a space big enough to hide in. It was all she had time to do.

When she next parted the stalks, the men had spread out across the grassland and were closer. Her only hope was that their lethargic search, despite the watchful eye of the Interahamwe officer, would miss her. She lay flat and tried to squeeze herself into as much of the hollow as she could. A blade slashed at the grass a few feet in front of the log. She heard the man's heavy breathing from the exertion and smelled the odour of sweat and beer. His blade thudded on the wood, and the force jarred her wounds. He must be able to see her, but she would be just another body to him, she hoped.

A shout came from over by the roadblock, and the jeep's engine roared. The blade stopped moving, and the man was still while the sound of the vehicle faded. He sighed and muttered an oath, then Liliane heard the grass part as he made his way back to the road. She waited a few minutes until it was quiet around her, then disengaged herself from the hiding place. The grass had been flattened around the log, and she saw the men were now back at the makeshift roadblock.

The zeal of the Interahamwe for eradicating Tutsis was not replicated by the ordinary Hutus. This group seemed to just want to be left in peace to sit and drink beer. "Hutus are born to be lazy," Father would say, and the words tugged at Liliane's emotions as she lay in the grass to recover, her nerves shredded by the thought of what they would have done to her. She would have to wait until dark. Realising that this would be just the first of many such lookouts deepened her sense of hopelessness that there was nowhere to go.

She had to rest and sleep before attempting to cross the road, and when the light faded, she crawled back to the nearby village. The Hutus had torched it after slaughtering the inhabitants, but one of the huts was still largely intact. Its straw walls contained only one room. The sky was visible through gaps in the roof where fire had eaten away at it, but it gave her enough shelter, and there was a stained mattress to lie on.

It was dark when she woke and silent except for the buzzing of insects and the yells of hyenas out in the woods. Her limbs were stiff from the cold and bruises, but it was the pain in her head that had woken her. The wound was matted and rough with dried blood, and her temperature was high again. It was the damage beneath the wound that scared her. The embers of a fire still glowed in the distance, but otherwise, there was no sign of life at the roadblock. The outline of the hills was just visible, and a cockatoo started up a racket in the nearby trees. Dawn was closer than she thought, and it would soon be too late.

Vegetation had encroached over everything, but it gave her plenty of cover as far as the road. She parted the grass and stepped out, her eyes on the area where the men were. A shadow moved across the remains of the fire. It was still too dark to be seen, so she hurried across and into the undergrowth. By the time she reached the shelter of some trees, it was light enough to see a few men at the makeshift barrier. A line of lorries approached, and while the Hutus were occupied, Liliane hurried further into the woods.

A bit further on, the ground dipped and a pocket of mist hung in the valley beyond. She sat and rested and, as the sun's strength increased, watched the mist melt away to reveal a tea plantation. With no one to pick them, the plants had sprouted in the rains into wild thickets and spread over the gaps between them. The silence was disquieting, and she shuddered at the emptiness of the land. She didn't recognise this valley but knew there would be a village nearby for the workers. She had to find water soon, and food.

The track descended into the valley and over the tops of the trees, she could see the roofs of the plantation buildings. The storerooms and offices were abandoned, and the big metal doors of the warehouse lay flat, almost covered in weed and scrub. A rank smell hit her as she reached the workers' huts.

She stopped and listened to an unfamiliar noise that came from behind the furthest shelter. As she got closer a thick, dark cloud of insects rose out of the undergrowth. The dense, spreading grasses and bushes were reclaiming the village and its inhabitants.

She hurried as fast as she could through the village and sank down by a stream that flowed from the woods and under the dirt track. Holding her mouth under the cool water, she drank and washed the taste of death from her throat. Her pace slowed after that, and as the pain in her head worsened, the slower her progress became. She foraged berries and fruit, found water where she could and hid frequently to avoid Hutus who still scoured the land.

Although time meant nothing anymore, on what she thought was her third morning, she came to another road, bigger and busier. Now well-practised, she lay in the grass while a convoy of lorries drove past. They were battered and dirty, and there were small, round holes in the canvas of one of them. Just as she was about to cross, two large vehicles, bigger than jeeps, came along the road. Nothing seemed unusual about them, more Interahamwe, she assumed. She eased herself down into the grass and waited in her familiar death pose. The vehicles stopped close to where she lay and the engines died. Doors opened and boots crunched in the dry earth and stones at the edge of the road.

ELEVEN

There seemed to be only one of them on Liliane's side of the vehicles, although she could hear the murmur of voices further off. His boots, brown and scuffed, were only a few feet from her head, and she felt the spray from his urine spatter the back of her neck. His breathing was low and steady, and the smell of tobacco was strong around him. He struck a match, took a long, deep pull on a cigarette, then sighed. It reminded her so much of Father, who would stand in the yard in the early morning, the smoke curling through her window, his satisfaction evident in the studied intensity of his silence.

"Feel better now?"

Even in her confused and delirious state, Liliane knew the words were English, even though she had only ever heard Anna speak it.

"Nearly. God, I needed a smoke after the last village we came through. The stink." He struck another match, and the two men stood silently while the smoker concentrated. It was

English, but it didn't seem possible that the UN had come back with so many Interahamwe still around.

"We should get going, Frank." It was the non-smoker, a younger, excited voice. "This place gives me the creeps."

"Wait till we get to Kitabuye, man. If the stories are true, you'll want to be back here in the clean air. They say it's worse than anything we've seen so far." They lapsed into silence for a while.

"Do you think they are? The stories…"

"This isn't like anything I've seen before in Africa, Nick. That's why we're here. It's like a sickness has taken hold of the whole country."

He flicked his cigarette to the ground. It landed close to Liliane's face, and the smoke drifted into her nostrils. Her fingernails dug into the earth, and she gritted her teeth.

"They reckon it was at the church, don't they?"

Her throat burned and the pressure built in her head.

"Obvious place to gather them, I suppose."

She pressed her face into the grass and held her breath.

"It wouldn't be the first time we've heard of that happening."

The pressure became too great, and Liliane's cough seemed to hang for a long time in the silence of the bush.

"Shit, there's someone out there." It was the younger one, the confidence gone. Boots came closer.

"Frank, don't. It's not safe."

The smell of smoke and sweat was stronger as he parted the grass around her head and placed his fingers on the side of her neck. She was sure he must be able to hear her heart, not just feel its beat.

"We won't hurt you." His French was poor, but she understood him. "Come and help me, Nick. This girl's alive."

Strong hands gripped her and rolled her over. She opened her eyes, sure now that they weren't Interahamwe. They were white, although the older one's skin was brown and blemished from the sun. He had grey, wiry hair, and his wrinkled forehead and quizzical stare reminded her of Uncle OK. It was a kind face, she thought, and he was smiling and nodding as if to reassure her.

They weren't UN, nor even soldiers and there was too much concern and pity in their faces to be frightened of them. The one called Nick seemed embarrassed by her wounds as if he hadn't been close to any of the bodies yet, and he looked away as the other one ran his fingers over her scars. She had been just another dead body until the cigarette had landed close by.

"Nick, tell Joost to bring the medical bag. And the water," Frank called after Nick as he jogged back to the vehicles. He had a strange accent, so different to Anna's English. It reminded her of some of the whites who came to the plantation in the old days. She watched him as he examined her, how his eyes narrowed as he explored the injury on the side of her head and gritted his teeth as he followed the line of matted blood that ran down to her breast.

"You're safe now," he said as he looked into her eyes, and she forced a weak smile. She might be safe, but the fever was on her worse than ever, and her skin felt as if it would be too hot to be touched.

Nick returned with a green canvas bag, followed by two other white men who helped Frank to sit her up while Nick knelt beside her. "Have you found out where she's from, Frank?" He held a bottle to her lips. The cool water soaked into her parched mouth and throat like rain on dry ground.

Frank gave a slight shake of his head. "She's nearly dead, Nick." He sounded weary and angry at the younger one's enthusiasm. "Let's get her to the car and see what we can do for her." He stood and supervised the others as they lifted her out of the grass. "Joost, take a look at her," he said as they settled her in the back of one of the vehicles. Fingers probed her wounds again, and she felt warm liquid and soft cloth on her skin. His movements were quick and efficient, but he seemed unwilling to meet Liliane's gaze as if his eyes might betray what he could see.

"She needs proper medical care, Frank. Soon. You felt her. She's burning up." It was Joost who spoke. He had a way of talking that was different from Frank and Nick. She wondered who these strange men were and what they were doing in Rwanda at such a time while the one called Joost continued to swab her wounds.

Frank looked up at the sky. "If we get a move on, we can make the border by tonight. It's not far now to Kitabuye."

"No!" The cry escaped from Liliane's lips before she could stop it.

Joost pulled his hands away from tending her as if he had hurt her. "I'm sorry, my dear, I need to clean these."

You can't take me back there, she wanted to shout at them, but the words wouldn't come. All she could manage was to shake her head while the pressure built beneath the wound as if it would burst open.

Nick pushed in front of Joost and looked at her. "It wasn't you, Joost." His face was flushed. "She understood." He looked around at the others. "She knows where we're going. Look. She's scared." He bent low, his face close. "You're from Kitabuye?" She nodded. "Were you there? At the church?" He was excited. Another nod. "Don't be afraid of us. We want to help to find the truth." He turned to the open door. "She was there, Frank." She saw the look they exchanged, and it frightened her. They wanted something from her. Men always did. She felt vulnerable and powerless despite their sympathy and attentiveness.

"Guys, we have to go." It was the fourth man. His voice was strident. "What are you doing with her?" They all withdrew from the car, and she could hear them arguing in the road, arguing about her.

"We can't take her. She's half dead, man." One of the others shushed the speaker.

"Frank?" It was Nick. "She was there. She survived. She could be a witness for the work. Think about it. Plus, we can't just leave her to die. Not now we've started to help her. It would be like us killing her now. Let's make it one less death." His words were urgent.

"It's getting late, guys. We'll be out in the bush in the dark if we don't move." The voice was insistent.

"Frank?" It was Nick again. They were silent for a while after that. It seemed like Frank was their leader. Liliane waited. She would have to see the shadow around the church again.

"Joost, sedate her." It was Frank, his voice strained as if he sensed his decision was life or death for Liliane. "We'll need two hours there at least. Maybe more. We can leave her in Kitabuye with the RPF. Nick, sit with her. Let's go."

The decision seemed to galvanise the men and they hurried to get into the cars. Nick eased himself beside Liliane and edged close to her. She could feel his warmth through her dress, and it comforted her. Something in the way he looked at her reminded her of Patrick, who, as she grew into a woman, would stare at her as if he couldn't believe what she had become.

When the engines started, she glanced up and noticed the driver for the first time. He was Black but not a Rwandan, maybe from Uganda. She caught his glance in the mirror, and his eyes narrowed, whether in pity or acknowledgement, she couldn't tell, but he continued to stare. She felt uneasy as if he was trying to tell her something, warn her maybe.

The door next to her opened and Joost was at her side with the green bag. He fiddled with a needle, rubbed her arm and pressed it into her in one smooth movement. The door slammed and she felt the vehicle move as warmth embraced her and darkness washed over her. No pain, no fear; this must be what they meant to be safe, she thought as she lost consciousness.

When her eyes next flicked open, the sun was too bright, and she had to close them again. She thought she had been with her family, but then it might have been Alice and Kenzi, and she was sure Uncle OK had been there at some point. And Patrick. But as her head cleared, she felt lonely and frightened. She was in a strange vehicle, and she wondered why she was alone.

Blurred shapes moved nearby through the car window, but she could hear no sound and a great black shadow lay over the land despite the sun's brightness. This confused her, and she concentrated hard to clear the fog in her head. She saw a white man with golden hair. It was damp and plastered to his skull, his skin deathly pale, and when he wasn't holding a white cloth to his mouth and nose, he spoke into a camera held by another man. Two more white men came out of a building of red brick, stepping carefully, as if they might trip over the shadow that seemed to be all around them as well. But it was the smell, thick and rank, that lined her throat and reached deep inside her. It was a smell she knew, the smell of death. It was the smell of her people as they melted into the ground.

The men had promised her safety, but all they had done was to bring her back to Kitabuye. As she looked around, she felt as if she had descended into hell again, for surely that was what Kitabuye had become. From the bottom of the hill where the vehicle was parked, the shadow seemed bigger than when she had lain here, the bodies still heaped across the grass, frozen in the agony of their death. She wanted to close her eyes and shut out the sight but forced herself to look. The church and its grounds had become a crucible of hatred—great evil had been done here. She knew she had to confront her fear and look, to remember every detail: the shattered skulls and twisted, broken limbs, already more bone than flesh. She felt Uncle OK's presence again, heard his words in the night and knew it was important to remember this sight and how it had happened.

While the men moved around and recorded with their machines, Liliane committed the scene to her own memory until, at last, the sun lowered, and the shadow of the church once more fell on the Tutsis. The white men then hurried to their vehicles and loaded their bags. Only then did she rest her head back against the seat and allow her eyes to close. She would bury the sights and smells and memories deep inside her, somewhere no one could find them. Until she was ready.

TWELVE

There was too much activity around the vehicle for Liliane to rest, and in any case, the wound on her head pulsed, not with pain, dulled as it was by the white man's needle, but with rage. Her family, her friends and neighbours had been reduced to this vile stench that was almost visible above the tangled mass of bodies. The white men continued to cough and retch as they continued their work. At that moment, it wasn't justice that she wanted, it was vengeance. She wanted to make Malabanda and Gatsinzi pay for what they had done. It was these feelings that had, she knew, sustained her while she lay further up the hill. At various times in the last few days, she had felt angry, even ashamed, that she had survived. Now that she had been brought back and seen the true awfulness of what those men had done, she knew why she had lived.

She would make Malabanda pay for this.

A figure stumbled out of the church and headed to the car. She recognised him as Nick behind the cloth over his face. He looked so young and vulnerable among the carnage. Who were these men who had risked their lives to come here, who showed such outrage and compassion for her people? They had tended her wounds and seemed intent on saving her when she was just one woman out of a whole race.

The vehicle rocked as doors opened and equipment was loaded behind her, and as the hot air rolled inside, her stomach churned, and she had to grit her teeth and screw her face tight while the men coughed behind her. They gathered at the back of the car and seemed to be waiting for something to happen. The shadows were lengthening, and Liliane sensed their anxiety that darkness would come quickly.

"That took longer than we thought," she heard one of them say.

"It was worse than we imagined," another said, the voice shaking with emotion.

"You can't imagine this."

"We got what we came for, and no one else is close to getting this stuff. We'll screen in a couple of weeks if all goes well," Nick said.

"How can you care about that, man? Just look at all this. It's inhuman." It was the man called Piet. They were silent again as if trying to absorb the sights of a century of hatred unleashed in just a few hours of brutality.

"Jeez, where's Frank?" Joost's voice was tight. "It's getting dark. We'll have to stay."

"No fucking way, man. Here?"

"I'd rather sleep with ghosts than run into Interahamwe thugs in the dark." Joost snapped back. "Look, here he is now."

"The RPF commander thinks we should stay." Frank seemed uncertain as he spoke.

"Not here, Frank. For God's sake."

"God?" Piet said. "Don't think he stuck around to find out."

"The country isn't secure yet. You all know that. We took a risk to be the first ones in."

They didn't seem to know what to do until Nick broke the silence. "What about her? She was here, Frank. She saw it all."

"She's ill, Nick. We haven't got what she needs. Best leave her with the RPF. She's one of them, after all."

"But if we go now, she's still got a chance. She'll die if we leave her. They haven't got the resources. They trashed their own hospital—ransacked everything. You can see that. Frank, think of it. An eyewitness. It would make it even more powerful."

"She could be dead by the border anyway, Nick. She's burning up in here." She felt Joost's hand on her forehead.

"Frank?" Nick again. "Look, none of our lot hung around to stop it or even observe. She was attacked and survived. She's a witness, Frank. We can bring someone to justice if we take her and she lives. She must know who started it; give us names."

Whoever they were, they wanted justice, just like Uncle OK. And Liliane could help them. She didn't want to die in the bush in the back of this car. The time to die had been in the field with her people, but she had felt Uncle OK's presence, which had motivated her to survive. She would continue to fight now to live and one day come back, she was sure. Then there would be a reckoning. There would be justice. And vengeance.

"We go. We'll make it. Jammy, Amin, get us out of here." Frank's voice was firm, and the rest responded.

Liliane tensed as the engine roared and laboured up the broken-down road out of town. She winced as the jeep bounced in and out of holes and Nick took her hand. It was soft, unlike Patrick's coarse, rough skin, yet it was strong, and she felt reassured at his touch. She kept her eyes shut, and he made no attempt to talk but dabbed her face and neck frequently with a damp cloth.

She wanted to stay awake, fearful that she would never wake again if she allowed the drugs to claim her now, even if by doing so, the scars she could feel inside her were as painful as the wounds on her body. It was while she was fighting the fingers of drowsiness that were pulling her down into the darkness that the awful realisation came to her. The RPF must have got to Kitabuye soon after the slaughter of the Tutsis. Just a few days more and they would have been safe. Malabanda and Gatsinzi would have been taken, her family would be alive, and Patrick would still be hers, freed from the dreadful choices he had been forced to make.

***

The two vehicles drove on through the hills and forests while the night wrapped itself around them, pierced only by the light from the headlights that was swallowed after a few yards. After a long drive, the lead vehicle stopped, and the change in tempo broke Liliane's uneasy stupor. She watched as Frank jogged back from the leading vehicle, then closed her eyes again. She didn't know what being a witness meant, but she didn't want to be bothered by any more of their questions. Let them think the medicine still had her in its grip. Nick got out to speak, his door still open, the engine running.

"How is she?" Frank asked.

"I think she's slipping away, Frank." He sounded upset. "How far now?"

"Another stretch of forest, then it's the border. There's a medical centre been set up. We can leave her there, then go on to Kigali." Frank paused. "She might be better off dead. How can she live with the memory of this?"

"We need her, Frank."

"It's not just about the story, Nick!" He sounded angry. "Poor girl. Look what she's been through."

"But she's our witness. For justice as well," he added.

"Justice?" Frank laughed. He sounded bitter and tired. "Since when did that ever come to Africa?

Nick settled back into his seat and the fever tightened its grip on Liliane; her chest was sore, her breathing rattled, and she slipped into a fitful sleep until the sudden braking of the vehicle jolted her awake again.

Her vehicle was in the lead now, and from the headlights, she saw a roadblock ahead where a group of men in ragged clothes stood behind a barrier of logs. Their fire cast shapeless shadows which danced and flitted in the trees on either side of the road.

"Jammy, come with me." Frank wrenched the driver's door open, shouted in, then turned back towards the blockade. Jammy's shoulders dropped. His hands gripped the wheel, but Frank waved him forward, an urgent gesture that reflected the fear Liliane could see in his face. Slowly, Jammy slid out of his seat and followed. Piet stood by Nick's door. Sparks flew up from the flames and fireflies flitted around the glow, but beyond the shadows, the rest of the forest was invisible. It was the danger the RPF commander had warned against.

Everyone was silent as they watched Frank talk to the men,

Jammy translating for him. They didn't seem to be Interahamwe, but their guns were the only authority they needed out in the forest. The country appeared to be lawless now, and it occurred to Liliane that another civil war must have broken out if the RPF had got so far. When the flames flared higher, for a moment, she saw crates full of bottles that must have been looted from a nearby bar. The white men had told her she was safe, yet here they all were, surrounded by a dozen or more armed men. She knew what a prize she would be for them and wondered if the white men realised that she would be worth more to them if they traded her for their safety rather than retaining her as a witness. They seemed to care about her survival, but what if they had no choice? What would they do? She closed her eyes and concentrated on what was happening.

"Don't think they're Interahamwe, just a rabble," said Joost, but no one answered, their attention on the apparent leader who gesticulated and grew more agitated the longer the conversation went on. Jammy was doing all the talking now. The leader waved his arm again and a few of his men stepped over the barrier.

"This is trouble." Piet's voice was tight with the tension. "We'll need to give them cigarettes or whisky to make them go away."

"Not whisky," said Joost. "They're already pissed."

"I've got the money here," said Nick. The large camera they had used to film him in Kitabuye was on his lap, and he cradled it like a child. Liliane watched him finger some buttons and saw the side open to reveal a slim, plastic box inside. He took it out, stared at it, then slipped it back in and pressed the side shut. "Give them anything except the camera."

"They'll shoot us and take it all anyway."

"Fuck you, Piet." Joost piled some cartons of cigarettes on the front seat. Frank and Jammy walked back, surrounded by the rabble.

"They want to search the vehicles. Just show them what they want. Give them the cigarettes. They're all high, and they've been drinking."

"What about her?"

"Jammy told them she's sick with AIDS. That's one thing they seem to know they can't beat."

At that moment, Liliane's door opened and one of the Hutus leaned in. She felt hot breath on her neck and the sweet odour of khat mixed with beer. He shook her, his words slurred as he demanded she wake up. In the commotion that followed, Nick protested, but Jammy's shout persuaded the man to leave her alone.

"Easy, Jammy," Frank cautioned as their driver continued to remonstrate.

"I told them it's on her skin, boss," Jammy replied.

Behind her, the back door of the car was opened, and Piet groaned. "Shit, they've found the whisky."

She heard the seals on the bottles break and the sound of greedy drinking. She felt Nick's hand on her leg, and she placed hers on top of his to reassure him she was still with them. He was shaking, but she felt glad to have his touch on her.

"Give them some dollars, Nick." Frank was at the door. There was an urgency in his voice that she hadn't heard before.

Liliane dared to open her eyes while the Hutus' attention was on the whisky. The fire flared brighter for a moment, but she didn't need to see the white men's faces; she could smell their fear. They were alone and unarmed. Another bottle was opened, and the men cheered. Now they were milling around the cars, jabbing their guns and shouting. Jammy came to Nick's door. "You have to get out, mister."

"What do they want, Jammy? There's nothing else to give." Nick clung to the camera, but when a gun poked in the door, he pushed it to the floor and squeezed his legs over it. "Watch that, Jammy. All our work's on that tape."

The white men lined up, their faces damp with fear, and for a moment, Liliane thought the Hutus were going to shoot them, but the rabble were just interested in what they could pilfer. They pulled bags from the rear of each one and ripped them open. They were just ignorant peasants in tattered rags, but they were drunk and had guns, so they were unstable and dangerous. They paused to drink from the bottles and passed them around while they piled the cartons of cigarettes in their camp and rooted through the holdalls.

The camera on the floor next to her was the only thing they hadn't yet found. They were reluctant to come near her, but she knew the whisky would soon embolden them to return to her door. She bent down and dragged it across between her feet, suppressing a cry when the side slid open. She ran her fingers across the top of the plastic box inside the slot. It seemed to be important in their work and maybe in their fight for justice. She heard hands scrabbling at her door and protests from the whites, but this time, they were ignored. She lowered her head again and waited. Hands rummaged on the floor in the dark until they found the camera and pulled it from between her legs. A ragged cheer broke out in the clearing. The man took a last, long look at Liliane, but the others called to him. They wanted to see the object the white men prized so highly.

"Shit. The camera." Liliane lifted her head and saw Frank and Joost restraining Nick while he twisted and contorted his body, his voice high-pitched. "It's got all the filming on it." He sounded close to tears. His reaction seemed to confirm to the Hutus that it was valuable, and he stood quietly while one of them turned it over in his hands. He called to Jammy and pointed at the camera and then to the whites.

Jammy turned to Frank. "They want the camera, then we can go." The flames flared behind them, and their shadows were long on the ground. "All that filming. All the evidence." Nick's distress seemed to please the Hutus even more.

She heard Frank's voice. "We can't tell a story if we're dead." He turned to Jammy. "Jammy, tell him it's very valuable and they can have it."

The driver translated. They then beckoned the men to get back into the cars. The Hutus lifted the logs out of the way as the engines started.

"Fuck me, Jammy. Get us out of here." It was Piet.

Nick slumped into his seat and groaned as he watched the men pass the camera around. "They don't even know what to do with the fucking thing." He was distraught at the loss of their work. He seemed to have forgotten about Liliane. She put her hand on his leg and when he turned to her, she slipped the plastic box into his hand.

London

1997

THIRTEEN

The tea plants stretched into the distance, the orderly rows curving along the gently undulating lines of the valley to where the hills rose again in terraces of lush vegetation, a scene of tranquillity. It seemed like a place where nothing bad could ever happen. Liliane stared at the picture on the end wall, as she had every day since she first came to The Equator, a small café in West London. It dominated the room, a vision of paradise, just like the pictures in the books she studied at night as she tried to remember the place she no longer belonged to. Every morning, she studied it, sure that she had stood somewhere just like this in her old life. Then she would turn away, unsatisfied, knowing that the memories of her past life were always just out of reach, no matter how long she looked at the wall.

The doctor said her mind would never be the same, that her memory might be gone for good. The operation to save her life, even without the injury to her head, was enough to wipe her memory out. But it couldn't be true, she told herself every morning. She still felt things inside her, the shapes of people she thought she knew or sudden lurches of emotion, of love or fear or pain. Occasionally, she had a sense that there was something she had to do, as if she had something unfinished in her life. Then, just when she thought her head would clear and she would see everything, the feelings would melt back into the fog in her mind and leave her with the same emptiness and lack of belonging.

"I can't even remember my own mother or whether I had brothers or sisters," Liliane had complained not long after she had left hospital.

"It might be for the best," Geraldine replied as she finished dressing the wound on Liliane's head. "It's better you don't know what happened. You can build a new life without the burden of the past."

Liliane pulled away from the woman's touch. "Knowing my family wouldn't be a burden." Her voice rose as she spoke, but Geraldine gently pushed her back onto the chair as if the outburst hadn't happened.

"I didn't mean them, my dear." She fell silent as she concentrated on wrapping a brightly coloured silk hijab around Liliane's head and neck. She was still learning the technique of assembling a garment that she had never come across before. Once satisfied with her efforts, she added, "I just meant…you know…what happened to you." She smoothed the silk on

Liliane's head and neck and added as she did, "Here and here." She patted the scars that were hidden now, along with Liliane's past. "I know you wish you knew more, Liliane. But you can't pick and choose what you'd like to remember." She cupped Liliane's face in her hands. "If it's still there, that is. You'd have to see all the bad things as well." She brushed Liliane's forehead with her lips. "Best that it stays hidden, like your wounds."

Nick's mother, Geraldine, had welcomed Liliane into her home as a favour to her son, treating her initially as a curiosity to be indulged, a good deed to increase her standing in the village. "We all have to do our bit for these poor people, don't we?" she had told the vicar when he came to see Liliane. It was when she had watched Nick's documentary and seen Liliane's wounds that the shadow of the genocide darkened the calm, organised world she inhabited behind the high walls and gates. After that, she accepted Liliane as her own daughter. And Liliane loved her in return, although not without a feeling of guilt as she wondered if her own mother, who they told her was dead, would resent her transferring her affection to another woman.

The ache in her head behind the wound was always with her, a constant, dull throb as ever-present as the low rumble of traffic that passed by the café at all hours. If any of her memories were still there, they seemed to be behind an impenetrable barrier in her mind. Everything she wanted to remember, everyone she knew, as well as the person she had once been, were on the other side. She put her hand to the silk that covered the ugly, red scar that disfigured her skull and massaged it, wishing she could piece her head, and her memory with it, back together. With a sigh of resignation, she stood, ready to face another day, grateful for the life that had been hers for three years now.

She heaved on the café door with a grunt of annoyance until it came free from the tight grip of the frame and the lobby filled with light, then stepped into the street. The old stone building, which was once a bank, now housed The Equator. It comforted her, and she felt anchored by its solidity and endurance. Mr Sentwali, the owner, had made her manager six months ago, and the job had been much harder than she had imagined, even though everyone told her she was a natural at it. But she was more confident now and felt at home and safe in a way that thrilled her still as if she had never felt this way before.

It was still early, but the clear sky cast a crisp light over the street, and after the rain, the buildings looked as if they had been washed and polished overnight. She breathed in the still, clean air and leaned against the stone pillar next to the frosted glass window. Berto, who owned a delicatessen over the road, was already out enjoying his early morning smoke and waved across the road at her. He pointed up at the sky and stuck a thumb up. A day like this meant good trade.

"Morning, boss." Adele interrupted the moment of peace. "Planning more pain for us today?" Liliane took a playful swipe at the girl and then led her inside.

"That bloody door will be all yours when I'm gone." Adele made a sad face and then set about her first job—to start the large coffee grinder. This was Liliane's favourite time of the day when the early customers would come and inhale the rich, fresh aroma of the Umushanana beans. Office cleaners on their way home would rub shoulders with the workers going to make them dirty again. The rituals of this strange but friendly country amused Liliane, and she liked to watch these people, who never spoke or mixed, sit and appreciate the taste of that first cup.

Isabelle and Zee arrived as Liliane filled the till tray from the sturdy safe in the office. They worked well as a team, all of them orphans and survivors of the genocide. Yet through the cruel vagaries of war, while the others, outwardly unblemished by the violence, tried to forget what they had seen and suffered, their scars hid deep inside them. Liliane couldn't remember even the smallest fragment of her past life and chose to hide the scars that disfigured her body beneath colourful silk.

They had become family to each other, and the three staff regarded Liliane as a mother figure to replace the families they had all lost. It now seemed more than three years since

Geraldine had pressed the advert for a waitress in a Rwandan coffee shop into Liliane's hand and persuaded her she was both well enough and capable of starting a life for herself. It was time to create new memories to fill the void left by the old ones. With much trepidation, she braved the Underground on her own and navigated her way to the café with the help of a battered A-Z. As soon as she arrived at the row of shops, she knew which one was The Equator. The gaudy red, yellow and green of the Rwandan flag on the door and windows were stark against the neat greys and prim pinks of the shops around it.

"A lot of the other shops objected to the colours at first," Sylvestre, the previous manager, told her on that first evening as she admired the façade. "But now they all feel sorry for us and come here for their lunch instead. The only one who spoke up for us was Berto, who runs the deli." Liliane didn't know what a deli was but had noticed a smart shop with cakes and pastries in the window over the road with his name over it. "His family were refugees from Italy after the war. They didn't have it easy either. You'll meet him."

Already feeling at home, Liliane had relaxed into a scuffed, saggy leather sofa and surveyed the place while Sylvestre made her a coffee. "Mr Sentwali, the owner, got everything cheap from a club that was closing down in Piccadilly," he shouted from a cloud of steam behind the high wooden counter. "Not very Rwandan, is it? But apparently, this sort of furniture's trendy around here, so people keep coming. And the coffee's exceptional, which is why we really want them to come. Here, try it." The mug was decorated in the same colours as the shop front. "It's a cappuccino," he explained as she stared at the foamy white cloud brimming over the top of the mug. "I'll show you how to make one." Liliane wrestled herself forward out of the low seat and sipped at the mug, exclaiming in surprise when the first hints of coffee seeped through the froth. "It's Mayaguez. Like it? And we've got Umushanana on next week as well, from a new co-operative in Gitarama. We're trying to support what little economy is still left in the old country."

The sun streamed through the two windows behind her that rose almost to the ceiling and bathed the café in a translucent early evening glow. "I love it. And all this." She waved a hand at the posters of wooded mountains and lakes on the walls. It was when she noticed the picture of a tea plantation on the end wall and looked away, feeling a sudden stab of anxiety in her stomach that was alien to her. And every day since, the feeling had grown that she had once lived somewhere like it. In the years that followed, the picture had become a comfort to her, an attachment to the beautiful country she had once lived in. Every morning before opening up, she would sit with a coffee and stare at it. She felt sure that if only she could step into the frame, she would be able to walk down the hill to the town that she was sure was there and that the secrets of her past would be revealed.

The day had again passed quickly in a blur of faces, clouds of steam and the din of conversations that filled the café all the way to the high ceiling. "We're going for a drink after work. Coming?" Adele asked while they put the takings in the safe.

"I'm meeting Geraldine. Cinema tonight." Adele rolled her eyes at the idea as they went back to the café. "I enjoy it. It's the cultural education Geraldine has decided I need before I can go to university in the autumn."

"We'll have more fun, though." Although Adele was coping better with the memories of the past than the others, Liliane was increasingly worried about Zee. Recently, he had been drinking more, and she imagined she would have to pick up the pieces the next morning.

She rapped a glass ashtray on the counter. "It's another record today," she announced. "That's the third this month." Mr Sentwali had promised them all a bonus if the takings continued to grow, and she smiled as she heard Isabelle and Zee chatter about what they would spend it on as they wiped tables and swept beneath them.

"Be careful what you wish for, Liliane," Adele said from behind her. Liliane's gaze, as it often did when it was quiet in the café, was on the picture on the far wall. She had once confided in Adele about how she hoped that the picture might jolt her memory and had been shocked at the emotion in the girl's reaction.

"You can't imagine what the three of us have to go through night after night. You suffer one night of my dreams, and then we'll see how keen you are to know it all." She sounded so like Geraldine at times. Adele's concern was partly selfish because Liliane's ignorance of the horrors the others had endured was the rock on which they were rebuilding their new lives. They needed things to stay that way.

Liliane gave her a quick hug of reassurance and chased them out of the café, secretly wishing she was going with them as they strolled down the street, arm in arm, their laughter rippling back to her. Looking at the clock, she rushed to her rooms to shower and dress up the way Geraldine expected her to. Isabelle had burned a tray of croissants at lunchtime, and she wrinkled her nose in distaste at the lingering smell, mixed with stale coffee and over-steamed milk, that clung to her clothes and skin.

It was after a shower, while she stared at the ugly scars that disfigured her head, neck and chest, that she recalled Adele's warning. In the mirror, she could see her books piled up in the next room, open at photographs of bodies, disfigured and heaped in contorted piles. Her fingers traced the contours of the cavity on the side of her head, and she tried to imagine again the blade slicing through her bone. What pain I must have endured, what terror must have convulsed me, she thought as she stared back at herself in the mirror. Her eyes were wide with fear and shock as if they had just seen again what they had witnessed once before. She relaxed her grip on the basin, stretched back and kicked the bathroom door shut. The books were beginning to get inside her head and gnaw away at her sensibilities. She must have witnessed such scenes in Kitabuye, where Nick told her she was from. Maybe she, too, had lain in a pile of bodies like in her books. She traced the scar on her neck with her fingertips and wondered again which wound she had suffered first and how she had survived even one of them.

Geraldine and Adele were right; no good could come from knowing. She turned away from the mirror with the familiar unease that always gripped her when she scrutinised her scars like this. The memory of what had happened was still somewhere inside her, she was sure. If it came back, it would change her comfortable life forever.

FOURTEEN

The front of the café was bathed in evening sun as Liliane leaned against one of the window ledges and waited for her bus. The warmth of the breeze felt fresh on her face after the heat and steam of the café. She realised her bus must be stuck somewhere back in the stationary traffic, giving her a chance to draw breath and enjoy the ordinariness of the world around her. She watched the passers-by, preoccupied with their own thoughts, their lives lived to the full without the fear and repression that had blighted her own country. At times like this, still feeling like an intruder into these people's lives, she wondered if they too could be coerced, threatened and frightened into turning on each other in the same way she had read about her own people. Sometimes, she tried to imagine how her customers would react if she failed to don her hijab one morning and let them witness the reality of why The Equator was a refuge for the people who served them.

Then the traffic became unblocked further down the road, her bus trundled into sight, and Liliane lost herself in her science book.

***

"Liliane, you'll never guess." There was an edge to Geraldine's voice despite the affectionate kisses and a flash of anxiety in her eyes. "Nick's going to join us for a drink. He was nearby. Just for one," she added rather too quickly while she scanned Liliane's face and, seeing no response, leaned forward to pat her hand. In Geraldine's world, this always made everything all right. Then, as if it had been carefully choreographed, Nick was at the table and flopped onto the sofa next to his mother, his eyes fixed on Liliane's as he leaned over to kiss Geraldine's proffered cheek.

"Hi, Liliane, you look great,' he said with a brief wave of his hand and a flash of the smile she remembered from her first few months living at his parents' house. It was a smile that had made her feel like she was the only person that mattered to him. "Lovely scarf," he added, and the smile broadened, inviting Liliane to join him in the joke.

"It's a hijab, Nick, as you well know, considering where you've just been," Geraldine chided him. Geraldine never seemed to understand her son's gentle mocking of her or chose to ignore it. Liliane had never known which it was but flashed a complicit smile at Nick as Geraldine rose to the bait. She was proud of the silk-patterned garments she had specially made for Liliane. "I suppose all the women wear these where you come from," she had said when she first unwrapped some, but Liliane had still never seen anyone dressed like her in the books she looked at.

Nick's hair was longer than Liliane remembered, bleached a pale gold, his skin burnished by long days in the sun, and he had the unkempt, lived-in look of someone who had not needed to bother about his appearance for a long time. The look suited him, she thought as she told him how good it was to see him and added, for Geraldine's benefit, "It's been too long." There was a maturity about him now, some inner confidence that he had acquired in the few years since she had last seen him. The old cocktail of desire and dislike was confusing her all over again.

He was, Geraldine announced, as if she had been studying Liliane's assessment of her son, not long back from a big assignment abroad, and Liliane smiled at the emphasis. Since his documentary of Rwanda aired and shook the nation, Nick Heggarty didn't do small assignments.

"I hear things are going well for you, the café, studying and…" he paused and, when Liliane didn't respond, shrugged his shoulders, "everything else," he added, an acknowledgement of how little he knew about her these days. Liliane let the silence between them stretch and watched his face redden beneath the brown glow of his skin. In the early days at The Grove, the walled, gated manor where the Heggartys lived, she had found the ease with which he blushed endearing. She had mistaken it for vulnerability until she scratched the surface of his character and exposed the ruthlessness upon which he had built his career.

"Liliane has done very well for herself while you've been chasing your stories around the world." Geraldine spoke like the proud mother she thought of herself as to Liliane.

"Your mother has made it all possible for me," Liliane added, with a pointed look at Nick, "since I left The Grove." Geraldine shifted in her seat and stretched across the low table to pat Liliane's hand again.

"Well, that was all a long time ago. And I'm taking no credit, by the way," his mother said with a glance at him. "She's done incredibly well in the circumstances." Liliane wondered if she meant for a penniless, broken refugee or for the way she had fled life at The Grove. She took Geraldine's still outstretched hand and squeezed it with affection.

"You've been like a mother to me." Geraldine's face glowed while the closeness that had developed between the two women during his lengthy absences seemed to make Nick uncomfortable. Now he leaned forward and hooked his arm around his mother's shoulders and, with that smile again, reclaimed her from Liliane. As he sat back, his scent, heavy with shades of leather, wafted across the table.

"Nice perfume." It had been an intimate joke between them once, in those weeks when she was taught how to live again, coaxed into speaking and coping without the memory of her past life.

"It's cologne," he replied, as he was expected to, but his smile slipped, and he suddenly looked vulnerable and nervous. "I haven't worn it since the night you left," he added, and for a moment, none of them seemed to know what to say.

Why tonight? she thought. Isn't just seeing you enough for me to cope with? But it was too late; the connection was already made. It all came back so easily despite her having ignored it for so long. It was that night again. She had known he was in her bedroom even before he had latched the door shut. His scent, mixed with the sour smell of the cigar he had smoked with his father, was already around her. The first time he had come to her room, a few weeks earlier, was to apologise for having taken her to his editing studio to show her images of Kitabuye in a vain attempt to shock her memory to return. He had sat on the floor with his back against the bed and told her about everything he had seen and experienced in Rwanda. She remembered now how she had been scared when tears dripped off his cheeks as he told her of what he had seen. He came a few more times in the weeks after that, at first sitting on the floor, then the edge of the bed.

She had no memory of sleeping with a man, but that night, when he touched her, she recognised the longing that stirred inside her. She had experienced this before in her hidden life. And she also knew that she had enjoyed it.

"Nick?" she whispered, but he was already at her bedside. She saw the lighter shade of his hand in the darkness reach for the lamp. "Don't." She stretched across, wrapped her fingers around the switch and felt his own close over hers. "My head," she said. He had seen her wounded and bloodied when he found her, but she felt shame and embarrassment now and feared he would never look at her again if he saw her as she now was.

"Can I?" She felt the edge of the sheet lift, and she slid across the bed to allow him in. She felt comforted by his closeness, a thrill as he touched her. It was, she realised, part of who she was and who she had once been. Yet with the desire came an undercurrent of uneasiness that grew in intensity with every button of her nightdress he undid until its pull was too strong.

"You'll never want for anything, Liliane. I promise you. I'll protect you always. Give you a new life, the best of everything." His mouth kissed the side of her head as he whispered to her.

She tried to push him away. His words panicked her as if

an old, primeval terror had been disturbed. It flooded through her until she felt it would burst out of the scar on her head. When Nick pulled at her nightdress, she screamed to release the fear and loathing; their intensity obliterated all the desire she had felt. She beat her fists on his head, then his upturned face, and he fell to the floor as Geraldine, followed by Charles, rushed into the room. Liliane moaned and rubbed and clawed at her stomach as if it were on fire while Nick protested as Charles pushed him out of the room. Geraldine had driven her away from The Grove for the last time the next day.

"Liliane?" She could tell that Geraldine knew where she had just been; it was in the woman's voice, her eyes, even in the way her hands rubbed at the non-existent creases of her silk blouse. "I said we must get going, or we'll be late." Liliane beamed her best smile first at Geraldine, then Nick, to reassure them. She still remembered the bewilderment on his face as he looked back at her from the doorway. She had never been able to explain it to him because she hadn't understood herself what had happened. Now, with Nick sitting opposite her, his eyes telling her that he had been living that night again as well, the same confusion fogged her thoughts.

"Let's meet up. Soon. For a chat. Drink, maybe." Liliane's words tumbled out of her, and she felt the tension in her head ease. Nick's face brightened.

"Great. I'm around for ages now." He leaned forward as if the offer had broken some invisible barrier between them.

"How lovely." The relief was palpable in Geraldine's voice. "I'll go and pay." She reached for her bag. "Then we must go."

"It was Mother's idea." Nick's arm swept over the drinks when his mother was out of earshot. "Sorry. I can see it's been awkward for you."

"I meant it. The drink. We should talk. Just us." It was impulsive, but she felt pleasure from having said it.

"I'll call you," he said quickly. Geraldine was weaving her way back through the tables.

"Come to the café."

"Right, are we ready?" There was a flicker of triumph on Geraldine's face, and Liliane could tell she had been watching them. In the years since Liliane had left for London, Nick's mother seemed to have forgotten, or forgiven, what she had witnessed that night. Liliane allowed Nick to kiss her cheek when they parted, and his smell was still on her skin as they sat in the back of the taxi. She felt trapped again between the man who had saved her life for her memory and the woman who had rebuilt her life and was desperate for that memory to never come back. The happy, settled life she had, though, came at a price. Geraldine and Charles were such dominant characters. Whenever she thought of breaking free from her compliance to them, something told her that this was how her life had always been, how it was always meant to be.

***

The cinema was a small, what Geraldine described as an 'avant-garde' establishment, which showed the sort of films she thought Liliane should see before she went to university. Charles had insisted that education was what she needed to better herself, and Geraldine had helped arrange the college courses for her.

"You'll be mixing with some very clever, sophisticated people, you know," she said on their first visit. "You need to be able to hold your own."

"Show them I'm not a savage, you mean?" Liliane had quipped and immediately regretted it when she saw the hurt on Geraldine's face. "You're very kind, and I'm going to enjoy my cultural education. And," she had added to mollify Geraldine, "spending time with you."

It had taken her a long time and many embarrassing moments to learn how to live among the people of this new country without offending them. Geraldine had been very good with her, tutoring her and giving her the confidence to live. It was only when she left the security of The Grove that she realised the Heggartys lived in a part of society that was sparsely occupied. It had been three months before she even set foot outside the gated grounds of their house and realised that the rest of the country was different. Although London had initially been another steep learning experience, she felt more at home in the ordinariness—the earthiness of the customers who came to The Equator. She often wondered who had taught her English and how she remembered how to speak it. Nick had told her that she understood him and the others when they first found her and that there had been a number of European charities supporting health and education across that part of Rwanda.

Tonight's film was a classic crime thriller from the fifties. "It's a bit 'noir'," Geraldine explained as they took their seats. Liliane was glad Nick's mother couldn't see her smile in the half-light as she settled into the luxurious armchair. She loved Geraldine as if she were her real mother and had learned to accept her as she was. After three years in London, she had also come to understand the country into which she had been thrust. She had soon realised the elevated position the Heggartys occupied in society and her fortune in having access to their generosity, even if it was a relief to live in her cramped little apartment above The Equator.

Relaxed in a chair more comfortable than anything her café had to offer, Liliane found it difficult to stay awake. The film was slow to get going, and she struggled to understand why she was meant to like it. There had been too many scenes in shadowy places, too much arguing, too much violence against a woman who had been left bloodied and crying on the floor of a dark room.

She grew more uneasy as she watched the violence being inflicted on the woman, and the scar beneath the silk protested at her stress. She closed her eyes but could still see clearly. There was a curtained window on the far wall and a sliver of light on the floor below the door. She seemed able to feel the woman's pain and the discomfort of the position she had been thrown into. Geraldine nudged her, and she nodded to reassure her she was awake.

"This next bit is famous," she whispered. Liliane gripped the padded arms of her chair and tried to swallow the tightness in her throat. The door of the room opened to reveal someone silhouetted against the light behind. Liliane shrank down in her seat, made herself smaller as if to be invisible, and grasped the arms harder. She shut her eyes, but still the figure came closer. An alien smell burned in her nostrils as if they had been singed; her body ached. She could taste blood in her mouth and feel it scabbed on her face. When the man bent over the woman on screen, she screamed, then stood and rushed through the door into the lobby of the cinema. She had to get away from him.

"Liliane. Liliane." Geraldine followed her out and now pulled her close. "It's only a film. Don't worry. I jumped out of my skin the first time I watched it." She rubbed Liliane's back as if calming a child after a nasty fall until her shaking lessened and her breathing calmed.

"I'm sorry. I'm sorry. It's just…" She pulled away from Geraldine. "I want to go now. I can't watch it."

"Stay here. I'll get our coats."

Liliane was waiting on the steps outside when Geraldine returned. Although the evening was still fresh and bright, it couldn't dispel the dark mood that had descended on her.

"That was me," she said before Geraldine could deliver any further reassurances. "It happened to me. Just like in the film." She stared back at the cinema. "It's how…" Her hand was upon the silk that covered her throat, and she ran her fingers down the puckered skin that felt as ugly as it looked.

"It's just a film, Lili. It's meant to make us feel part of it. It's why it's so good." Her confident words were betrayed by the tremor in her voice.

"I was in a dark room just like that. I could smell something…incense and candles. I was lying on a rough mat. I had blood on my face. And then… I don't know. This." She touched the side of her head. "And more…"

"You can't know that, Lili. That's all gone now. You know it is." This was Geraldine's worst fear, and she seemed to be trying to reassure herself as much as Liliane. "Don't think about it. Whatever it was will go if you don't dwell on it." She shook Liliane as if she could dislodge the thought from her mind.

"It was real, Geraldine," she insisted. "I'm scared. What if…what if it's true and it happened like that? And what if I remember what happened next?"

"Do you want to, Liliane? Do you really? Do you want to undo the last three years? The happiness you've got? The future, going away to college?" She paused to catch her breath, then tried again, her words more measured. "Don't risk it, Lili. Just forget it. Don't concentrate on it." Geraldine spoke now like the mother she wanted to be, stern, reproachful, as if the finality of her tone was enough to banish the memory back behind the veil that had kept it hidden. "Anyway, you don't know that it really was like that. It's just…it's just…oh, I don't know. You just imagined you were the lady in the film. That's all."

A few people stared at them as they passed by. Geraldine, unused to making a scene in public, lowered her voice. "Let's go for a drink. I think we both need one."

Liliane let herself be guided to a bar further up the street, and an uneasy truce was established. Neither of them was sure what more could be said to bring closure to the incident. Eventually, Geraldine tried again. "Look, Lili, I don't know what happened tonight, but I'm sure it's nothing to do with your other life. That's over. This is your life now. It started three years ago. That's all you need to know."

"I know, Geraldine," Liliane replied with all the confidence and brightness she could muster. "I'm sure you're right. You've been very good to me. I won't dwell on it, I promise."

Later, as she waved to Geraldine as her cab pulled away, she wished it was all that simple, that she could bring the same order to her own life as Geraldine seemed able to with hers. But the sense of foreboding that had worried away at her since the cinema refused to leave her as she pushed the stiff door open with her shoulder and picked her way through the darkened café. At the door leading to the stairs to her apartment, she paused and turned. Her eyes narrowed against the gloom. A bus passed by. Its headlights shone on the far wall and illuminated the picture. Someone was sitting at the table below it. Lovers' Corner, Adele called it. He stared at Liliane, motionless, the whites of his eyes accentuated by the jet black of his skin. She had seen him before. He belonged in the life that Geraldine said was over. The bus passed. The light faded from the corner. She stretched her arm behind her and flipped the switch. There was no one there.

Liliane ground her palms against her eyes and looked again. The café was empty, as she had known it would be. Yet that face, in that brief burst of illumination, had been familiar. She had seen it before. She had known him once. She had known him very well.

As she turned the lights off, a sense of desolation came over her. She didn't know how, but she recognised it as the emptiness of loss where once there had been, she was sure, love and desire. She stopped at the foot of the stairs. Grief had, in that brief moment, entered her life.

FIFTEEN

The strip of grey light between the curtains and the rumble of an early bus was enough to break the last flimsy strands of Liliane's sleep. The sweat that soaked her nightdress was evidence of where her mind had wandered in the night. The heaviness in her limbs and the stiffness in her neck were just the dregs of the distress that coursed through her on the occasions when she knew she had returned to Kitabuye. It had always been the same dream because the church was the only place she knew about. She would always be standing in front of the red brick building, staring at the shadow that spilled out of its door, across the grass and over the wall until it lapped at her feet. The longer she stared, the more she noticed the grotesque shapes that poked out of the darkness—arms and legs twisted in knots and faces frozen in shock. She would see the flesh melt in the heat of the day until people came and piled the skulls in neat rows, just like in the books on her table.

As she sat in the café, earlier than usual, the optimism that had suffused her the day before was gone. Where there had been a lightness in her spirit, an upsurge of joy for the day ahead, she now felt listless, and even her coffee sat cold in front of her. The events of the night before, Nick, the cinema, and the dream, had left her confused and frightened. Then, there was the figure in the corner in the darkness, the figment of her disturbed imagination. It pushed her other concerns aside for a moment, and she felt absorbed by grief again.

She tried to reason with herself, just as Geraldine would have. Her over-excited mind was still a bit unbalanced after her 'little turn' in the cinema. Then there were the two large gins Geraldine had insisted she drink 'just to calm her down'. It was no use. She couldn't think like Geraldine. There was another explanation, one that she had been trying not to think about.

"Hopefully, she's through the worst of it now." Liliane could still remember the sombre tone in the doctor's voice as he spoke with Geraldine and Nick in the corridor outside her hospital room. It was the start of her new life.

"But her memory? She says she doesn't know anything. Not even who she is. I had to tell the girl her own name, for God's sake." Nick's voice rose to a shout. "I brought her back to be my eyewitness."

"Nick. Nick. At least she's alive. It might still come back." It was his mother, cajoling and mollifying.

"I asked you if this might happen if you operated before I'd had a chance to speak to her. I wouldn't have..." He stopped, and there was silence for a moment until the doctor spoke again. His words were calm in the face of Nick's anger.

"She would have died if we hadn't operated when we did." As the door was pulled to, his words crept through the last of the gap. "It's no longer about her memory, I'm afraid, Mr Heggarty. I'd be more worried about her brain deteriorating. The trauma…"

The brief snatch of conversation and Nick's outburst of anger had frightened Liliane as she lay alone and scared in the strange room. She didn't know who or where she was or who these strangers were who spoke about her chances of life or death. Yet as her health had settled and she was guided step by step into a whole new life, the fear that her brain was damaged receded. It was only when the decision was made that she should go to university that it reasserted itself.

"What if it's too much for me, that my brain can't take the stress, or my brain goes bad?" She had said to Charles and Geraldine in the face of their determination to see her better herself.

"Your mind is perfectly fine, Lili. Apart from the obvious, that is. And anyway, Charles has pulled the strings now, so it's all settled." And for Geraldine, it was. Liliane was, it seemed, their project. She knew they loved her but often wondered if they wanted her to succeed to show their friends what good benefactors they were and how they used their money for good causes.

She roused herself for the day ahead, even more unsettled than when she had woken. Her brain must be waking after a long rest. That had to be the answer. It was as if a veil had momentarily been lifted the night before to reveal glimpses of the past. She would have to find a way to lift it higher and stare harder for longer at the images she was sure were behind it. The alternative was too awful to think about.

She already felt drained by the time she unlocked the front door, daunted by the prospect of the long day ahead then college all night. Adele and Isabelle were in high spirits when they arrived, still laughing about the boys who had chatted them up. Adele already had a boyfriend, yet she courted attention wherever she went. She seemed to need the constant reassurance of admiring looks and brief dalliances to compensate for the lack of a family and the separation from her past. Liliane worked hard to ease her insecurity and knew that making her manager when she left for college would be another step along the painful path, despite Adele's own doubts.

Isabelle had been very quiet and reserved when she was introduced to Liliane the year before. The damage of what she had seen, her parents and siblings dragged into the bush while she hid in a small roof space, was still evident in the frightened look in her eyes and the mistrust of anyone who tried to help. She eventually told Liliane how friends and neighbours, people she had known all her life, had joined in the killing. After hiding in the marshes of a local lake, she was rescued by an RPF patrol and handed to a charity. More beautiful than Adele, she was tall like Liliane, and her poise had engendered a loyal band of customers, mainly young men, who would hang back until Isabelle was free at the counter. She seemed glad to let Adele make the running with the boys, but Liliane would smile at how Isabelle often ended up with the best-looking one.

Liliane could cope with the antics and love lives of the two girls. They were easier to counsel and guide away from the horrors of their past. It was Zee who she worried about most. He was already in the corner preparing food, but she could tell from his laboured efforts that it had been another night of too much drink and sleep ravaged by the nightmares that he seemed unable to shake off.

"How are you doing, Zee?' She laid a hand on his shoulder, but he just shrugged.

"I'll be fine, thanks, Liliane." She knew his eyes would be bloodshot from drink and lack of sleep, but today, she could still smell the drugs on him. He was resorting to different ways to dull the pain and forget, but soon, he would have to face his demons and overcome them on his own. She gave his shoulder a pat, then turned back to the café.

Zee told her once how he had hidden in a cupboard while his family was killed. He had listened to the screams until one by one they fell silent. "I was scared they would smell my shit, Liliane," he had said. "It was running down my legs." He tried to make a joke about it, but there were tears in his eyes as he recounted the story. Yet it was what he told her next that chilled Liliane. "Mind you, some of those Hutu priests were bad, Liliane. Ours hated us. He gathered us at the church and then started it all. I watched him do it. He killed people himself." He still looked bewildered that such a thing could occur. Later that night, she searched through her books and found more examples of massacres at churches which had been inspired, sometimes led, by priests. The church was the only part of Kitabuye she knew about.

Nick had found her on the patio as she enjoyed the solitude of an early morning at The Grove. "Come over to the stables, Liliane. There are some people I'd like you to meet." She took his outstretched hand, surprised at the pleasure she felt at the contact. It had only been a few weeks since the last operation, and she still felt dizzy when she stood.

On the way through the garden, bright with blooms and heavy with their smells, he explained how his parents had paid for the old stables to be converted into an editing studio for him. While this meant nothing to her, she was still impressed by the array of machinery and screens that filled the room when he guided her in. Three men were gathered around one of the screens.

"Liliane, you won't remember, I know," he said and paused, clearly hoping that she would, "but this is Frank, Piet and Joost. You met…well, they were with me in Rwanda. They helped me with the filming, in Kitabuye," he added.

The men seemed uncomfortable, and their nervousness transmitted to Liliane. She stayed rooted at the door until Nick pulled her further in. They told her it was good to see her again and how well she looked. Then there seemed to be nothing else to say, and they fell silent and waited for Nick, who seemed to be in charge of the meeting.

"Liliane, I thought if you met the guys and we chatted about…well, about when we found you and then the journey to Kitabuye and everything, it might help you remember things, you know, jog it all a bit." His words seemed to unsettle the others, but none of them objected. "Then you might be able to help us with some information we need for the documentary." He guided her to a table in the centre. Its chairs faced a large screen, and she turned to see Frank at her shoulder. His face was brown, and his brow creased with deep lines when he frowned, as he did now. His eyes seemed sad as if they had seen too much sorrow, but they brightened when Liliane smiled at him.

The large screen flickered, and she turned to Nick,

confused at first, then frightened as the image of a church, the red bricks bathed almost to pink in the brightness of the day, filled the screen. There seemed to be a shadow around the church. As she looked closer, she saw it was bodies, hundreds of them, that had cast the land around the church into darkness. She felt Frank pull at her chair and turn her away from the screen while Joost stood in front of it. Nick started to object, but before he was on his feet, the door behind him slammed into the wall, and Geraldine stood in the entrance.

"What's going on here? What's Liliane…" Joost moved, and Geraldine saw the screen. Nick seemed to shrink into his seat as she stood over him. "We agreed never to show her. You promised!"

The dream had started after that, always the same, but as she had settled into life in London and gathered her new life and friends around her, it had lain dormant—until last night.

"Are you all right, Liliane?" It was the usual mid-morning lull, and Adele was behind her. Liliane looked up at the mirror behind the jars of coffee and noticed for the first time the smudges of tiredness under her eyes. "You look like the one who was on a big night out." There was concern behind the humour, and when she turned, she saw Adele's brow creased with concern.

"I…I didn't sleep too well, that's all." Her weak smile felt less convincing than her words had sounded.

"Is that all? You look sad." The doubts and fears of earlier in the day pressed down on her again, but she couldn't, she wouldn't burden Adele with them.

"Come into the office while it's quiet."

The back room, with its large safe and Liliane's desk, also acted as a storeroom. With the bars on its windows from its days as a bank, they often joked that their coffee was the safest in the city.

"I saw Nick last night. Geraldine invited him for a drink before the film." The swirl of conflicting emotions boiled in her again as she spoke his name.

"Ah, I see." Adele didn't know everything that had happened in those early days, but enough to know the impact it would have on Liliane. "And?"

"I suggested we meet for a drink."

"And now you're regretting it." Adele took Liliane's hand. She could cope with Liliane if she had man-troubles. Adele had enough experience herself. "Don't. It's time you two sorted yourselves out. Maybe it's meant to be, Liliane." Everyone knew Nick had rescued Liliane, and Adele just wanted a romantic ending to the story.

"It's…it's not that easy, Adele. I can't explain. It's complicated."

"It's three years," Adele interrupted. "It's time enough."

"Well, he's coming over for coffee anyway. Satisfied now?"

The girl's eyes widened. "Here? When? I'll reserve Lovers' Corner." Liliane laughed despite herself. She had led Adele far away from her real fears, even though creating this false trail would bring its own problems. She would worry about that another time.

As they left the office, Adele turned. "There's nothing else, is there?"

Liliane swallowed, shook her head, and smiled. The other girl's eyes narrowed as if they were peering inside her mind. "You can't put the sauce back in the bottle once it's out, Liliane," Adele had warned her once. She wasn't to know that a few drops had leaked out already.

SIXTEEN

Liliane was thankful for The Equator having another busy day. The continuing fine weather had brought tourists and residents alike out in force early, and she was too busy to think. It was only when she sat in the office in the early afternoon that the implications of the previous night sank in.

The equilibrium of her life, disturbed only occasionally by her attempts to prompt her memory, had been unsettled in the darkness of a cinema. Now fear and pain, love and grief were intruding on this new version of herself. Geraldine had shaped and guided her like a puppeteer, yet Liliane always had a nagging feeling that her destiny had already been shaped. Her past, she was now sure, was the key to the future life she was meant to lead, even if, by picking away at the threads that had already been revealed, her comfortable present unravelled uncontrollably.

She stared at the wall, at her desk, then back to the wall, unable to concentrate. Her eyes, unfocused, landed on the scrap of paper Nick had slipped into her hand. If anyone could be the catalyst to unlocking her secrets, it was surely Nick. He had been with her in Kitabuye, had seen the things she had experienced. She dialled the number before her doubts got the better of her. He answered on the second ring as if he expected her call and was immediately solicitous.

"Mum told me about the cinema. She's worried about you. Thinks you're looking for things that don't exist, can't exist." His tone was neutral, always the journalist, weighing up both sides. He waited for her response. She wondered if he was taking notes or taping their conversation.

"Can we talk about it? Tomorrow at three, here?"

He was silent for a moment, used to being in charge, controlling the conversation. "Sure, Liliane, if it suits you. Maybe better face to face." Another silence. "Are you…are you okay? I mean, upset or anything? Sounds like a bit of a shock." She felt a glow of pleasure at the concern in his voice. Last night had stirred his emotions as well.

"I'm fine. It's just…more complicated than your mother thinks."

He laughed, not unkindly. "Most things are. You know her well now. I could see it last night."

"We are close. You should try. With her, I mean," she added hastily.

"With you both. Until tomorrow then." He was gone, but Liliane kept the phone cradled to her chest. When she rested it back on its cradle, she experienced the familiar cocktail of excitement and trepidation whenever Nick was involved in her life. Such a dominant and forceful presence in her early months as she tried to make sense of the life that had been thrust on her, he had tried to control her in the same way that Geraldine now did. At times, it was comforting, as if she had known before what it was like to have her movements watched, her life influenced and managed.

As she sat in quiet reflection for a while longer, she knew it was the sadness she had felt the previous night, a sense of lost love that was something new in her life. She often felt that a part of her was missing, some integral piece of her without which she could never be complete. But this new sense of emptiness was different. She had been in love with, and loved by, someone. Her past might well be hidden behind some impenetrable fog, but it still seemed capable of injecting plenty of confusion into her present.

She roused herself and headed up to her flat. There were only a couple of hours of serving time left. Adele and the team could cope now that the residents had gone shopping and the tourists had headed off to the sights. She stuffed her college books into her bag and headed back down to the café before she could change her mind.

"I thought I'd head to college a bit early. Maybe take a walk in the park. Clear my head."

After a quick look around the room, Adele shrugged and said, "We'll cope."

Once outside, she leaned back against the wall for a minute and let its warmth seep into her. Even the fume-laden air seemed to refresh her after the stuffy atmosphere of the café. She decided to get off the train early and walk to the park near her college.

Whenever she descended an escalator into the huge caverns beneath the city, Liliane could never help wondering about the differences between this country she now called home and the one that had been home but which she only knew from books and the few films she had seen. What was it about these people that had driven them to such heights and depths, and yet her people still lived in mud huts and so easily shook off all the trappings of civilised life? Still pondering such weighty issues, she realised her train was at the station she had decided to alight at. She had intended to read through the work she had to submit that night whilst on the train, but instead, her thoughts had again strayed into trying to understand how her country had turned in on itself so viciously.

The shouts of some youngsters ahead of her caused her to look up, unaware she was already on the escalator, so absorbed was she in her thoughts. She enjoyed travelling the Underground and got some vicarious pleasure from watching her fellow passengers. She tried to guess what they were doing, what sort of people they were, where they might be going and what they would do when they got there. She looked across to the down escalator, now busy with early office leavers. In the rushing tide of faces, one, further up but approaching fast, stood out. The man's jet-black skin was accentuated by the shiny white band at his neck. They were about to cross when he glanced up from his newspaper and looked over at Liliane, as if he sensed he was being watched. Their eyes met. His were large, magnified by thick lenses in heavy black frames. They narrowed as if trying to recognise her or confused by the intensity of her stare.

Liliane felt as if she had been punched in the stomach. She grabbed at the handrail. He was past now but turned his head, and their eyes locked again. They were close to her now, and she could taste his breath and feel the quiver of his lips on hers. His hands were on her shoulders, and she felt the strength in him as he pushed her down to kneel in front of him.

When she came to, a few people were standing over her. One of them held her bag as she sat propped up against the wall while the crowd pushed past, some slowing to look down at her. A grey-haired lady knelt beside her and felt for her pulse.

"It's all right, dear. I'm a nurse. Looks like you fainted there. How are you feeling? Dizzy? Sick?"

Liliane forced as strong a smile as she could manage, wanting only to get outside, be on her own, away from these kindly strangers. "Neither, thank you. I just felt hot all of a sudden, you know." The lady nodded in sympathy and let go of Liliane's hand.

"Can you stand?" She nodded to two men, one in the uniform of the Underground, and they assisted Liliane onto her feet. "I'll walk you to the fresh air; make sure you're okay."

Liliane took her bag and the nurse's arm and repeated her thanks and apologies a few times to the other helpers. The nurse was right; she did need fresh air, but to clear her head of the memory that had shocked the breath out of her.

Once she was seated on a bench in the square across from the station, the lady left her and disappeared back into the ticket hall. Liliane's shins were scuffed and sore where she must have fallen onto the next step, but it was the pain in her scars that was worse. The sight of the priest had scared her. It had only been a few seconds, a moving face in a crowd and all she could now recall was the colour of his skin, the white collar, his eyes. Above all, though, it was what he had made her do that still disoriented her. She rubbed her shoulders and felt again the pressure of his grip as he forced her to kneel, his breathing quick, his eyes wide with anticipation. There was also the smell. She had been in the same room with him as the one she remembered lying in at the cinema the previous night.

SEVENTEEN

Liliane couldn't say how long she had been slumped on the baggy sofa under one of The Equator's high windows. The room was quiet and incomplete without the bustle of its customers. The trepidation that had been like a persistent undercurrent in her since she fainted on the escalator remained undiminished. Despite the security of the café, the strengthened glass and thick walls of the old bank building which muffled the sounds of life from the street to a muted murmur, her hands still shook from the experience. The journey home had been a blur of fear and isolation, and Liliane had pulled an old bottle of brandy down from one of the high shelves when she got back. The liquid rasped her throat and set fire to her chest, but eventually, she felt a warmth spread through her, which seemed to ease the tension.

One corner of the room, high up, still gathered the last of the sun that was sliding behind the high roofs opposite. She sank lower in the seat and watched specks of dust swirl in its beam while shadow crept up the wall until the last bright patch gave way to the gloom. In that moment, it felt to Liliane that, with the sight of the priest and the spark of a memory, a shadow was also descending on the happy life she had built for herself. He was from Kitabuye, she was sure. Where else could she have known him from? And how else could she have remembered something so degrading? No, he was here in London. She was sure. The gloom in the café deepened and reached into her soul. The memory that had been prompted by the sight of the priest kept playing over in her mind, as if on a continuous loop. The priest, the room with its distinct smell, his eyes and what he had made her do.

For years she had accepted that her past life was hidden, her mind suffused by a weightless, all-embracing fog that blanketed everything she wanted to know and sucked her attempts to pierce it into its shapeless mass. The sight of the priest had been like a sudden blast of wind that ripped a hole in the shroud over her past and allowed her a brief glimpse of what lay beyond. Then, just as quickly, the fog billowed and obscured it again and left her unsure of what she had seen or whether she had seen anything at all.

The incident that had revealed itself, freighted with revulsion and terror, had caught her off balance as if the escalator had suddenly stopped and pitched her headlong. Now, alone in the darkening café, Liliane forced herself to do some jobs to keep her mind occupied. She emptied the dishwasher, polished the glasses, put them on the shelves, cleaned the filters on the coffee machine and refilled the grinder. It was when she had written cheques for the unpaid invoices in her office that she glanced up and saw Nick's number, now stuck on her pinboard. She lifted the phone then set it down. Her fingers drummed on the dial; her lower lip clenched between her teeth. He would help, she knew, then he would take control and tell her it was nothing, just a mistake. There was, though, really no one else she could turn to. She sighed, grabbed the handset again and dialled quickly, almost frantically, as if reporting an emergency.

She was about to hang up, annoyed yet relieved, as it continued to ring when he finally answered.

"Nick." The rehearsed words wouldn't come. It was all a mistake.

"Liliane? This is a surprise. I was just on the way out." Still her words wouldn't come. "Liliane, are you all right? Is it about tomorrow?" He sounded disappointed.

"Can you come over?" It was all she could manage. Her voice sounded small in the high-ceilinged room.

"Now? Is something wrong? What's the matter?"

"I…I don't know." It sounded pathetic. She tried again. "Yes, I think there is."

"Tell me."

"I can't. Just…just come. Please."

"Okay. Okay. I need to make a call. Half an hour. Okay?" But she wasn't, no matter how many times he said it.

"Thanks."

She put the phone in its cradle and felt an irrational pang of jealousy as she wondered if it was another woman he was calling. Anyway, why did she care? She hadn't seen him for three years. She picked a couple of bottles of wine from the shelf above the till and put them in the fridge, then sat and waited while her mind replayed what she had seen and felt. In the quiet of the café, doubt gnawed away at her confidence. It had only been a few seconds, a brief glance. She couldn't really be that sure, could she?

She had left the front door ajar. When she heard the scrape of wood on the tiled floor, she wiped her hands on a tea towel, checked herself in the mirrored glass, adjusted her hijab and wiped a speck of mascara off her cheek.

Nick stood awkwardly by the swing door from the lobby, and she saw in his stance the wariness that she had sensed on the phone. Geraldine had once explained how her last night at The Grove had left its mark on him too. She understood his hesitancy and moved towards him, smiling. She needed him to listen without being cynical, and she allowed him to greet her with a kiss.

While he explored the café, she poured the wine. "It's really good, Liliane." There was genuine admiration in his voice. "I'm impressed." She watched him lift the lids on the tins of the different coffee beans and sniff approvingly, his eyes shut as he savoured the aromas. He prowled around for a few minutes to satisfy his curiosity while she sat at one of the tables, still unsure how to express what she had experienced.

"You've done well. We're all really proud of you." Liliane wondered if he meant that the Heggartys were proud of what their money had achieved in reconstructing her life, but he seemed genuine, and she regretted the churlish thought. She smiled and passed him a glass of wine. "Cheers then." He sat opposite her, smart in an ironed shirt, pressed trousers, clean shoes, and she wondered if her guess was right after all. "I was off to a book launch. It's not important," he said, as if he had read her thoughts.

"I'm sorry, Nick. I just…something happened. I couldn't think who else to call."

"I'm glad you did." He reached for her hand, and she let him hold it for a few seconds. "I guess I owe you one." The colour rose from his neck, and Liliane looked away to spare him. That night was still off-limits.

"I saw someone. Someone from my past." Her words tumbled out. "On the Underground. The priest from Kitabuye. I knew him. I recognised his eyes, his glasses."

"Slow down. Slow down." He held up his hands as if surrendering. "Let's start again. One step at a time, Liliane," he said, but now that she had allowed the incident back into her thoughts, her words continued to spill out unchecked.

"There was something else." She stared into her glass. It was too shameful to tell him. "I remembered something. With him. The priest."

"You need to calm yourself, Liliane. I don't know what you're talking about. I can't help you like this."

Liliane took a deep breath. "I saw a priest. He was on the opposite escalator. He wore glasses, dark frames. He looked at me. I knew him. It was his eyes that prompted everything. I've seen them before."

Her chest was too tight to carry on. Nick sipped his wine and waited. She took another breath as if she was about to submerge herself in deep water. "He looked away and then…then it was as if he was next to me. His face was close. He made me kneel and…" the rest of it was stuck somewhere inside her. "I fainted, and people helped me," she said finally and drained her glass.

He refilled her glass, and they drank in silence for a while. He had taken a notebook out earlier, but it lay, still blank, in front of him. She stared at the end wall. In the subdued light of the room, the picture's lines were less defined, as if the sun in the picture had itself set for the night.

After a while, he leaned forward. "So you could only have seen his face, especially his eyes, for just a few seconds before you fainted." If he doubted her, his true thoughts were hidden behind his impassive features.

She sighed and nodded. It was what she had already challenged herself about. The silence became too much for her. "I didn't need long to recognise him. As soon as he looked up and stared at me, I knew. I felt it, Nick." She beat a fist against her chest, but her voice carried less conviction.

"So that made you think you knew him, and because it was a priest you saw, you assumed that he was the priest from Kitabuye, and that's how you know him?" His calm logic cut through her furious certainty.

"How else could I know him?"

"It would be pretty strange for someone like that to turn up as a priest in London, all the way from a small town in Rwanda."

"Well, I'm here. And my staff. Why can't he be?" Her response sounded petulant, and they lapsed into silence again. Liliane sipped her wine and waited, but he seemed far away, as if he was recalling his own time in Kitabuye.

"It's just…" He paused like her doctor had before he told her about her injuries. "You see, we did a lot of research about Kitabuye, Liliane. We had to as part of our planning for the documentary. It helped our credibility to have as much background as we could, to show we'd checked our facts." He paused. "It's why we wanted your testimony. Anyway, the thing is…" She could see he was going to say something she wouldn't like. "The thing is," he repeated, "the Catholic Church told us the priest, Malabanda was his name, is dead. He was killed, but whether by the RPF or the Interahamwe, they couldn't say." His smile was all sympathy and sadness. "That's why I asked you how he could possibly be here. He's dead, Liliane. You couldn't have seen him."

It was dark outside now, and the solitary light that had been adequate earlier cast long shadows across the café and created pools of darkness in the far corners. She felt helpless in the face of his facts. He took her hand, and there was tenderness in his touch. "I'm sorry, Liliane. I'm sure you did see a Black priest on the escalator. There are plenty of them in London. I think maybe you've been reading too many books." He squeezed her hand. "And watched too many scary films with my mother." She knew he meant it as a joke, to try to lighten her mood, but it just deepened her depression and sapped her desire to fight for what she was sure she had seen and felt.

"But it was the eyes. The glasses. They sparked something in me. I have looked into them before. It was as if he…" Her voice tailed off as she didn't know what it was she wanted to say. Finally, more confidently, she said, "He was close to me. Like you are to me now. Closer. I could smell him. I even felt his hands on my shoulders."

"It was your imagination, Lili."

"It was a memory," she snapped back. "How could I imagine something so…so vile?"

He recoiled at the sudden vehemence in her voice and stood as if to escape her fury.

"Well, you must have…"

"I've never done that. I've done nothing at all since…since I've been here." He leaned closer. "He's dead, Liliane. Dead! Dead! Dead!" His hand thumped the table with each word. The sound pounded in her head, and it reminded her of the familiar beat of a drum that she was sure was from her past. She could see he was upset by the argument. His face was pale, his hair stuck to his damp forehead. For a moment, she imagined she could see tears on his cheeks and a black shadow all around him. It was a glimpse from another time, a different place. The stress of the day pressed heavily on her.

Nick went to the fridge and found the second bottle of wine, and this gave Liliane time to reset her thoughts. He pulled his chair closer. As they drank in silence, the last of her fight ebbed away.

"Liliane, I don't doubt that you've had some sort of a flashback. I believe you saw a priest with glasses. But that's where the coincidence ends." His own belligerence had subsided with the drink. "His eyes or the glasses might be similar to Malabanda. I don't know. There were no pictures of him that we ever found. But he's gone. Believe me."

She wanted to describe the wrench of fear that overwhelmed her as she looked into the priest's eyes. Such emotion, though, was no match for his cold facts. Her certainty had dissipated, and she felt unanchored. Her scars nagged at her and sapped her energy to argue anymore. He was talking again now, and she forced herself to listen.

"Did I ever tell you the Catholic Church owned the plantation in Kitabuye?" He was looking at the wall behind her.

She didn't know there was a plantation in Kitabuye, but she was sure she knew what it looked like. She didn't need the picture. She was standing on the edge of a clearing, looking down on the bushes. There was a big shed behind her, and an old man with grey hair was calling to her. The image thrilled her for some reason.

"Liliane, are you okay?" Nick squeezed her hand, and she roused herself, forcing herself back into the room and away from the hilltop. "We were surprised how much land the Church owned across the country. They had a lot to lose if the Hutus didn't keep control." She didn't tell him she knew all this from her books. Her life was her own now. His voice droned on for a while about the war in Rwanda. Then he told her about his recent assignments. They were on safer ground now, and Liliane told him about the staff and Zee's drinking exploits, which made them laugh. They both seemed relieved not to be talking about why she had called him.

With the wine finished, Nick checked his watch and stood. "Best be off. Early start." They moved to the door and stood in intimate silence until Liliane shivered and broke the spell. Nick stared at her, and she braced herself to be kissed, but he stepped onto the pavement. "Let's do this again, go out one night. Find a bar. Have a meal after."

"That would be nice. Call me." She kissed his cheek and stepped back into the safety of the lobby, where she turned. "Thank you for coming. I'm sorry I ruined your evening. I'm sorry that…" She shrugged helplessly.

"You really do think you saw him." It wasn't a question, yet the confusion on his face was strangely comforting. She felt an urge to sink against him, feel the protection of his arms around her and share with him the fragments of memory. "But why would they lie about it?" He shook his head as if bewildered by what he'd heard. "I must have another look at all the research," he said to himself. He stopped as if to speak again, but all he managed was a nod and a smile.

She leaned against the front door for a long time before she closed up, relieved to be alone at last, wearied by the events of the evening. Her college bag was still in the café, the work to hand in still in it. After seeing the priest, she had forgotten that she was on her way to college. Her hand hovered over the light switch, reluctant to let the darkness in. For the first time ever since she had lived there, she went back to the front door and rattled it, just to make sure.

"What if he is here? What if he recognised me?" she had asked Nick on his way out, but he had waved the question away. Reassured, she turned the lights off but hesitated at the door to the stairs. The seat in the corner was empty.

"Come back, whoever you are," she whispered. "I need you." She needed the intimacy she knew they had shared. She wanted again the passion that she felt within. But it was grief that overwhelmed her, a remembrance, a feeling of love lost and the gap it left—a hole she realised could never be filled.

EIGHTEEN

The rooms above The Equator were Liliane's sanctuary, a place where no one was allowed. It was where she indulged her secret. The books she borrowed from college were spread over the drop-leaf table in the living room, and both of its flap extensions were up to accommodate them all. It was where she tried to prompt her mind to reveal the person she had once been. Unable to sleep, she ranged around the small apartment, from bedroom to kitchen and back to the living room. Her fingers, as restless as her feet, flicked through the pages she knew so well.

She pulled at her hijab in frustration and it slid over her shoulders to the floor where the silk pooled around her feet. Back in the bathroom again, she splashed her face in the basin. Once sensitive to water, time had strengthened these permanent reminders of the madness that gripped her country, scars that she chose to hide to avoid awkward silences and embarrassed stares. The surgeon had transformed the deep, jagged gash in her head into a shallow cavity, but it was still ugly bone and red scar tissue where no hair would grow. She was able to look at it dispassionately these days, inured to the shock of its appearance. On the surface, it seemed no different now than the first day she saw it. The doctor told her the damage beneath had probably taken her memory, but he couldn't promise her health wouldn't deteriorate one day because of it. She had always ignored his words since, but the possibility refused to leave her alone now. She had told Nick most of what she had seen and felt and had been adamant in her certainty. He had listened with kindness, then told her she was wrong.

Maybe her brain was deteriorating and had concocted a fantasy out of a random face on the Underground. Even if he hadn't died, there was no reason why the priest would, or could, be in London. The logic was brutally clear, yet it still couldn't dispel the sense of foreboding that nagged away at her.

She splashed her face again as if doing so would wash such fears away, then prowled around the living room until she finally settled at the table. She stared at a photograph of the hills of Kigali in front of her, certain that she had stood on them in the past and looked down on those red walls and roofs. The desolation of being alone in the world weighed on her more than it ever had. All this talk of Kitabuye had awakened in her the sense of loss for the family she no longer knew. Adele organised a 'birthday' party every year to celebrate the date when she had left the hospital. It marked out her new life, which had been carefully arranged by Geraldine and in which Liliane felt she just had to play the role allotted to her. The clothes in her cupboards, the job at The Equator, the night classes, the university course, each step in her new life seemed to have been carefully choreographed for her. She was an orphan, just like Adele, Zee and Isabelle, yet unlike them, she had never been able to grieve. There were no faces of her family to recall, no happy memories to make her smile. Yet she was supposed to be the lucky one because she had survived without the horror of remembering.

"You're the daughter she lost," Nick told her once as he tried to explain his mother's fixation on making everything just right for Liliane. "It was before me. She died after a few days. That's why they are how they are with me as well." No matter how much they might want it, Geraldine and Charles could never replace the mother and father she had lost. And what was Nick meant to be to her? A brother or a lover? She felt an overwhelming certainty that she had once had both in her life. She pressed her knuckles to her forehead, as if she could squeeze the past to the surface. She had loved, and been loved by, someone. She could feel it. But there had also been someone else, someone whose absence had shrivelled a part of her. She closed her eyes and tried to picture the girl she once was, the woman she had grown into and the relationships that had shaped her, but still, only vague shapes would come.

She headed down to the café and paced around the tables until she was in front of the picture. It was as if it had drawn her towards it. There was a plantation where she lived. Maybe this explained the attraction the picture had for her, why she felt comforted yet sometimes disturbed by it.

The leaves shimmered on the plants. Straps dug tight into her shoulders. A basket was heavy on her back, and her muscles complained as she straightened. The girl next to her said something, and Liliane turned towards her. She was very beautiful, Liliane thought, as she spoke again, her voice low.

"Have you got to go again tonight?" The girl's brow was furrowed with concern.

Liliane hated to be asked about it. The shame weighed on her worse than the wicker basket strapped to her shoulders. She nodded and bent back to the bush in front of her. Yes, she did have to go. Her father would take her to make sure she went in.

The image faded, and the girl was gone. So was the weight. Only guilt remained from that brief glimpse of her past, if that was what it was. She knew something else about herself, something that only her friend seemed to have known. Her past was full of secrets and a father who was complicit in her shame. She turned away and headed back towards her rooms.

***

Before she had gone to bed, Liliane had paused over an open book, a familiar one. The pictures were of rural churches, some little more than wooden sheds, part of the fabric of the country. They were more than churches; they were gathering places for the villagers. In each photograph, bodies lay outside the church, just like in Kitabuye. She knew by heart the accounts of priests and nuns who had lured Tutsis to the church for safety, only to let the Interahamwe turn on them. It all still shocked her. It was not so much the extent of evil that depressed her. It was more the fact that, in many cases, it had been priests who turned away from everything they should have stood for.

The priest, Malabanda, was, she now felt, in some way, the key to her own past, yet none of the turmoil that had shaken her world would have happened if he hadn't turned to look at her on the escalator. She could recall little about his features. He wore a dark suit and collar; that much was clear. Beyond that, it was his eyes behind the heavy glasses. The only thing she was certain about was the sudden dread she felt, as if someone had tipped her headfirst down the escalator. It was only a second until he looked away, as Nick pointed out. Had the priest also recognised her? Did he see something in her eyes that surprised or concerned him? The thought made her uneasy. A fitful sleep left her feeling slack and unwell, and the events of the day before were on her even as she woke. She had seen Malabanda. Malabanda was dead. Cold logic dictated one way, her emotions the other. And in between these two conflicting thoughts, there was the prospect that her wound was finally claiming her. It was going to be a long day.

***

She had removed the evidence of Nick's visit to avoid awkward questions, but her attempts to be cheerful with the staff and customers gave her a headache. In the first lull, she retreated to the office on the pretext of sorting out the coffee order and was sat, head in hands, when Adele peered in.

"Sorry to disturb, Liliane. Berto needs a few packs of coffee. Want me to go?" The boxes were stored at the back of the office, and Adele came further into the room.

"I'll take them." It was a good excuse to get the fresh air she needed. "He's got a query on his last invoice. I can do that as well."

"Okay, boss." She was about to go, then turned. "What time's Nick coming?" Her eyes were wide with anticipation at the prospect of romance in Liliane's life.

In the momentary silence, Liliane felt panicked. "He…he called last night. He can't make today. Hopefully later in the week." It sounded a bit lame, but it was the best she could do. Adele pulled a sad face. "Don't worry, nothing's happened. Some work came up. You know Nick." Smiling so much was making her headache worse.

It wasn't in her nature to deceive her staff, but the alternative would be too stressful at the moment.

***

"Liliane, you coming in or what?" She had been staring across at The Equator for a while from the steps to Berto's shop. The café had been her life, had given her the stability to become who she was. Now, it felt as if the ground beneath her was shifting, taking her to a place she might not like.

She turned and flashed a smile at Berto. Sometimes, she wondered if he exaggerated his accent to remind his customers they were in a real Italian deli. Yet, no one could mistake his appearance—the thick, dark hair, his tan-coloured skin and black soulful eyes—for anywhere else. He waddled down the steps and gave her the usual embrace, his whiskers tickling her cheeks. "Us refugees have to stick together," he would often say to her, mostly when he wanted a favour, even though he had been there forty years. Behind the genial smile and the bumbling friendliness was a shrewd businessman. Even while he held the door open for her, she felt him scrutinise her.

"You spent a long time admiring your café," he said as he guided her into the back of the shop. "I thought you not love Uncle Berto no more." His voice was light-hearted, but his eyes searched her as if his suspicions were already aroused. "Here, have some of this. It's new, I'm trying it out." Berto loved his grappa, and Liliane braced herself for the harsh, sour kick in her throat. "You look like you need it." He poured a little into two glasses. "Kubuzima bwazi." He had surprised her in the early days of their friendship by learning a few words of her language, which had endeared him to her.

"Saluti." She tipped the glass and tried not to shudder as it lit a fire in her empty stomach.

"Is business not good, Liliane? Are you worried about it? You seem…preoccupied."

"Business is good, Berto. Too good, we're so busy all the time. I might need more staff before I go."

"That's because you steal all poor Berto's customers," he said with a twinkle in his eye at telling such a blatant untruth. The drink had found the tension she hadn't realised was in her, and she relaxed. They were sat at a high-top table at the rear of the shop. Berto would often perch here and watch the customers come and go, many of whom would stop and chat with him. It was a quiet corner where no one could overhear them, and as Berto poured another shot, Liliane wrestled with the temptation to tell him what had happened to her. He pulled a pile of paper napkins from a shelf and began to fold them while Liliane sorted out the invoice with him. She toyed with her glass, aware that it was still early and she hadn't eaten.

"When do you leave us then, Liliane?" Berto looked more mournful than usual. "We'll miss you."

"October, if I finish my college work in time," she told him.

"I have confidence, Liliane. You're smart."

"Well, I haven't been that smart this week." Berto's eyes narrowed at the bitterness in her words. "I played truant last night. Didn't go." She sipped again at her drink. As its warmth spread, she realised she wanted to tell him. She needed someone who wouldn't judge her, who would just listen and give some wise, unconditional advice. "I had a shock on the way to college. I saw someone. Someone I thought I recognised." She pulled the napkins towards her and straightened the edges to avoid looking at him, intent on keeping her voice even.

He was silent for a moment. "Someone from the old days? Was that the shock?" It hadn't taken him long, but he asked without the scepticism Nick had shown the previous night. She continued to fiddle with the napkins until Berto pulled them back across the table. "I could tell you were troubled when you came in, Liliane. We know each other too well. Both of us have suffered in our own way." Something in his voice made her lift her head. "I have my own memories, Liliane, from the war. I saw my father and brothers lined up against a wall and murdered by the Germans. I was only a boy." He took her hand, and she felt the pulse of emotion in him. "For years, I buried it deep," and tapped his head, "but it still leaked out one day when I wasn't expecting it. I knew it was always there. You never know," he hesitated, and he glanced at her head, "it might still be there."

"He was a priest. I mean, he is. The man I saw. It was on the Underground. It hit me like an electric shock, Berto. I knew him. He was in my life. In Kitabuye."

He considered this for a while, and she waited, comfortable in his silence.

"It would be strange for him to end up here." He looked at her, eyebrows raised, but there was no judgement in his look.

"I've had other memories since, like mine are leaking out as well. And I wasn't ready for them either."

"You think the sight of the priest triggered them?" His smile was fixed, but there was no mirth in it. "That this is just the start?" She could see he was reflecting on his own experience. "There's no going back, Liliane. Be careful." He sounded so like Adele in his warning.

"So you think you knew him then, back in Kitabuye? This priest?"

"Yes, I did. I'm sure he was the priest in my town. But that's all I'm sure about." His acceptance of her admission had caught her off guard. "His name is Malabanda. Or it was then. Except he's supposed to be dead. The Church said so a few years ago when Nick made his documentary."

"I see. So he thinks you're mistaken."

"Or mad." For a moment, she couldn't hide her bitterness.

"I could make some enquiries. There can't be many Rwandan priests in London, after all." Berto was very active in church. He made it his business to know as many people as he could.

"I don't want to bother you. I might be mistaken. Probably am."

He shook his head as if pitying a child. "We know each other well, Liliane. You wouldn't be telling me this if you didn't believe it. I can see now why you hesitated. If you think it's true, well," he shrugged, his hands out, "that's good enough for me."

"Thank you." She leaned across, kissed his cheek, then stood before he could offer her more grappa.

She paused outside for a moment and watched well-heeled ladies in beautiful clothes come and go from the shop. It was a different world to the Rwanda, to the Africa, she knew from her books where people starved, and delicate cakes and pastries were unheard of. How was it that she lived in this place of peace and plenty? It was all too immense to contemplate, so she hurried back over the road. As she stood outside The

Equator, she knew that some of the ties that had anchored her new life had frayed in the last few days.

It was that time in the morning when there was a lull in trade, the workers all in their offices and shops, the tourists and shoppers yet to arrive. She walked through the swing doors. Geraldine was there. Whatever conversation had been passing between her and Adele was finished. Their stares rebuked Liliane, and she suddenly felt very tired.

NINETEEN

"What's going on, Liliane? What are you trying to do?" Geraldine's voice was on the edge of being strident. Liliane knew she wasn't expected to answer. A storm was coming, and it was best to let it blow for a while and hope it didn't carry her away. "Twice in two days now, you've invented silly stories about things from before you came here." She held up her hand, and Liliane swallowed her protest. "What else could they be but inventions? That ridiculous outburst in the cinema I was prepared to overlook. Now you're getting all upset over thinking you've seen someone who's dead, stirring Nick up on some wild goose chase."

Liliane resisted the urge to shout back and defend herself. Instead, she forced herself to concentrate on what Geraldine was saying. She was already regretting having had a second glass of grappa with Berto.

"After everything we've done for you. All of us. We've done it all for you, Liliane, to help you make a new life for yourself, safe from everything that harmed you, shielded from the past and all the hurt." She looked around the room as if searching for other causes of disapproval. "Charles is very disappointed, Liliane. He's done so much for you, as you well know."

"I do, and you both know how grateful I am, Geraldine." But the woman swatted the words back at her with a swipe of her hand.

"You're upsetting the settled life you've got here, and for what? A face in a crowd on an escalator. A few seconds. No more." Her voice rose as the words tumbled out, her knuckles white on the back of the chair.

Liliane felt her cheeks burn with anger. Nick had betrayed her. Now, Geraldine was trying to force her back into the life she wanted her to lead. Her head thrummed with anger and resentment. She was tired of being compliant to Geraldine and ever grateful for Charles's generosity. It was her past and her future. She didn't want to be a bit part player in her own life. And she didn't want to be an emotional crutch for her staff anymore.

The two women glared at each other. Liliane felt a terrible urge to rage at the woman opposite, to grab her and shake her. The feeling was so strong it frightened her. Something dreadful might happen if she lost control, and she would lose the family she had been given. Instead, she kept silent and pushed the anger deep down inside her. Geraldine, too, was quiet now. She suddenly seemed older, more vulnerable. Her voice cracked.

"I don't want you to risk your future by dragging up the past. It doesn't exist anymore. It doesn't need to. And it won't help you. Stop looking for it. Your future's bright. I'm worried that you'll…that you'll make yourself ill if you find out what happened." She stopped and took a breath. "I've lost one daughter, Liliane. I don't want to lose another." The last few words seemed to be trapped in her chest, and Liliane could barely hear them. In that moment, the surge of blood to her head that had threatened to push the anger out of her receded like a wave pulling sand down a beach. It was Geraldine who would be crushed by the revelation of her past. She couldn't inflict it on her. She had been here before with someone else who had been unable to bear the burden she had placed on him. It was a momentary feeling, but it was enough. She knew now that her past was there, within reach, and it would shape her future and who she would be. It was her responsibility alone to find it, whatever the future might then bring with it.

***

There was a bench in a square a few minutes walk away, close by the railings and set near some overgrown shrubs. It got overlooked by those seeking the sun for their sandwiches, but it suited Liliane, and she often came to this spot when she needed some space. The shade hid her, and she leaned back on the cool metal in relief. The seclusion and the fresher air eased her tension, and her head felt lighter now she had escaped. In the office, her scar had pulsed in distress, but now the ache had subsided, she could think clearly again. She should have known Nick would tell all to his mother and that Geraldine would descend on her. She chastised herself for having gone to Berto's, and she worried now that she had confided too much in him. It made her nervous to think that Malabanda, if he really was in London, might get to hear that she was too because of Berto's enquiries.

The only person she could trust was herself. It had been left unsaid, but Liliane could see that part of Geraldine's concern was driven by whatever the doctor had told them all those years ago. She was afraid of losing another daughter. It would be a shame if the things she was experiencing were figments of a damaged, deteriorating brain. In the meantime, Liliane refused to believe it. But she knew that to own her past, she had to find Malabanda. The urge to do so had been growing in her since the previous evening. The conviction was even stronger now. She had to find him, but on her own.

***

It was late when Liliane got back. She fumbled with the front door, confused and irritated, until she found the right key, then shoved it with her shoulder and ended in a heap in the lobby when it opened more easily than normal. She sat down on the nearest seat and leaned forward, the wood of the table cool on her hot brow. She stole a glance at her watch and groaned. It would be time to open up again soon.

It was Zee's fault, she told herself, or maybe Adele's, but deep down she knew it was herself to blame. Geraldine had said enough to Adele to worry her, and, of course, it got passed on to Zee and Isabelle. It had taken a lot of reassurance during the afternoon but what had struck her was the depth of love her staff had for her. The burden of responsibility weighed heavier with each conversation and the idea of a meal together had seemed the best way to cut through the gloom. Mr Sentwali had given her some money to reward the staff, and this seemed like a good reason to spend it. The day's tension had affected everyone, and each had downed their first drink with the studied concentration of people determined to enjoy many more.

Aware that she would fall asleep if she didn't move, Liliane wove an unsteady path through the tables and, when she got to the door, made a conscious effort not to glance at the picture or peer into the gloom of the corner. She needed sleep. Upstairs, she managed to pull the curtains before the spinning room got too much. A book, open at a picture of the hills of

Kigali, was on the sofa. She stared at it then swiped it onto the floor and flopped onto the cushions.

When she woke, the sun was bright on her face. She looked up to see a cloud pass across the sky, its shadow on the hill opposite. Father pulled her close and hugged her so tight it hurt. They played a game, trying to be the first to pick out her school and their house in the city spread out below. As they walked, he talked to her about their country's history and why things happened the way they did.

"We Tutsis used to run this country, but now we're second-class citizens, Liliane. Many Hutus hate us," he told her.

He was always serious on these walks and treated her like an adult as he tried to educate her, but today, his voice was different, and when she looked at him, there were tears on his cheek. His stories about the past had never upset him like this before, and this worried her. She fished a handkerchief from her sleeve and wiped his face, but he wouldn't look at her and kept his eyes on the far hills. Further up the road, at the top of the hill, she saw a house set behind high, pink walls. A guard stood at the gate, but he seemed to know Father and let them pass into the large garden. It was laid out with lawn and lots of beautiful plants with colourful flowers, which she recognised as japonicas and bougainvillea from nature studies. The red bricks were clean as if they had been scrubbed, and the large windows, with views over the city, were so bright in the sun that it hurt her eyes.

"You must be very respectful, Liliane. Mr Akayesu is the Minister for Finance, and I work for him," Father explained. "I shouldn't really have my job because I'm a Tutsi, so I have to ensure I work harder than the Hutus and always do what he tells me. And so must you," he added.

"His daughter is in my class, Father. I've seen him there."

"I know, Liliane. He's seen you too. He always asks about you."

"Will Miriam be there too? Are we going to play?"

He seemed about to say something, but after a silence, he said, simply, "No." He pulled a brightly wrapped package from a bag. "This is a present for him. From you. His favourite sweets—Turkish Delight. He'll be very pleased. With you. And me."

His words were quick, and his nervousness transmitted to Liliane. "I shall be waiting in the garden for you." His skin was damp, and her hand slipped out of his just as the door of the lobby opened. Akayesu is such a massive man, she thought. He was taller than Father, with a huge stomach covered by a dark suit, and she wondered how someone as small as Miriam could have such a large father.

"Come and stand here, Liliane. Let me see you," Akayesu said when they had entered his large study and twisted his hand for her to twirl around. "This girl will break many hearts, Iwo, yours included, no doubt." Father laughed with him, but Liliane noticed how he fiddled with the brim of his hat with nervous fingers. At a signal from Father, Liliane stepped towards Akayesu, the gift held in front of her.

"Thank you, Liliane, thank you." He pulled at the paper, and she was surprised at how excited he seemed over such a small gift. Father looked happy too. "Come and sit with me, Liliane," he said, and his hand pushed her further into the room. Behind her, the door closed. "Here is one of Miriam's books. You can read it to me."

His legs stuck out on either side of his large stomach, and he pulled Liliane between them until she felt his breath on her neck. His grip was tight, and she could no longer blink back her tears. She wanted to get away from him. Her head was sore and when she reached up to rub it, she was surprised to find that her fingers sank into a rough hollow. Her breathing was loud and erratic, and her blouse clung to her back as if she had been running. She struggled off the sofa and stared around her in confusion. The hills of Kigali lay in a book at her feet, not through a polished window. She was alone, yet her skin still felt the prickle of pain that had woken her. Her brain was scrambled with tiredness and alcohol, but it was no dream. It had been too real for that. She rubbed the top of her leg and tried to erase the imprint of his touch. A lorry horn sounded in the street, but she heard only the angry bellow of Akayesu.

One thing was clear to her now. She knew who her father was. She knew the worry lines chiselled on his forehead, the tick at the side of his mouth, the way he avoided looking at her. And yet…and yet there was another Father to discover as well, she was sure. Twice now, she had seen him. Each time, a residue of disgust and shame soured her mood. He allowed bad things to happen to her. She sank back onto the sofa as if the realisation had sapped the strength in her legs. He was a Tutsi among Hutus, a frightened man, aware of the power of life and death they wielded over him.

Kigali and Kitabuye. Akayesu and Malabanda. She had seen herself hit Akayesu and knew now that her impulsive action had cost Father his job. And Malabanda? She touched her scars as if they might transmit their memories through her fingertips, but they were mute, unresponsive to her touch. Yet the answers to her past and the signposts to her future lay beneath them.

She was too tired now to piece the few shreds of memory into anything coherent. They hung around her like gossamer filaments. One day soon, she was sure, there would be enough of them to weave into the picture of her life.

***

"I hear you had a visit yesterday." Liliane had sought refuge in the office at the first sign of a break in trade. Everything seemed an effort that morning, and the headache from the day before was back. Now Nick. She had answered the telephone distractedly. The image of her hand striking Akayesu, as a red mist blotted out her senses, still occupied her thoughts. That was the reason why they had left Kigali. It was her fault they had ended up in Kitabuye. Akayesu first. Then Malabanda.

"Thanks to you, yes. Are you calling to gloat, or did you want something?" She no longer cared if she upset him. He was silent for a long time, then seemed to gather himself.

"I was worried about you, Liliane. We all are. All these episodes. It's concerning."

"I seem to be the only topic of conversation in your family."

"We're your family as well, Liliane. We care. We love you." He paused again. "I love you."

"Is that how you show it?" Her voice was raised.

"Don't shout, please, Liliane. I wanted to check you're okay and to apologise. I should have known better. She's really stressed about you. You must have seen that." He spoke quickly, as if he sensed her patience was limited. "Look, Mum hasn't told me to call you. This is me, Liliane. You're getting carried away by things you think you've seen or remembered. The man you thought you saw is dead." That was why he had called. It was impossible to argue against his facts. "And these other things you've imagined—"

"I haven't imagined anything," she shouted. "It's all still here in my head. I know it is." The telephone cradle rattled as her hand slammed on the table. "You brought me here because you wanted to use me, use what I knew."

"Liliane. Listen," Nick protested, but she was in no mood to relent.

"I'm grateful. You know that. I owe you my life. That doesn't mean you own it. My past…or my future."

"If you've got any sense, you'll accept you don't have a past. And you'll wreck your future if you go looking for it."

"You were happy to use my past once. Now that it's no use to you, I'm supposed to pretend it doesn't exist. I thought a priest back from the dead would be a good story for you."

He was silent for so long that she thought he had hung up.

"Look, let's meet again. Properly this time. I'd like to see the café when it's open." They arranged a time, and he hung up. It had all ended too quickly. She wished she hadn't mentioned the chance of a story. Nick Heggarty could never resist a challenge.

TWENTY

The Equator was shut on a Sunday, and Liliane allowed herself to stay in bed until she felt a desire to get up. Saturday had been her day off, and she had enjoyed shopping and exploring London by herself. Two nights of sleep, uninterrupted by promptings from her past, left her refreshed and energised. The solitude allowed her to think, to get things in perspective, and it was with renewed determination that she rummaged through her bags of shopping. If she was going to find Malabanda, it was on her own. She would shape her own destiny, even if it all proved pointless.

The map seemed bigger in her room than it had in the stationer's shop and almost covered the wall behind the door to the stairs. She set a small table in front of it and placed a box of pins on it along with the slim booklet she had found in an old bookshop. She didn't dare count how many names and addresses of churches it contained. It was a start, and she was in control at last. It was her secret, and no one could tell her what to do or how to do it. There were four months until she went away. Four months to find Malabanda. And her past. If it was all fruitless, she would turn away and step into the future that was planned for her.

The idea had come to her as she wandered past a Roman Catholic church. She stared at it. There must be a notice board, something to say who the priest was. Finding nothing outside, she had tried the door. It was unlocked but something made her hesitate. She knew all the bad things that had happened at churches in the war. This was different. It was personal. Malabanda again. She had remembered how she would see him on the steps of the church in Kitabuye, watching, waiting for her. There was a board in the lobby. No African priest was mentioned.

She pushed her first pin in the map and crossed the name out in her book. It gave her a small sense of victory, a first step in her hunt for him. It would be so much easier if she could enlist Berto's help in her search, but she still harboured misgivings about already having told him too much- and who he might talk to.

That night, she sat in the café, as she often did on a Sunday, and planned for the week ahead. The light was failing as she completed her preparations. She closed her notebook and looked up at the end wall.

The earth was soft beneath her feet. The double doors of the shed were open, and she was climbing over some packing cases with another girl while an old man inspected the contents of an open crate. She ran over to it and looked inside. There was a green dress on top, too big for her, but she held it against herself and waited for the man's approval. Beneath his grey, frizzy hair his face creased in pleasure. "One day, Liliane," he said. Then the sun set, and the café was in darkness.

She bit her lip in disappointment. She knew instinctively she had loved that man like he was her father. There was a void in her where he had once been. No matter what the rest of her life brought, it could never be filled. This was grief again, she realised. She sat for a long time in the dark and imagined the old man was with her for company. She felt comforted by having seen him. His appearance in her life seemed to revitalise her, to give her strength to find Malabanda. She no longer felt on her own.

***

"Nick's here," Zee announced with a grin, and he seemed genuinely pleased for her. Over his shoulder, she saw him seated by the window where they wouldn't be disturbed, a table all on its own. Lovers' Corner. It was laid for lunch. Even Adele was pulling the strings of her life now. She waited and watched Nick as he rifled through a file of papers, absorbed in his work. He had looked so young and vulnerable when she woke from her operation, his distress tangible as he realised she didn't know who she was. He wore the confidence that success had brought him so easily now, yet there was a hardness in him that she guessed came from the war zones and killing fields that were his workplace.

"He had nightmares for months after he got back from Rwanda," Geraldine told her some time after she had moved to London. "Not that I'm justifying what he did, of course, but we had to get him some help in the end," which was quite an admission from Geraldine, who normally never acknowledged weakness in her son.

He stood when he saw her weave through the busy tables, and she allowed him to kiss her cheeks. She felt nervous at his touch, and she saw in him also the conflicting emotions she still seemed to arouse in him. They talked for a while about The Equator, her studies at night school and going to university in the autumn. Adele brought coffee and food and fussed around until Liliane chased her away.

"Mum says you're coming down for a weekend sometime." He seemed pleased and surprised. She hadn't told Geraldine why she was going or what she wanted but would be counting on his support when the time came. They stayed on the safe ground of idle chatter until they had eaten, then Nick turned to his papers. She could see he wanted to tell her something.

"Since I saw you last time when…" He seemed unsure how

to describe Liliane's claim of having seen Malabanda. "Well, I've had some time off and dug out my old papers about…about that time." She nodded her acknowledgement and he carried on. "I was so angry at the UN. Everyone was at the time. They abandoned your country, stood by and watched as it went mad. Our governments in the West were no better. I had all the evidence in front of me: the ethnic hatred and tribal savagery compounded by Western complacency and politics. It was all in my documentary. Everything I felt. I think it was what made it so successful. It was angry and it touched a nerve." He looked up from his papers and she saw the anger burning again. "I identified all the bad guys, so I thought." His hand slapped the file that separated them. "But maybe I didn't have all of them." He pulled on a yellow sticker. "Look at this. There were scores of massacres at churches, all organised by priests, all offering sanctuary and then…" She knew about this but let him tell his story.

"It was so easy, Liliane. Get them all together in the one place they thought they'd be safe. Great way to make sure none got out alive." He screwed his face in apology. "Sorry, that was a bit blunt." She shrugged and he resumed. "I found all these reports of priests and nuns killing people." He tapped the thick file again. "The Catholic Church was a partner in government with the Hutus. It had power over people's lives, over their minds, and it had a key role in the colonisation of your country.

There was a lot of wealth at stake if the Hutus lost power." She sensed his frustration for missing this angle at the time. "Their fingerprints are all over the genocide, Liliane." In his intensity, it was no longer 'that time'. "They helped plan it. And they helped execute it. I didn't see it at the time." She expected him to carry on, for his excitement to burn brighter, but he flopped back in his seat and slammed the file shut.

She reached across the table and squeezed his fingers. "You believe me then? About Malabanda? Is that why you've been looking at this?"

"I'm sorry I was so… I learned the hard way not to discount even the most outlandish things." He smiled in apology. "You seemed pretty sure, Liliane."

"I still am." This wasn't the time to tell him how much else had leaked out, how much more she knew about herself.

"You did get me thinking, I must admit," he said but the energy seemed to have gone from him. "Some of this stuff's come out since, of course," he continued, but this fact didn't seem to lift his spirits. "Except no one's interested. It's a few years ago, the world has moved on and they've got enough people to put on trial over there. It's all about reconciliation and rebuilding now. This just stirs the trouble, the memories." He swept a hand over the papers and sounded bitter. "I'm three years too late. It's not about the story, Liliane." He looked defiant. "There are people who should have been brought to justice.

The word jarred with her. It was important to her, but she couldn't tell why. She used his silence to focus her own thoughts. Justice. Was that why she needed to find Malabanda? It was all so confusing.

Eventually, he carried on. "I confronted the Church, here in London, with the evidence that showed that Catholic bishops and priests in Rwanda were involved in planning the genocide and in the killing." He leaned forward, his face flushed. "Churches were used as traps to lure the Tutsis. I saw it in Kitabuye. But the same happened in many places, Kibuye, Nyarubuye, Ntarama." With each name, he jabbed his finger on the pile. "There's so much information about priests murdering, of nuns killing Tutsi children, always at the church. It was everywhere, Liliane. It was evil, it was wrong, and someone needs to be brought to account. I showed them all this."

"So what did they say, the people you saw?"

"They just denied it all. They conceded that a few priests did some terrible things, but they were the sinful acts of a few individuals, acting out of fear, rather than the collective, organised action of the Church." He sat back, frustrated. "They just stone-walled, even when I showed them all this, evidence that their Church in Rwanda was part of the government, part of the planning for the genocide. They shrugged and said that the Catholic Church has a role to play in the government of many countries but that doesn't mean it goes around killing people."

He was angry, but with himself or with the Church, she couldn't tell. "Did you ask them about Malabanda? About him being in London?" He was silent for a while as if choosing the right words to use.

"I asked if they were sure the priest of Kitabuye was dead." She could see he had been embarrassed to ask. "They just pulled out their papers and showed me his death certificate. They were adamant about it, I'm afraid. So I don't know who it was you saw." He sat immersed in his own thoughts for a while and Liliane let him be. Eventually, he roused himself but with the air of a man who knows he's beaten. "I've been to the government with it, but they're not interested. It's all Serbia and Kosovo and bombings of Americans in Africa and Islamist terrorism." He looked up at her. "I wish I'd nailed those bastards at the time." She thought of what Geraldine had said about the nightmares and, for a moment, saw the memories of Kitabuye weighing on him again. She took his hand. He had risked his life to tell the world what was happening. Now, it was old news. She wished she could help him out of his misery.

"If…if Malabanda was alive and here in London, would that change things?"

"It would change things. It would mean they knew what was going on, what their priests were doing and that they condoned it." His enthusiasm flickered briefly. "It would mean they were knowingly engaged in hiding guilty priests, giving them new identities." He shook his head as if such a thought was madness.

"This isn't like you, Nick. You've got all this information on what they did in Rwanda, but you still trust them because it's England."

"You find him, Liliane. See if you can bring him back from the dead." He packed his papers away, and they arranged a date for dinner.

Zee was at the door. Nick high-fived him and they embraced. Liliane watched in surprise at how well they seemed to know each other, their heads close together while they talked.

"I didn't realise you and Nick were such good friends," she said when Zee came back. The prospect made her uneasy for some reason.

"Just bumped into him once, had a few drinks," he replied but he turned away as he spoke. Zee's face always betrayed what he was thinking, and she knew he was hiding something from her, but Isabelle interrupted them just then, and Liliane dismissed the thought.

"Berto brought this for you, Liliane. Said it was important," she said. Liliane took the envelope and put it behind the till. It could wait until they were less busy.

TWENTY-ONE

Liliane woke to the rattle of rain against the window and an unaccustomed chill after the oppressive heat of the last few weeks. She checked her clock then pulled the bedclothes tighter. It would be quiet this morning and a few more minutes wouldn't do any harm. She had been back in Kitabuye in the night, rooted in front of the church. She had grown used to these nocturnal visits and no longer woke up drained and on edge. The church was the opposite of everything she had seen in London: rough-hewn bricks of red clay, not smooth marble; gaping holes for windows to let the breeze blow through, not intricate stained glass; a small metal cross above the entrance, rather than an ornate carving. It was becoming familiar, and these days, she could clearly recall memories of walking through the grounds to the old doors, in the days before the killing left the shadow around it.

At quiet times like this, she had learned how to summon up memories. Sometimes, they slipped easily from the clutches of the fog but often she would catch just a tantalising glimpse before it would slip away from her. Today, when she concentrated, she was inside the old brick church.

"Inyenzi," he shouted again. His hands gripped the small rail in front of him so hard his knuckles blanched. Liliane shifted in her seat as Malabanda railed against the Tutsis and felt her mother's hand tighten on hers. The priest's eyes were wild, spittle was flecked on his chin as his voice rose and even the Hutus seemed to cower beneath his venom. "Inyenzi, you will burn in hell unless you submit to your Hutu masters." He looked at Liliane as he said this. She turned to her father, but his gaze was fixed on the priest, and he was nodding enough to catch Malabanda's approving look. She leaned closer to the boy on her right and felt his comforting strength through the thin fabric of his shirt. He was her twin. His face had revealed itself a few nights previously. It was like looking at herself. The next morning, she bunched her hair behind her head and saw him in front of her in the mirror, the same high cheeks, the pointed nose and full lips, the oval eyes. He was Bernard. In the church he stared back at Malabanda, defiant and contemptuous.

The alarm broke her concentration and the memory disappeared. She got out of bed and stood in front of the mirror. Bernard stared back at her, so alive it was hard to believe he had really gone. His death had left a hole in her life that she was only now able to identify and rationalise. They had been together, inseparable since birth, now parted by death. How could she not have been with him when the time came? She knew enough about those days to know death didn't come suddenly. The Tutsis knew. They waited. She should have been there. She had no death certificate, no eye-witness accounts, yet her books told her that Kitabuye was one of the towns where the killing had been so systematic and efficient the RPF had recorded few Tutsi survivors. She was alive. Her family was dead. She had a gilded life in London. Her family suffered a brutal death. How could they not have done? Now that she knew them, the guilt of being alive was squeezing the life out of her.

She needed to understand. Her future depended on her knowing. Knowing everything.

***

It was time to open up. The present was demanding Liliane's attention. She had some small pieces of her past but still too few to see any sort of picture. It would have to wait for now. Life in The Equator resumed its normal pace. Her incident with Geraldine faded from being a talking point to old news, and everyone avoided any mention of Liliane's past. Even Adele's questions about Nick became infrequent in his continuing absence.

Liliane used her free time to visit churches, and the number of pins began to multiply on the wall, although she was no further forward in locating Malabanda. His face was more distinct to her, beyond the vague features of that glimpse on the escalator. She was sure it was the same man, the man who was supposed to be dead.

It was, however, a conversation with Isabelle one evening that changed everything. Adele and Zee had left early after a quiet afternoon. Isabelle had been distracted all day and Liliane sensed the girl wanted to talk. When the café was swept and tidy, she made two milkshakes and beckoned the girl to a table.

"You've been quiet today. Everything all right?" She had learned that silence was the best way to get people to say what they might not want to. Isabelle concentrated on her drink until the straw sucked on air. When she looked up, her eyes brimmed with tears. Liliane reached across. "It's okay to talk. If you want to."

"I…I can't tell Adele. She'd try to ignore it." Liliane let her take her time. "I've been seeing a counsellor." She didn't need to explain why. "She said it might help if I talked about it to others. So that they know."

"Talk about what, dear?" Although she already had a sense of what was coming.

"About being raped…when the Hutus came for us." Liliane squeezed her hand and smiled. There was little else she could do. "I've met a boy. He wants to… well, we both do, you know. But I'm scared. I can't bear it when he touches me…down there. I panicked. He was really nice about it. He understands, as much as these people can."

Liliane nodded but she was back in the bedroom at The Grove, remembering Nick's confusion at her own panic.

"I was too, Isabelle." She didn't know where the words had come from, but she heard the conviction in her voice.

The girl looked startled. "You've remembered?"

"I know now. Inside me. I haven't remembered, but I feel it now. Nick wanted to once… we both did." It was the only explanation now. "It ended the same way."

They clung to each other for a long time as if their lives depended on it. In that moment, it came to her. It was Malabanda.

Isabelle's mood was lighter when she left. Liliane was carrying the burden for both of them now. She sat back in the café and tried to absorb the fresh awakening within her. When she closed her eyes, she could see the room again—the same one. She felt the skin on her back snag on rough bricks and her stomach burn from its violation. His eyes were wild behind the thick glasses. It was Malabanda she was with when her family died. This changed everything. She wasn't trying to find him just for justice. It was personal now.

***

She sat at her table later in the evening, unable to focus on her books. Adele and Geraldine had warned her. Now she knew. Malabanda had raped her. She was sure he had attacked her, caused her injuries but… but something was still missing. She felt drained and too tired to work and went to her bedroom to undress. The wardrobe door was open.

She didn't remember putting the green dress on, but still, it really did look good on her, and she twirled from side to side to admire her mother's sewing skills.

"Very nice, Lili. You look quite the woman now." She turned away from the oval, wooden mirror that stood in the corner of the shop and saw the man she had seen outside the shed in the clearing.

"Thanks, Uncle. I'm going to show it to Patrick."

"Mind he keeps his hands off it, now." The old man grinned. "Your mother will be mad if it gets creased. It's meant to be for your sixteenth birthday, not parading around town."

Liliane pulled a face then turned back to the mirror. She didn't think her mother had meant for her breasts to be so exposed when she altered the dress, and she marvelled again at how big she now was. She smoothed her hands over them and pulled the material down, her head on one side, until she was satisfied.

"I think every woman and girl in Kitabuye has stood in front of that mirror to try a dress on. I'd be driven out of town if I ever did sell it."

Liliane stepped across and hugged him. "Thank you, Uncle OK. You're like a father to me. I sometimes wish…"

"Don't, Lili. He's a good man. He does his best. You'll understand one day. Of that, I'm certain, I fear." Liliane kissed him and left, aware of the men watching her from the sidewalk as she went. She hurried her step, eager to show Patrick before it was dark. He would be waiting, she knew, where he always waited, away from the disdainful looks of his family. She hurried past the church lest Malabanda see her and on up the hill to the little dip where Patrick was lying on his back. He scrambled up as she got closer and stared at her, open-mouthed. She turned round to show him and felt his hands reach behind her and lower the zip.

"Careful," she said as he pulled the dress down her shoulders, and she wriggled her arms out. He put a finger to her lips, laid the dress on the grass then eased her down into the dip with him as the sun set behind the hills.

In the mirror, her scars were more obvious than ever, the beauty she had just witnessed now ravaged. She kicked the door shut, angry at everything that had been taken away: her family, her memory, her looks. And Patrick. That was the boy's name. He was a Hutu, a strong young man, and she shivered as she remembered his fingers on the skin of her back. It must have been forbidden love for a Tutsi girl to sleep with a Hutu boy. The thought prompted uneasy feelings in her. Was he still alive? What choices had he made?

Such thoughts weren't welcome, but they wouldn't leave her. She had lost him, but not to the knife, she was sure. When she finally slept, she saw him again. He was in a crowd of men. The last she saw of him was when he turned away from her.

***

She was up early the next day, her sleep interrupted by so much turmoil. The appearance of Patrick in her life had alternately thrilled and disturbed her, just like the effect Nick had on her. The similarity of emotions confused her. She began to tidy the papers that had accumulated behind the till, receipts no longer needed, notes of orders long ago served and an envelope with her name on it. It was from Berto. She remembered now. Isabelle had given it to her, but she had shoved it behind the till until the café was quieter. There was no note, just a slip of paper with the address of a church.

Her A-Z was in the office, yellowing Sellotape holding the spine together, dog-eared from use. She found the reference in the back, flicked to the page, and stuck a finger on the square. On the opposite page, in the top corner, was her college. It was where she would be tonight. She tucked the note in her pocket, excited yet nervous. He must have found a church with an African priest. Yet it would be late after college. And she knew she shouldn't go on her own. Now that she had a real lead, part of her wanted it not to be Malabanda. It was easier to hate him and plot her revenge on him when he was still an indistinct sighting on the Underground. If he really did exist and she was face to face with him, what then? Her impulsiveness had got her into this. She had never thought about the implications.

***

The sky was leaden, and rain sluiced down the big windows of The Equator when Liliane was ready to leave for night class. The café seemed to be in perpetual gloom all day as the bad weather of the last few days continued. It was a night when sensible people stayed inside, but her studies were too important. She was losing focus and falling behind. She checked her bag, then her money and found the slip of paper in her pocket. She put it back behind the till, turned away, then went back to retrieve it. It might just be worth checking where the church was. That would be all.

The class was hard that night and she had to concentrate. At the end, she chatted to the others, forced herself to smile at the jokes and fought off suggestions for a drink. She knew some of the boys liked her. She enjoyed watching them compete for her attention, but tonight, she was distracted and aloof and they drifted off to the pub. She hesitated on the steps of the college and watched them go. It was only a few minutes to the church. Just have a look. The others would be in the pub until late. She could come back.

It took longer than she thought, but she eventually stopped opposite the church and looked back along the deserted, tree-lined avenue, the branches still dripping after the latest sudden downpour. The temperature had dropped with the rain, and she shivered. The church was visible through the branches, its features dominated by the dull grey figure of Christ hanging on a stone cross embedded in the front wall of the squat tower. His blank eyes watched over anyone who entered through the wooden doors below. The stained-glass windows on either side were dull red. The stone had blackened with age, and the church looked closed and unwelcoming.

She hesitated, relieved now that it appeared to be locked and empty. There was a noticeboard outside, and after waiting for a solitary car to pass, its headlights deepening the grey of the evening around her, she picked her way through the puddles to stand in front of the board. Apart from service times, there was no other information, and the name of the Priest in Charge had long since been painted over. There had been a service that evening, but it would have finished long ago. Now she was closer, she could see the stonework was stained with damp patches, and green streaks bled down the walls. Water trickled out of a broken gutter onto the head of Christ and down his face, as if he was weeping.

She flinched as a large drop of rain spattered on her forehead and turned to go, but the shower was sudden, and soon the rain was bouncing off the paving stones around her. There was a wide stone overhang above the doors, and she flattened herself against them after she ran up the steps. The street was devoid of life, the houses and trees indistinct shapes through the rain. The gutters overflowed in sheets of water onto the steps around her and pushed her further against the door. It suddenly swung open under her weight to reveal a windowless vestibule, the pale light from the doorway swallowed by the darkness within. Swing doors led into the church, but the small panes of glass revealed little of the inside. One of the doors shifted as she pushed on it, and the creak of the hinges seemed louder in the stillness. Nothing stirred in the church, and unable to hold her breath any longer, she eased the door ajar until she could squeeze through it and winced again as it groaned shut.

The daylight outside seemed to falter once it reached the stained-glass windows, and two candles on either side of the aisle provided the only other light. As her eyes adjusted to the gloom, the rows of pews became visible ahead of her. Beyond the candles, there seemed to be an impenetrable barrier of darkness, except for a red light suspended in the air. A smell of stale incense wrinkled her nostrils and irritated her throat, and for a moment, she was back in the darkened room.

Treading carefully on a carpet she could not see, she walked past the candles. They flickered brighter as she passed and illuminated the dark wood of the closest pews. She waited until they were still again, her breath shallow. The flames cast small pools of light on the floor, and in the red glow of the sanctuary lamp, she could make out the altar, a crude wooden table, unadorned. To her left, the Virgin stood watching her from the shadows.

The silence and gloom felt threatening, and Liliane yearned to be back outside, away from the suffocating stillness of the church. It suddenly occurred to her that someone must still be there for candles to be lit and the door to be unlocked. The dark corners at the front continued to withhold their secrets, and she wondered if he was there, watching her, waiting for her to come closer. No one knew she was here. Her friends would never know where to look if she disappeared.

It was time to go, she decided, when behind her, the candles flared and hissed and lit the altar for a moment. There was no sound, no breath, just a slight disturbance in the air and a different smell. Someone was behind her.

She turned quickly. The thump of her heart seemed loud in

the silence. He was still in shadow, but the red light shone back at her from his glasses.

"Can I help you? I'm afraid we finished an hour ago." He stepped into the light of the candles. His skin was black, but the lenses were thin, the frames made of wire. He wasn't Malabanda. "I've just come to lock up and put the candles out." He seemed to be expecting some sort of explanation for her presence in his church.

"I was sheltering from the rain," she mumbled. Her hand grabbed the end of the nearest pew. The brief surge of fear then relief had left her weak.

"I didn't mean to surprise you. I didn't see you until I was close. Can I help you?" he asked again.

"No, thank you. I hadn't meant to come in. I'm sorry. The rain."

"You're always welcome. Try us on a Sunday. Here, take this." He handed her a service leaflet, and her hands still shook as she folded it and put it in her coat. "Where are you from?" he asked.

"Rwanda," she told him and without meaning to, she added, "Kitabuye." His eyes narrowed, and she saw him take in her hijab.

"My details are on the leaflet. If you want to talk. It can't be easy facing life after what happened there."

"Yes. It is hard. Sometimes. Thank you."

"I'm from Gitarama." He seemed to need to associate with her pain, her past. "We have both seen more than we should have."

"I…I don't remember." She touched her head and he nodded.

"Then you are blessed." His words reminded her of Geraldine. Had her actions brought a curse on her? A curse of knowing, gradually, imperceptibly seeing everything. She thanked him again and left.

The clouds had passed, and the last of the evening sun, low in the sky, shone along the avenue of trees, and the road glistened. She felt reprieved. It had been foolhardy to go in alone in the dark, but she knew that she hadn't really expected to find him. Even now, she was still unsure that she really had seen Malabanda on the escalator. Back in The Equator, she sat for a long time. The church clock in the nearby square struck midnight. The window above her head rattled as a bus rolled past, and its lights shone on the picture. If Malabanda was in London and the Church was sheltering him, she needed to be smarter, more careful than she had been tonight if she was to find him. It was no longer about her own curiosity, a need to satisfy herself with what she had or hadn't seen. There was a growing certainty inside her that she had been saved for a reason.

TWENTY-TWO

Liliane had just finished wiping down some tables as the early morning rush subsided when one of the regular customers caught her eye and called her over. He was in his late twenties, she thought, dressed as always in a sober suit and tie with a newspaper spread across his table.

"Another coffee?" she asked, although she had never seen him stay longer than for one.

"No, no thanks. Very nice, though. Best for miles around, all of it," he said and looked around the café. Liliane flashed him a smile of thanks and waited for him while he ran a finger over his paper. "No," he repeated and looked up at her. "You're all Rwandan, right? You? Your staff? You all came here after the…" He hesitated, as most people did, unsure what word would cause the least offence. "After the war?"

"We came to escape the genocide, yes." He nodded and seemed relieved not to have to say the word.

"I'm a lawyer," he said in a lower voice, as if ashamed to admit it. "International law, in fact."

"Must be interesting," Liliane replied, unsure where the conversation was going.

"The point is, I've been helping gather evidence, put the prosecution cases together for some of the trials. To bring some of those men to justice." His last word stirred something inside her; it was important to her but still she was unsure why. Her face must have betrayed her confusion because he added, "In Rwanda. Sorry. I just thought you might be interested." His finger stabbed the paper on the table. "Men like this." There was repressed anger in him, she thought. She bent lower to read the title of the piece. 'Paymaster of Rwandan genocide sentenced to death.'

"This guy, Akayeysu, was Finance Minister. Channelled money to the Interahamwe. They were…"

"I know what they were. And what they did," she added, aware of a sharpness in her voice.

The man nodded. "I guess so. Anyway," he folded his paper and reached for his bag, "I worked on this one. Nasty guy."

"I know," Liliane replied and regretted it straight away. She had sparked his interest in her.

"You knew him?" He unfolded his newspaper again and held it towards her. "This guy?" His voice was a mix of disbelief and respect, but it was Akayeysu's voice that echoed in her head, "Come and sit and read to me," and she could almost feel his clammy fingers on her leg. She remembered again the fleshy face, his broad shoulders and extended stomach, partly hidden by an expensive-looking suit jacket.

She pulled the other chair out and sat, her head close to his as Adele hovered close by. "My father worked for him for a while. We…left Kigali for Kitabuye a few years before the war started."

"Out of the frying pan," he said with an ironic laugh, then held his hands up. "Sorry, that was crass." His skin coloured, just like Nick's did, and she felt drawn to him, endeared by what he was doing for her people. "That was one of the worst, wasn't it?" She knew people couldn't resist the connection between the massacres and what lay beneath her silk, and she smiled when his gaze fell on it.

"It's not very nice," she said, and he averted his eyes.

"You survived," he said. "One of the lucky ones."

"Apparently," she replied. "In fact, I remember very little still." Her hand touched her head.

"But you remember him." She could see he was thinking about it all and his own connection to Akayeysu. "Your father must have been good for them to tolerate him in a position like that. Did you meet this guy?"

She hesitated, then looked away from him. "Yes. Yes, I did." She heard the certainty in her voice. "He wasn't a nice man." The face on the table rekindled the memory. "I'm glad you helped convict him. Thank you." She held her hand out. "Liliane," she said.

"Adam." They were both silent for a while. He had something on his mind and waited while he deliberated. He was a serious young man, she could see, no doubt accentuated by the work he did, but when he had smiled, she saw a softer side to him.

"You mentioned Kitabuye." She nodded her encouragement as she saw he was still wrestling with his thoughts. "It's early days, please keep it to yourself, but we're building a case against a guy called Gatsinzi. He was a sort of mayor in the town." Another name, another piece in the puzzle.

"I think I can remember him." The words came slowly as she picked away at the strands of memory. As bits of it unravelled, she saw a fat face with cruel eyes and moons of sweat on his shirt. She was in a narrow corridor with him. "Yes, yes, I can." It was Malabanda and Gatsinzi—together. "Will he…will he die as well?" She supposed there should be some sense of satisfaction that these men were facing justice, but all she could feel was anger for all the wasted lives and for the way these men had been allowed to let it all get that far.

"I hope so." Adam's serious face was on again. "Look, Liliane, do you…do you remember anything about him, about the day when…?" He shook his head as if in despair at the thought. Zee's account of the deaths at his village church had triggered her own memory in a quiet moment a few days ago. As the memory had unfurled itself, she found herself looking down on her own church from a hill, peering through the branches of trees. There was a glint of metal in the sun, like sparks flying, as it arced downwards. She saw the knife stab a man in the chest. It was Malabanda who wielded it. It was the first death. Then it was over. She saw nothing else.

"No, I don't. Sorry." It was too soon to talk about. It was locked away still, too raw, too hurtful for her to cope with.

"Here's my card." Adam stood, the picture of Akayeysu folded away now. "If you remember, that is." They shook hands very formally. He looked as if he was thinking again, but this time, evidently decided not to say whatever it was, just smiled, then was gone.

Liliane stared at the swing doors long after he had pushed through them. The shadow of the genocide had fallen for a moment over The Equator, and she shivered as if its presence had sucked the warmth out of the room. Adam was engaged in a fight for justice for her country, for the people in her town, and for her family.

"Liliane?" Adele was at her shoulder. "What were you two talking about for so long? He comes here a lot, doesn't he?" The girl was bursting with curiosity.

Liliane scanned the café. It had gone quiet. She called Zee

and Isabelle over. "That man, Adam, he's a regular. He's doing some very special work. He's helping to prosecute the Hutus who led the genocide. I think," she paused and looked at each in turn, "I think it's difficult and demanding work but he's doing it for us, for our families, for justice. Just…just be nice to him. And give him a free coffee every day."

She fended off their questions, told them as much as she thought able to and caught snatches of their excited chatter as a rush of customers descended on them. The ground had just shifted beneath her again. It was a constant, nagging concern to her that the things she was experiencing, of people and events in her past, were just made up by a damaged mind to taunt her. But Akayeysu was true. The photograph matched her memory, as did his job. And although the memory was true, so was the reality that came with it. Her father had taken her to Akayeysu and left her with him. It was hard not to feel bitter towards her father, even harder to excuse him for the fear he must have endured daily. She remembered his face in the church, compliant, eager to please Malabanda, while next to her, she had seen Bernard, contemptuous, hostile, unafraid. Her own father had betrayed her to Akayeysu and then traded her to Malabanda to save himself. Maybe Akayeysu had given him the idea, or Malabanda, like Akayeysu, had given him no choice. Whatever the truth was, her beauty, she now knew, was a weapon he had wielded in his fight to avoid the blades that he knew, from his privileged position in government, would come one day.

That sadness stayed with her all day. In the evening, in the quiet of her flat, she concentrated on reassembling all the pieces of her past that had so far come to her into some sort of incomplete jigsaw.

Liliane. Bernard. Patrick. Three friends, yet more than that. Bernard and Patrick loved each other like brothers. The images came to her as she sat in the dark. The faces of two young men, always together, arm in arm, laughing and fooling around, playing football, drinking in a bar. Lots of small flashes of memory, as if a film was being fast-forwarded in her mind. She could differentiate now between her love for Bernard, whose absence had left a void that no other man could ever fill, and for Patrick, whose presence in her life had aroused such a different type of love in her. She missed them both and tried to coax more memories of them back to her. She saw herself, still young, running the tracks around the town looking for them, wanting to share their fun. Then, when she was older, she was watching them from outside a bar. She saw them climb on a table to see the screen over the men's heads and fall off in the melee when someone scored. There had been some happy times in her life among the sad memories that seemed to escape more easily.

She tried to keep the film running, but it came to an end.

Her mind wasn't ready to give up all its secrets yet, and she balled her fists in frustration. The telephone rang, and she reached for it absentmindedly, the images still bouncing around her head like dodgems.

"Liliane, it's Nick." It was so unexpected among the emotion of seeing the boys that she couldn't find any words to greet him. "Just thought I'd see how you are," he said, but she sensed there was more to his call than that. There always was with Nick.

"I'm fine. Having a quiet night. Catching up." She wished she could confide in him, seek his help in piecing everything together, but there was still so much she didn't yet understand.

"I've been doing a bit of digging around since our last chat. It got me thinking. I was wondering, Liliane, the priest you saw on the Underground, did he have a scar on his cheek?" She lowered herself into her chair again, unsettled by the question yet unsure why. She had only really seen his eyes; it had been so brief. Anyway, his face wasn't fully turned to her, the left side not visible. "Just a long shot," he added, a trace of irritation in his voice at Liliane's continued silence.

"I'm thinking, Nick," she said, but in her mind, she saw the face in the church and then again, close to hers, in his room. "No, I don't think so. His face wasn't fully turned towards me, though." She needed to tell him. "I do remember his face from the past. It's come to me a few times now, sometimes close up, like the first time." It sickened her to think. "Same glasses, same eyes but no scar. I'm sorry, Nick. Is it important?"

"It would help," he replied. "Not to worry, it might have happened later. Look, I know it's mostly blank, but if he was the priest from Kitabuye, although he was a Hutu, do you think he might have been the sort to defend the Tutsis, maybe even die for them, as the Church says?"

She saw the wild eyes, the blanched knuckles as his hands gripped the wood. "He called us Inyenzi, cockroaches. This was in church. He hated us."

"But no scar?"

She sighed. "No." He seemed to accept that she could recall things now, and it gave her confidence to carry on. It might be important. "Malabanda started it at the church. I've seen it. Enough of it anyway to know."

"Are you sure?" She could tell this was important and told him everything she knew. "He was in it with a man called Gatsinzi, the Burgomaster," she said. It all made sense now after seeing Adam earlier that day.

"How do you know about him?" His voice was quiet, as if afraid someone would overhear.

"I think I can remember the two of them now." She didn't feel as if she wanted to tell him about Adam yet because she was afraid it would all come back to Akayeysu. "What's going on, Nick? What are you going to do with everything I'm telling you?"

"I'll tell you all about it when I see you. Listen, thanks for the information."

He was gone. His story, whatever it was, was everything to him now. Liliane sat back, her eyes unfocused, confused by the day's events. It was all getting too much too quickly. She imagined how Adele would berate her if she knew. Too much sauce had been spilled. Maybe it was time to tip the rest out.

TWENTY-THREE

"Malabanda has got a scar! Nick. Nick. Pick up. Speak to me. I know now. I can explain. Call me. Please!"

For a third consecutive day, Liliane had called to speak to Nick and finally felt compelled to leave a message. She had wanted to tell him in person, to hear the excitement in his voice, but he seemed to be away and had told no one where he was. It had come back to her a few nights previously, the smell of incense still on her skin after sitting through a service in a church that was on her list and was now a pin on her map. The board outside had the name of an African priest, but it was an early evening Mass, and she felt safe in the large congregation.

The priest wasn't Malabanda. She saw straight away but was hemmed in on either side and had to endure the whole service. The incense was shaken close by her, and she had to grit her teeth and dig her nails into her palms to stop herself from retching. It was a smell that triggered bad memories. She scrubbed her skin in the shower when she got home, but it seemed to have seeped through her pores, and at some point in the night, the smell was even stronger. The skin on her back was on fire, and Malabanda had her pinned against the wall, his breathing ragged. But this time, it was different. She remembered more. Her fingers closed on a metal cross on a shelf above her head. She brought it down on his upturned face and saw the sharp edge tear through his skin and heard his roar of pain. He had grabbed a knife. She watched him bring it down on her.

The street lights were out, and it was too early for traffic. Liliane lay rigid in bed, tensed for the blow, but it didn't come. Her scars felt as if they had been scalded. There was a terrible ache in her stomach. She reached up and felt the wounds on her head and neck. They were intact, the rough skin and jagged edges comforting to her. Now she knew for sure. Malabanda had inflicted the dreadful wounds on her, but she had hurt him first. She had been overwhelmed with hatred for the man and what he had done to her for so long. Nothing else mattered. She felt that all-consuming loathing again. She had marked him. He would have to look at what she had done to him every morning when he looked in the mirror. Even now, it still felt like a small victory.

The next day was Sunday, and Liliane sat in front of the map, disheartened by the number of pins yet to be used. She called Nick a few times that day without success and then again on the Monday, slipping away to the office every few hours.

That evening, she phoned The Grove and spoke to Charles.

"We're looking forward to seeing you Saturday." He sounded genuinely pleased. It was a long time since she'd seen him.

"Me too, Charles. I've been trying to get hold of Nick. Is he with you?" She tried to keep the edge out of her voice.

"Not here, Liliane. I think he's working on something. You'll see him on Saturday. Any message if we speak to him?"

"Just to call me." She bit her lip and felt the sting of tears. Charles must have heard the catch in her voice, but he seemed to know better than to press her. They stayed on the safe ground of train times, and Liliane hung up. She had no other means of contacting Nick. She knew none of his friends, and so the next day left the message, her voice flat with disappointment and, for some reason she couldn't fathom, a rising sense of foreboding.

What if he's tracked Malabanda down? What if Malabanda had a knife? For a while, her imagination raced over all the dreadful things that Malabanda could have done. She pushed herself up and forced herself to go down to the café and get busy. He was away working. She could tell him to his face on Saturday. That was all there was to it.

Yet the constant drip of memories was now taking a toll on her, and she felt increasingly destabilised by the truth of her past that was emerging. Adele's advice was becoming uncomfortably correct. On days like this, Liliane wished she hadn't been so headstrong and inured to the warnings her friends had given her. She knew her family now, but she also knew the truth of her father's betrayal of her innocence and their relationship. And then there was Malabanda and what he had done to her.

The sauce was most definitely out of the bottle, and sometimes she could feel it pouring from her head and neck, over her breasts, her blood mixed with his. It was then that she knew without any doubt. She had been with Malabanda when her family died—when the Tutsis were massacred. And with that certainty came a new truth. She could have saved them. It was her fault they had died. She was the bargain between her father and Malabanda. If she had played her part, her family would have lived. The notion sickened her. The revelations were becoming increasingly hard to absorb. She felt like she was standing on the edge of a precipice, and one more memory would tip her headlong into oblivion.

***

The gradual change from the concrete, steel and grime of London to the now frequent patches of woods and fields went unnoticed by Liliane. Even as doors slammed at stations and people came and went around her, she saw nothing but the darkness of her reflection in the window, the pale unblinking ovals of her eyes and the red and green silk of the hijab that framed the outline of her face. Malabanda had stolen her innocence, and her scars were the legacy of his violence. She would not let him take her past from her while there was still a chance to salvage it from the wreckage of her mind.

But at some point, in the tunnel before her stop, her resolve dissipated. The defiance that had glared back from the mirror that morning had dissolved in the tears that glistened in her reflection in the window. She didn't have to do this. She could have submerged the idea, pushed it back into the fog where the rest of her memory lived undisturbed. But some inner desire still drove her on despite the unease that gnawed away at her. She straightened and smoothed the material around her face with her fingertips until they felt the ridge of jagged skin beneath her ear.

"It doesn't matter what you look like on the outside, Lili," Geraldine said when she saw the scars for the first time. "It's who you are on the inside that counts," she continued as she fixed one of the hijabs she had bought for Liliane in place. "No one need ever see them, not even Charles or Nick." She pulled her over to the sliding doors of her wardrobe. "See, you're just a normal young girl with a very pretty face and good taste in clothes."

Geraldine's love—so strong, so unconditional—was

precious to Liliane, and what she was about to ask of her would test it, maybe break it. Part of its strength was in their shared ignorance of Liliane's past, which had helped Geraldine to shape her future, and Liliane, who knew no better, had acquiesced. Up ahead, a slim crescent of blue sky was visible just beyond the red light. A small part of her own life had been shown to her and she felt again the urge to leave the darkness behind, no matter what lay beyond it.

The red turned green, the carriage lurched forward, and she screwed her eyes up as it emerged from the tunnel. Nick would be waiting for her. She would tell him now before Geraldine sapped her resolve and bent her to her own will again. She wondered if he expected this, wanted it even, so they could share again that first day when he had found her on the plains. The guard took her bag as she stepped onto the platform, slammed the door and blew his whistle all in one practised movement, then flashed a smile at her.

"Lovely morning, ma'am. Visiting the big house?" He set off down the platform, calling over his shoulder. "I remember you coming here, you see," he said in answer to her confused look. "Caused a fuss at first until we all realised." He turned, his free hand on the white gate, his eyes shiny. "They shouldn't have let it happen, should they? Someone should have paid for it. Where's the justice in this world, that's what I said to the wife." He stepped aside to let her pass. "Anyway, you have a nice day. Mr Heggarty is waiting."

"Thank you, I …" Over his shoulder, she saw the familiar grille of Charles's car. Then, with his arm raised and broad smile, he strode across the tarmac. Not Nick. She turned, unsettled, confused and reached for her bag. "Yes, I …will," she stammered to the guard, no longer sure that she would.

"Liliane. Lovely. Been looking forward all week." He even smells rich, she remembered as Charles kissed her cheeks and then with a sudden shout of, "Sod it, girl, give me a proper hug," he held her in a tight embrace, and she felt the affection that had once been so valuable to her. "Harry, well done. Thanks." She watched Charles shake the guard's hand—a crisp note left behind in his palm. She had read an article about Charles once, how he was a tough, fearsome opponent in business, ruthless in his deal-making, but that wasn't the man she knew. He was a big, friendly bear, almost comical in his red shorts, his belly hanging over the belt, his weight masked by his height.

She sank into the leather interior, flowers clasped in her hand, while Charles stowed her bag behind her. Maybe he's still working, editing in his studio or writing another script, she thought as the car accelerated up the hill and Charles chatted amiably. She knew how Nick hated to be disturbed. In her short time living with them, she had witnessed his parents tiptoe around him, their indulgence a far cry from how they treated the rest of the world.

"I suppose you're wondering why you're saddled with me, Liliane." He flashed her a broad smile, but there was an unusual restlessness in him. Nick had been so enthusiastic about her coming to visit. "He had a visit a few days ago. Some government chaps. Geraldine can tell you more. She was here. Wanted him to go off with them. Haven't a clue where, though. Or how long. Just packed and went." He checked on Liliane, but his words meant little to her. "He's been a thorn in their side for long enough. Maybe they want him inside the tent for a change," he said but couldn't disguise the concern in his voice. "Shame about all your Rwandan stuff he'd been working on, though. That priest of yours and everything. Proper scandal, if you're right." The car purred along the country lanes, Charles effortlessly flicking his wrist now and again to guide it around the bends.

Liliane could see the top of the house in the dip ahead of them. It would have to be now. She had to get him on side before Geraldine got to him and they ganged up on her. Without Nick, it would be so much harder.

"Charles, I …I want to ask you something. It's about why I came." He kept his eyes on the road, but his features had stiffened.

"Fire away, Liliane," but he was wary now, despite the smile.

"I want to see the video."

The car rolled to a stop in front of the gates, but they remained closed. Next to her, Charles was impassive, and she let the silence lengthen, giving him time to think. The trees were taller than she remembered, the ivy clinging to the honey-coloured walls thicker, but then it had been a few years.

"Why, Liliane?" It was what she expected; it was no more than she was already asking herself. "And after all this time?" He turned to look at her, but the bluff confidence she associated with him was gone, the ruddy complexion now pale. She imagined he was as much troubled by what Geraldine's reaction would be, as he no doubt was for her own state of mind. "It's this priest business, isn't it? You're that sure you saw him that you want to start all this?"

Liliane kept her eyes on the gates but nodded and wondered if Geraldine was watching them on the little screen in the kitchen, already full of questions. "It's started to come back, Charles. But it seems to be stuck on the bad things. I thought seeing it would help me find the rest, the good times, as well as the truth."

Charles took her hand, a slight tremor in his grip where there was normally firmness, but his voice was gentle when he spoke. "I wondered if this day would come; I was never sure myself it had all gone. Your memory, that is, in the operation." She could tell he was wavering, thinking it all through, weighing and measuring the implications, the consequences, like one of his business deals. "You'll only see more bad things, Liliane. Bad like you can't imagine. It made Nick ill, you know. After you'd gone, and before, I suppose. We had to get him help." It wasn't an excuse for his son, she knew. There was too much sorrow and regret in his voice. He let her hand fall back on the seat, pressed the button and waited for the gates to swing fully open. "If it doesn't…" She let him search for the right words, sensing he was still undecided. "If it doesn't work, Liliane. If nothing more comes and your mind retreats again, then…" He leaned towards her, his face close. This is how he makes his deals, she thought. "Then that's it. No more talk of priests, no more dragging up memories. Your past remains just that."

She nodded, but the look in his eyes told her he wanted to hear it. "Yes," she said, "I promise. Thank you." They shook hands, the deal was done, and he eased the car along the gravel drive until the house was near. He slowed, and she feared he had changed his mind.

"Leave Geraldine to me. Go up to your old room for something. Then let's get this done." His smile was easier now, the decision made. Time for action. Geraldine was waiting at the door, a quizzical look on her face.

"Train late?" she asked as she gathered Liliane close.

"Just the usual," Liliane heard Charles say over her shoulder as Geraldine clutched her tighter.

"It's so good to have you here again, Lili. Perhaps you'll come more often now you've..." The words caught in her throat, and she pulled Liliane close again.

This is going to be too hard, she thought, but over Geraldine's shoulder, Charles stood in the doorway, his smile reassuring. The hallway was as imposing as she remembered, the gleaming black and white tiles she always feared she would slip on, the winding staircase Nick told her he used to slide down, the high, domed-glass ceiling. It was still imposing but not as threatening as the first time she entered it, still disorientated from the operation, ignorant of who she was or where she was from.

"I'll just pop upstairs," she said, stooping to pick up her bag, not daring to look at Geraldine in case she betrayed the guilt that was already welling up within her. At the top of the stairs, she turned, but Charles was already shepherding his wife into the kitchen. Liliane shut her door and leaned against it; he would be telling her now, no delay once he was decided on a plan of action.

The room was as she had left it that last morning, everything in its place. It was as if she had died, and Geraldine couldn't bear to change anything. The bedclothes were still the same as when Nick had lifted them and slipped in beside her, his warmth comforting at a time when she felt lonely and empty. In the years since, she had regretted her action, unable then to understand what had made her do what she did. Only in the last few days had she finally understood. The terror Malabanda had inflicted on her was deep-rooted inside her, wired into her emotions. In those few months of recovery, she had come to depend on Nick, the emptiness of her mind beginning to fill with feelings for him. On that last evening, an animal urge for him had coursed through her. She bit her lip at the memory and slid one of the glass doors to unpack when she heard Geraldine's sobbing disturb the dreamy silence of the old house.

Back at the door, breath held, Liliane listened, but no more sounds of distress leaked from the kitchen. She imagined Geraldine held tight by Charles, her cries muffled in his chest while he told her what he was about to do. She leaned over the polished banister, undecided, for a few minutes, desperate to see Geraldine, to explain. She was still fearful that the emotion she would encounter would break her own resolve, and she would consign the search for her past and her quest for Malabanda back into the empty void of her mind.

Everything in the hall was in its place: the octagonal walnut table perfectly placed in the middle of the floor, the vase dead centre, the lilies, whose scent wafted up to her, reflected in the polished wood. All perfect, all as it should be in Geraldine's world. But she couldn't control the slow emergence of Liliane's past. A whirlwind was about to blow the remnants of the fog away and, in doing so, would cut a swathe through the cultured order of this house as well. As she watched Charles walk across the floor to his study, she felt the first breaths of wind stir within her. He reappeared and looked up to the landing as if he expected her to be there. He studied her in the heavy stillness that hung over the house again, then nodded. The tape was in his hand.

***

The journey back to London was interrupted by delays, but Liliane was immune to the frustration that upset her fellow passengers. The contents of Nick's programme had lost none of their power to shock, and Liliane noticed how even Charles, whom she knew only as a tough, self-confident businessman, brushed the tears from his cheeks.

Much of what she saw early on was already known to her from the books she had pored over. She had studied so many photographs in that time that the madness that unfolded on the screen held no surprises. It was when the team arrived in Kitabuye that she gripped Geraldine's hand tighter and had to massage the throbbing scar on her head, as if it, too, was about to relive the shock of the blade. The images had come quickly.

It had been difficult to assimilate all the memories that were dragged out of the deepest recesses of her mind. Geraldine fussed around her and treated her like an invalid again.

"You're not losing me," she'd told her when Geraldine expressed her fear that she was losing the Liliane she knew, "you're just getting a more complete me."

It was, though, with a sense of relief that she sank into the seat as Charles slammed the carriage door and waved until she was out of sight. She closed her eyes, not to relax and sleep, but to concentrate on the tumble of memories successfully released from their captivity. Adele had recently shown her how to try to win money by dropping a coin onto moving trays full of coins in the hope of dislodging more than she put in. Liliane's first coin had caused a whole stack of them to tumble over the edge, and that was how she felt at that moment.

When the camera had turned from the church and viewed the main street, it was as if she had suddenly regained her sight after a period of blindness. Of course, the hospital was there on the left, and then a row of small shacks that had been shops but now appeared to have been ransacked, the doors ripped off, cardboard cartons trampled into the dust. And there was Uncle OK's shop further down on the opposite side of the road. She knew that if she turned left just past his shop and followed the road, she would find the house with the gates where she had last seen Father and Bernard waiting for her and

Mother's tear-soaked face. Yet even as she absorbed the grief that had been aroused, a new, darker image assailed her.

She now knew, she realised, where Malabanda's house was, and she remembered again all the times she had gone there. She stared at the countryside beyond the glass, but all she saw was a young girl, her hair plaited in bunches on the sides of her head, her neck bare and unblemished. She was holding her father's hand while they stood outside the door of the red brick house where the priest lived.

"Please, Father, don't take me in," she cried as she tried to wrest her hand away, but Father slapped her face and dragged her along the path. She remembered how dark the lobby was and the murmur of voices behind a door. She remembered how she had wanted to press her ear against the door, but a woman was watching her from the shadows at the end of the corridor. The door opened, and Father came out, his face in shade from the lights in the room and squeezed her hand. When Malabanda appeared at the door, Liliane now knew what it was she was going to have to do. That was the first time.

Malabanda—he had dominated her life in Kitabuye from the very first day they arrived. She remembered how Bernard had rushed in from the yard to find Mother.

"There's a priest at the door, Mother. He wants to come in."

"Of course, he can come in. He won't harm us, Bernard."

For the first time since they had hurriedly packed as much as they could into Father's car, Liliane saw a smile crease her mother's face. She was a devout Catholic and had blind faith in the priest who ministered to them in Kigali. Liliane knew her mother would see the priest's visit as a sign that things would go well for them in Kitabuye.

"Mrs Iwo, welcome." He advanced across the room, and Liliane watched Mother take his outstretched hand, her eyes shiny. "I'm Father Malabanda. We're honoured to have such an important man as your husband here to help us." But even as he spoke to her, he was looking at Liliane.

"Thank you, Father. This is Bernard and this is Liliane—our twins."

"Well, I hope we shall see these two in Sunday school. And," he added, taking a step towards Liliane, his gaze fixed on her, as if taking in every detail, "I hold a Bible study for the young ladies of the town. I find they are so much more responsive to the words of our Lord."

Bernard shifted uneasily at Liliane's side, but Mother was already under his spell. As they carried on talking, Liliane wondered if her brother had also noticed how Malabanda's eyes had lingered on her.

"What a nice man," Mother sighed when he had gone, her hands clasped to her breast, "and what a lovely smile," but Liliane thought it reminded her of how a crocodile looked before it had snatched a young antelope in a film at school.

As the train moved closer to London, Liliane tried to block the thoughts of Malabanda from her mind. She had more memories now of Bernard and Patrick, of the times she had enjoyed with each, separately and together. And then there was Patrick. When she wasn't thinking about Bernard or Nick, Liliane's thoughts were invariably pulled back to the boy she had loved, maybe still did. He was bigger, stronger than Bernard but lacked the mental toughness and resolve of his friend. His size meant the other boys looked to him as a leader, but it was a role that Liliane knew ill-suited him. Patrick just wanted to be friends with everyone and hated any sort of conflict.

She closed her eyes and pictured the two of them, remembered them as boys and then as the men they became, old enough to be told to kill. Yet she knew now how much the boys loved each other, and as she searched through the part of her mind that was now open to her, she saw the three of them as teenagers.

The whole class was down by the lake, thrashing the water, screaming and laughing. Her unfolding memory told her it was the start of the holidays. Liliane clung to Bernard. She restrained him until he broke away and raced to the water's edge.

"Bernard, come back. Father says we mustn't go near the

water. I'll tell," she shouted but Bernard was already wading deeper, calling out to find Patrick.

"Hi, Lili." She felt Patrick's arm around her waist and leaned into him, aware that Delphine was watching from among a group of Hutu girls. "Where's Bernard?" he asked, and they both looked out on the crowd of kids.

"He must be in there somewhere." There was an edge in her voice, and Patrick let go of her and stepped forward, his eyes on the lake. "We've never been used to water in Kigali, and he doesn't like it. You know he does things to be like you."

They both saw him at that moment, much further out, arms flailing, his head slipping beneath the water.

"Bernard." The other children stopped playing and stared at Liliane as she screamed his name again. Patrick was already in the water, his arms thrashing him forward. He dived near where Bernard had been and disappeared himself. The children were quiet now, aware of danger, unsure what to do except stare. Then suddenly, they were up, two heads, arms and legs tumbling the water. Back on the grass, Bernard coughed up the dirty lake water while Liliane held him, and Patrick high-fived the boys in the crowd.

"You saved my life," Bernard said, his voice hoarse from coughing. "I owe you."

Patrick grasped his hand and pulled him up. "You'd do the same for me. Maybe not in the water, though." They laughed, and it was all forgotten. As she stared at the houses and offices that signalled the end of her journey, Liliane still felt the presence of the two boys with her. Then Bernard was gone and just Patrick remained on the edge of a crowd of men, a machete in his hand.

TWENTY-FOUR

The days that followed dragged into nearly two weeks. The satisfaction of unlocking such a large portion of her past paled as soon as Liliane reached her flat and saw the map, the little red pins not yet resembling the rash she hoped to impose on it. She called Nick's number, but the answering machine was full and as she took her coat off and unzipped her bag, her mood soured.

"People don't just disappear into thin air, Liliane," Geraldine had said when Liliane expressed her concern over Nick's absence, "especially when they're doing work for the government." But people had disappeared in Rwanda in the years before the genocide. Maybe it happened in England as well.

She just wanted Nick to come walking through the door of The Equator so she could tell him about Malabanda and what he had done to her, to explain what happened that last night at The Grove and why. She wanted to share with him the family she had remembered and tell him about Bernard and Patrick.

The gap Bernard's death had left in her life was, at times, unbearable, now she was aware of it. And what of Patrick? He was a Hutu. He must have killed. That meant he had lived. The love that had been rekindled in her left another, different type of gap in her life. She had wanted to share all this with Nick, to unwrap her hijab, show him her scars and reveal her life. But now he was gone, just another gap in her life.

As the days passed, it was Malabanda who slowly filled the empty spaces. She remembered so much now about the priest, about what he had done to her family, to Kitabuye, and to her. The thought that he was in London terrified her. She began to look out for him wherever she went and, unable to battle the rising dread whenever she thought about him, abandoned her visits to churches. If only Nick would come back. He would know what to do. She was sure he believed her now and that his certainty had sent him off on one of his investigations. He would make life difficult for the government, the Church, and anyone who he felt was dissembling and hindering his search for the truth, or at least the truth he wanted to find. Each night, she fought off the possibility that Nick had upset too many people once too often as far-fetched. Yet she couldn't understand why he wouldn't at least let her know what he was up to. And then her fears for him would turn to Malabanda again.

In the next few days, Adele fretted at Liliane's mood but

seemed cheered when Liliane told her that she was missing Nick. On the third day, she confessed her concern over his continued absence, but Adele brushed her fears aside.

"He'll turn up you when you least expect him. You can't control guys like him." Her face brightened, and she nudged Liliane. "It'll be worth waiting for by then, though." A lovesick Liliane was easier to cope with than the alternative. "I'm sure he'll be in touch soon. His work's important, Liliane. You of all people know that. He needs to concentrate."

Another week passed, and the staff became used to coping with Liliane's depression, still unaware that her mind had been opened. She spent her hours alone piecing memories together and turning her old life over and over to make sense of it all. One night, she woke with a dread sensation in her chest that Nick wouldn't be coming home because he had upset the wrong people. He knew about the Church's role in the genocide and was now intrigued by the possibility that maybe the Church was hiding priests who had committed atrocities in Rwanda. As she lay in bed, the heavy hand of guilt fell on her again, but this time for Nick, not her family. It would be too much to bear if she caused the death of another person she loved.

***

Liliane had taken to retreating to her office earlier in the mornings than usual and would sit hunched over her desk, head in hands. All the sounds of normality, the laughter and hubbub of morning chatter, the roar of steam, the bean grinder, washed over her. All she could think of was Nick being taken somewhere to stop him from getting answers to the questions she had planted in his mind. This isn't Rwanda, she told herself again, where people lived in dread of saying or doing the wrong thing or for just having the wrong blood in their veins. Such paralysing fear had seeped its way into her father's very core. Pleasing the Hutus and preserving his family's safety from the catastrophe he knew was coming became more important than the sanctity of his own daughter's innocence.

As her thoughts continued on this bleak trajectory, Adele tapped on the door and stepped in. She was tentative at first, yet there was suppressed excitement in her. "Hi, sorry to disturb you, Liliane, but…"

"It's busy, I know. I can hear it. I'm coming now," Liliane said, unable to stifle a sigh. She just wanted to be alone, to sit and think and try to make some sense of her life.

"Well, yes, it is. But not too much. We're coping. There's someone to see you." Adele paused a beat, her face brightened. "It's a journalist…" She took a step back as Liliane came towards her.

"Nick? Is it Nick?" Then her hope faded as she saw Adele's confusion.

"It's a lady, Liliane. From The Standard." She came closer and brushed her hand on Liliane's arm in sympathy. "I'm sorry. I didn't think. It's not Nick." She swallowed hard. "They're doing a series on coffee shops, and they want to do a feature on us. They like the idea that we're all…" She hesitated and looked embarrassed. "Well, you know, refugees. That we've survived and made a go of it."

Liliane stared, uncomprehending, but Adele hated the silence between them and carried on. "She's just taking a few photos, talking to the customers. Think of the publicity, Liliane. And we'll be in the paper. Imagine that."

Liliane could imagine nothing worse but knew she owed the team some payback for her moodiness that increasingly infected them all. She sensed a feeling of inevitability about this, even if her judgement told her nothing good would come from it. She felt Adele's excitement and could imagine Zee's delight at the prospect of his picture in the paper. Anyway, the journalist was probably already at work. If she was half as tenacious as Nick, Liliane knew the article would appear regardless of her reluctance.

"You'll only need to speak to her for a few minutes," Adele insisted as she led the way into the café and approached the journalist.

"Lucinda, this is Liliane, our manager," Adele said. She pushed Liliane forward to a lady in a smart, tailored suit. Her hair looked expensively cut, and her makeup was sophisticated. Liliane disliked her immediately, perhaps because she felt untidy, hot and tired. She took the woman's business card and set it behind the cash till then wiped her face with a damp tea towel, careful not to raise her eyes to the mirrored glass.

"This place is perfect, Liliane. It's got everything: the ethnic background, and you're buying the original Rwandan coffee to support the home country's economy. And you guys, the survivors who've beaten the odds. It's a great story." She beamed as she said this, and Liliane tried to remember where she had heard that phrase before. "This won't take long. I've taken some photographs, and I just need a quick chat with you. Our readers like to see pictures and want to know what's on the menu and what the coffee tastes like. You won't know I'm here." Lucinda raised a camera and pointed it at Liliane. The flash was so bright and unexpected that Liliane rocked back on her heels and winced as the cash till dug into her back. She felt unready and needed time for makeup, to compose herself, but Lucinda was already gone, bestowing her full attention on Zee, who talked animatedly, transfixed by the beautiful journalist who wanted to know everything about him. Even Isabelle, always so calm, was now similarly infected by the prospect of seeing herself in the evening paper. She hovered over Zee's shoulder then posed for a photograph with him. Liliane remembered she was so like Alice, the girl who had been too beautiful. Liliane's nights had been haunted since that weekend by imagining what must have happened to Alice.

The café got busier, and Liliane turned to make some coffees. We don't even need the publicity, she thought sourly, resentful that this woman had barged into her café like this, annoyed with herself for letting it carry on. Lucinda was talking to some customers, but when she saw Liliane watching her, she snapped her notebook shut and meandered her way through the tables to the counter.

"Is there somewhere quiet we can talk? I'd like your story for the article." Her bright smile and even brighter eyes antagonised Liliane. She was about to refuse when a thought occurred to her, and she nodded towards the office door.

"Do you know Nick Heggarty? He's a journalist like you." There was an aggression in her tone that she hadn't meant, and it seemed to take Lucinda by surprise. Her face coloured, and her confident manner wavered.

"I'm…I'm not in his league, Liliane. Trailing around trendy coffee shops, no offence, and doing restaurant reviews is… well, it's still journalism, I suppose."

"But do you? Know him, I mean," she persisted. She could see Lucinda was like Nick. Someone who wanted to be in control, to ask the questions, not to have to answer them.

"This is a great place you've got here, Liliane." Lucinda had regained her poise but seemed unwilling to look at Liliane, choosing instead to scrutinise the office, running her fingers over the boxes of coffee. "It'll be a good article. Show you in a good light."

"Have you, though, seen him recently? Nick." She felt the blood pool in her wound.

"But it's the human angle here, you know. It's you guys. That's what will really interest the readers. Particularly after—"

"Have you seen him around? Heard anything about what he's working on?" Liliane had hold of her arm and pulled her away from the boxes.

Lucinda stepped back from Liliane's, but her eyes were fastened on her. There was a hard edge to her voice now, the charm gone from it. "I know him, not well, though I've tried." The corner of her mouth ticked up, and Liliane saw the disappointment. "I'm not sure anyone does. He's very focused. You must know that. When he's got the sniff of a scoop." She shrugged. "He'll turn up when you least expect him." The sparkle was back in her again, the story the most important thing. "Anyway, Liliane, let's hear a bit about you. Going to be a doctor, I hear."

***

The next morning, the alarm went off earlier than normal, but Liliane was already awake, still upset with herself for allowing the journalist to disrupt so much of the day before. She had told Lucinda as little as possible, desperate to be free from her perfumed smile, irritated at the flash of jealousy that had sparked between them. For the rest of the afternoon, the staff had acted like unruly children hyped up on the adrenaline of publicity until Liliane could bear no more of the incessant chatter and closed up early.

In her room, she stared at herself in the mirror, shadows under her eyes, worry lines across her brow, her hijab stained and creased. If Nick had walked in on Lucinda's interview, she was sure she knew who would attract him more. She was jealous, and it was as if the feeling had travelled a well-worn path into a familiar spot inside her. With her eyes closed, she saw Delphine run her fingers down Patrick's arm, recognised the connection in their laugh. She felt again the surge of rage, of jealousy, for the woman who must surely have welcomed him into her bed and into her body when he returned home sated from the harvest of killing.

Even now, so long after, she experienced the shuddering intensity of her love for Patrick, her hatred of Delphine and the grim acceptance that the Hutu girl had won. When they were younger, she had fought Delphine in the field behind the school, rolled and kicked and punched in the dirt, watched by

Patrick and the others. Liliane had triumphed and claimed Patrick, but Delphine had bided her time and waited for the final reckoning. She had won the war.

Liliane splashed water over her face, but the stain of jealousy ran deep within her. When she finally raised her head, she knew it would take more than water to expunge the hatred and the shame that always followed after it. She had to go to her main coffee supplier, and Adele would open up that morning. She showered, dressed and gathered her papers in a trance and was glad she was only one of many buyers who had turned up for the meeting. She was able to endure the presentations and tasting without effort and made her excuses for leaving before lunch. Her mood, at least, was brighter as she approached The Equator after a morning spent with normal people, but it deteriorated as she pushed through the doors.

She could hear the commotion from the street, and the café was packed, but the staff didn't seem to be working. As she pushed her way to the hatch, she saw copies of The Standard. They were open at the same page on every table. She pulled one closer, and her own face stared back at her, her eyes wide in surprise. The article was spread across two pages, but she only saw the headline.

'Survivor of Kitabuye massacre flourishes in Knightsbridge'.

She should have been happy with the publicity and the resulting surge in customers, but it was meant to be about The Equator, not her. She read the article while the staff waited for her reaction. It wasn't what she had said. She hadn't told Lucinda any of this. She snatched the paper and took it into the office, aware that Adele and Zee had trailed in behind her.

"It's good, isn't it, Liliane?" Zee tried. "Great photo of you." But he stopped when Liliane turned to face them.

"Who told her all this? The journey to the border, the tape?" she demanded. Zee shrunk back against the door, but Adele stood her ground.

"We didn't. How could we? You never told us any of that. You must have told her." There was an unusual aggression in her voice, and Adele's eyes slid to the cloth covering Liliane's scars.

"But I didn't…" Her hand went to her head in a reflex action, and she heard the doubt in her own words.

Adele came closer, her voice softer. "It's a great article, Liliane. You look great. We all do. After all we've been through."

Isabelle poked her head into the room. "It's mad out here. Help, please."

"The whole place is buzzing. Come on." Adele turned at the door. "Customers are coming in with the paper, and lots of them are new ones. It's fun. God knows you need some of that in your life, Liliane."

Liliane sat for a few moments and tried to compose herself. It wasn't anger she felt, even though the staff's excitement was getting on her nerves. It was fear. Its fingers reached out from her stomach, and she felt them twine around her throat. She dry-heaved over the waste basket and rubbed tears from her eyes and cheeks. They'd even put a small picture of her on the top of the front page. Everyone in London would know who she was and where she lived.

There was no way they were going to shut early that night. They were rammed, as Zee put it. He spent the afternoon signing people's papers with his crude signature and having his photograph taken until the customers thinned and they began to tidy. Zee was about to close the door when a woman slipped in; her long, blonde, tousled hair was still damp from the late afternoon shower.

"No more, Zee," Liliane called and bent to the sink.

"Liliane?" She looked up to see the woman was now by the counter. "Liliane?" It was barely a whisper, and the woman was crying. She held the newspaper up. "I saw you…in the paper. It's me, Liliane. Anna…from Kitabuye."

TWENTY-FIVE

Just those few words and the woman's face streaked with mascara were like a thunderclap in Liliane's head. The last traces of cloud slipped away, just as they would in the morning over the hills of Kitabuye.

"Who's this, Liliane?" Adele asked, her eyes on Anna, suspicious.

"My older sister, Adele," Liliane said, no longer trying to stop her own tears. It was what Mother had called Anna, as the two had spent so much time together. The two women collapsed into each other for a long time until, at last, they pulled apart and stared at each other in shock and wonder. Anna took in the hijab and her brief nod told Liliane she understood.

Isabelle had chased the customers out, and now she hovered by the counter next to Adele. "Is this a celebration, Liliane?" Adele asked.

"Yes, Adele, it is," Liliane replied. "My dear friend Anna is here, and I didn't even know she existed." Her words faltered, but Adele was already opening a bottle.

"Where's Zee?" she asked as she lined the glasses on the counter. "Not like him to miss a drink."

"He was talking to someone outside as we were closing. He looked excited about something, but I didn't see him once the customers had gone," Isabelle said. "Probably a date with one of his new fans."

The two girls were excited to meet Anna and intrigued to know about her life in Kitabuye, but Liliane could tell that Anna, despite entering into the fun of the occasion, wanted to be alone with her. Eventually, Liliane was able to chase the girls out, with Adele shouting back at them, "You must come back, Anna, and tell us all Liliane's secrets." Liliane noticed how Anna's smile froze at this, and when their eyes met, Liliane could tell she must have known all along.

"Don't lock the door. I'll do it when Anna goes," Liliane said with relief as they left. Turning to Anna, she said, "Let me just tidy the flat, then I'll get some food for us." She then ran upstairs to clear the maps and pins away. It was too much to explain so soon.

"Isn't it lucky The Standard chose The Equator for its next review. We might never have met again despite you living in London," Anna said as they sat at the little table minus the books that had long since gone back to the library. "I've always thought about you, Lili." Her words caught in her throat. "I saw the documentary…about Kitabuye. I assumed…" She looked down at the table, and Liliane could see she had her own demons from that time and was afflicted by her own guilt. "It wouldn't have happened if we'd stayed. You wouldn't be…" The thought was too much, and Anna cried again for a while. "When I got to the hospital that morning, Doctor Le Paih took me to his office. He was upset. I thought it was because of the car. Then he told me what was happening. I didn't understand what he meant at first. Then he got angry, and I realised the UN were coming just for us, not to protect the Tutsis. I felt sick. I knew what would happen. We all did."

She took a sip of her drink, and strands of golden hair fell across her face as if trying to hide the shame she felt. "He got us all together. The others already knew. Sister Maria wanted to go and see Father Malabanda, but the doctor put a stop to that. It had to be kept quiet or there would have been panic." She couldn't look at Liliane. "They radioed to say they were near, that we had to be ready. We just stood and waited. It was wrong. The UN was supposed to be keeping the peace, not just protecting the whites." Liliane touched Anna's arm and gave her an encouraging smile. "The soldiers were rough with us, pushing and shouting. We found out later a group of Belgian soldiers had been hacked to death near Kigali. They were scared and just wanted to get us out before the Interahamwe got that far. Kitabuye was the last town they evacuated." She turned to look at Liliane. "I refused to go. That's when they… well, you saw."

"You had no choice." It was all Liliane could think of to help her friend, and for a few minutes, they were silent, both of them back in Kitabuye in the rain-sodden street.

Anna angrily pushed the hair out of her face, her eyes bleak, as if she had relived those moments many times in the years since. "That bastard really hurt me. I passed out in the lorry. When I came to, we were far from Kitabuye." The UN had taken them to the border with Burundi and left them, she explained. "They pulled the canvas across the back and told us to keep quiet. Everyone was sick from the bouncing, but they wouldn't stop." She turned to Liliane. "I was covered in bruises, so sore. Then I saw all the bodies coming down the river, and they didn't hurt anymore. One of the soldiers told me they'd done a deal. Just get the whites out and they'd be left alone. They were under orders not to stop the Hutus, even if they saw it happening." She finally looked up at Liliane. "I've thought every day about what happened after we left. I think I always will."

"It wasn't your fault, Anna. Don't." She pulled Anna's head close and stroked the golden hair that had caused such a stir when she first came to Kitabuye. Alice had thought she was an angel because she'd seen one in the Picture Bible in school and that one was white with yellow hair as well.

They ate in awkward silence for a while, in contrast to the noisy reunion in the café. Their every shared memory was from a place which had been devastated by the genocide and from a time when fear stalked the lanes and alleys of Kitabuye. Eventually, the question came, as Liliane knew it had to. She watched Anna push food around her plate and tried to decide how much to tell her and how much her shame wouldn't allow her to divulge.

"Do you remember…? Can you tell me what happened, Lili?" She pushed her plate away, and her hand brushed Liliane's arm. "If it's not too painful. It might help us."

It was Liliane's turn to stare at the table as she pieced together in her mind that last day, trying to join the dots from the jumble of new memories. She started with the death of Uncle OK and the children, pausing while Anna wiped her eyes. They agreed what a wonderful man he had been. Then she told Anna about Malabanda, and as she described the rape and then his attack on her, she unwound her hijab, revealing the wounds and watched the tears run down Anna's face again.

"Pancrace took me to the field where the bodies were. He was supposed to finish me off but couldn't." She told Anna a few details of her escape and survival and then tried to summarise her life since coming to England as quickly as she could. It seemed like a dream now as she described The Grove and Nick and his family, the years of empty memories while she made new ones at The Equator.

"So is this guy, this famous journalist, more than just a friend then, Lili?" she asked, leaning forward conspiratorially. Liliane hesitated, unsure what to say, which Anna seemed to take as confirmation. "Well, he's very lucky; if you are, that is," she added, then her face darkened. "What happened to Patrick? Do you know?" her voice almost a whisper, as if afraid to awaken the memories she had of him.

Patrick. Her lover. Her hope. The rock she had wanted to build her life on until he had crumbled into dust. She saw his broad, smiling face, a boy's face. And then a man's face, a machete in his hand surrounded by a mob of men.

She told Anna about that morning and why she hadn't been at home. For the first time, she faced up to how he had left her. And now, another man had walked out of her life without explanation.

Anna began to leave with promises to return after school the next day. "I haven't tried your coffee yet. I could almost taste it as I read about it," she said at the bottom of the stairs.

Liliane pulled her arm. "Come out the back way. I can't face the front door. It sticks, especially after this rain."

Back in her room, as she got into bed, Liliane felt a new emptiness in her, deeper and wider than the hollow feeling Bernard's death had left her with.

"If Patrick's still alive, it's because he killed, Lili. Even the Hutus were killed if they didn't join in." Liliane remembered how blunt Anna could be but knew she was right. Patrick must have done what they all eventually did. She curled into a ball like she used to as a child when she was upset or angry and cried for the boy she had loved, for the man who had betrayed her. Worn out with the sadness, the futility of it all, she was close to sleep, and yet there was something else that nagged away in the pit of her stomach until the worry forced her to sit up and swing her legs off the bed.

It was past midnight, and she sighed at the prospect of another sleep-deprived night. She was about to get up and make a drink when she heard the groan of the front door being pushed open. That was it—she hadn't locked it. She had let Anna out of the back of the café and forgotten that she hadn't locked the front door after Adele left. There was another grating noise as the door was pushed fully open. Her head throbbed, and she thought she might faint as she stood. Someone was in the café. She stumbled into her lounge in the darkness just as the stairs creaked. She held her breath and kept still, like she had on the hillside, waiting for a blade to fall. A shadow blotted out the sliver of light under her front door. The handle turned. Liliane backed into her bedroom as the door was pushed open. The light was behind him, but she knew the silhouette. She had seen it so many times as she waited for him in his room in Kitabuye.

He had followed the same trail as Anna. His fingers groped on the wall and flicked the lights on. His eyes were filled with hatred behind the thick lenses. A scar curved down one side of his face and she felt glad she had left her mark on him as he had on her.

"Inyenzi bitch." It wasn't the voice that used to cajole and flatter her in his room, nor was it the venom-laced voice that had denounced the Tutsis in the church. It was the voice that had throbbed with pain and anger as he told Pancrace to take her outside and finish her. He held a knife in his hand, just as he had when he sliced her head open, as he had when he started the slaughter. Liliane wanted to get into her bedroom, barricade the door, but his eyes transfixed her, kept her paralysed, in the doorway. It had always been like this, his power over her, his eyes holding hers, sapping her energy until she would sink to her knees in front of him.

He came closer, and she felt his smell in her nostrils and down her throat. He raised his hand, and the light reflected on the blade. But there were other sounds now that filled the room. The crashing of boots on the stairs and a cry of "Police!" A familiar voice was calling her name. Arms grabbed at the priest, pulled him away from her, back through the door. Malabanda roared and struggled, but there were too many of them, and as quickly as he had appeared, he was gone again. In his place, she saw Nick and Zee, and then everything went dark.

When she came to, they had laid her on the settee. A policewoman stood nearby while a doctor checked her pulse. Nick was speaking, his voice excited, but he sounded far away.

"I'm sorry, Liliane. It was the only way to flush him out. They're hiding priests across Europe. I found others in the past few weeks. It's where I've been. I knew he must be here. I told the Church we had a witness who had seen him in London and assumed they would tell him. He must have known it was you from the escalator, and then we planted the article in the paper to confirm it."

Zee started to talk at the same time, his face flushed with excitement, but Liliane couldn't hear what they were saying anymore. There was someone else in the room, she was sure, over by the window. His hair was grey and grizzled, and the lines on his face were just as deep, but he was smiling at her. He nodded. It was justice, at last.

Kigali, Rwanda

1998

TWENTY-SIX

Liliane turned as the first burst of orange broke through a gap in the black clouds that wreathed the peaks to her left. Shapes emerged from the darkness, and she could tell she had come to the right place. She was at the top of a steep lane bordered on either side by corrugated iron shacks with collapsed roofs and walls, alongside more substantial earth and plaster buildings, their walls pockmarked and gouged. The track snaked down past them until it disappeared into a pool of darkness below.

She stood, her face turned to where she knew the city lay and remembered another silent dawn in Kitabuye. But today, rather than silence, the trees were loud with the chattering of starlings and crows. She watched as the sun's rays slid down the valleys to reveal the terraces cut into faraway hillsides, all shaded green and brown and then, further down, reluctant to leave the shadow, red roofs clustered together, peaceful in the early morning lustre. She had forgotten how quick the dawn came here.

A noise below her brought Liliane back to her surroundings, and she watched a young boy hobble up the hill towards her. His crutches dug deep into the flesh under his arms while the wooden ends slithered for grip in the dust beneath his foot. Even after he turned into a gap between two orange-painted earth walls, his grunts of pain and effort hung in the air.

The bottom of the lane, where it struggled out of the wild undergrowth and merged into the road where the car waited, was visible now. The wide, red artery gouged its way down the valley until it disappeared into the mist that still hung over the city.

For the first time since they had arrived from England, as she looked across the hills that ringed Kigali, Liliane felt the elation that came with reaching a familiar spot—the sense of a homecoming. The hills rolled and tumbled into each other below and around her and then rose again in the distance, mottled by the shadows of clouds that the strengthening sun had sent careering across the sky. Single-storey huts and brick buildings clustered together among the foliage on each hillside. She had been here before and remembered this view. It was one of her few memories of the time before they had left.

Father would bring her up here early on a Sunday morning, just the two of them. They would watch the dawn arrive and marvel at the surprises that came with each new day as the sun worked its way over the landscape—every morning different. She felt his presence among the ruins and desolation. It was what she wanted, why she had come. Too many memories of those times when they talked and when she saw a different, better side to him were obscured by the man he had become. But with them came sadness because the father she had truly loved, the one she wanted to remember, had only existed in the mind of a little girl.

As the mist surrendered the city to the sun's warmth, Liliane saw in the distance the new tarmac road that carved the city in half, their hotel at one end of it, its white stone and glass jarring against the shabby buildings around it. It made her think of her friends, Nick and Anna and Geraldine, and the familiar feeling of guilt tugged at her as she thought of the letters she had written just a few hours earlier. They had been more difficult to write than she had imagined and taken so much longer as she searched for the right words for each of them. She had to keep checking the window in her room for early signs of the dawn. Inserting the letters into the envelopes and writing the names on each had seemed like the final act of betrayal—three denials of friendship.

Yesterday had been closure for her friends and the justice they had come to witness. For Liliane, it was the redemption she had craved even as she lay on the hillside, the forgiveness of her sins, the atonement for surviving. But she had always known there was more she had to do before she would have peace. She had known it when she had watched Patrick walk away from her with the machete in his hand.

She stared down at the city and scanned the rooftops, wanting, above all, to recognise their old house, but the city was too scarred, too changed. She thought she could see the school buildings or what was still standing of them, but the scars of war had distorted it all too much. Doubt gripped her tighter than ever, but she had made her plans. She had no choice. The boy on crutches reappeared and turned to her, hand out, palm upwards. It was time to go, so she walked down the slope towards him, felt for some coins in her pocket and pressed a few onto his hand. He curled the jagged stumps of his fingers over them and slipped them into his shorts then hobbled back down the alley.

She turned to have one last look at the horizon. So few memories were left of that time; she wondered now how the innocence in her had lasted so long, how she had not seen or felt the hatred that always lay just beneath the surface. She picked her way down the track, sidestepping the bricks, broken furniture and other debris. She was relieved to see the driver was still waiting for her as she rounded the bend at the bottom where the track joined the main road. Her feet sent a few stones scurrying down the last of the slope, and the noise must have woken him because by the time she reached the car, he had the door open for her.

It had been just a year since Malabanda had been caught, a frustrating period when Liliane found it hard to move on until after the trial. It wasn't one of the first, but the fact that Malabanda was a priest and the Church had provided him with a new identity had made big news in England as well as Rwanda. It had also given Liliane a focus in the media that she had not enjoyed, and she was glad to be able to slip back into the shadows and let Nick have the limelight. He was a household name again, a regular face in people's living rooms. His revelations in yet another documentary about how the Catholic Church had hidden killer priests in churches across Europe had shocked even the most devout. The institution was still reeling from the scandal, the trial giving it fresh impetus. "The oxygen of publicity," Nick had told her with that familiar glint in his eye.

She settled into the back of the car and watched the city come to life as they passed through it. The shutters on the shops clattered as their owners hauled them up; young men and girls on bicycles competed for the road with stray dogs and goats. On the surface, Kigali seemed a normal African city: loud, colourful, vibrant. But when she looked closely, the signs were there—the residue of war, the wounds of the genocide. Burned-out buildings scarred the streets, and bullet holes pockmarked the walls. Many of the shops were empty, and people stood on the street corners and watched the world come to life with little interest. The normality of life seemed to run only skin deep, much like their religion, the faith that was supposed to have stopped the horrors of the past from surfacing again.

Her fingers moved involuntarily to the rough skin on her neck and then to the hollow of her head under the silk. She saw maimed and disfigured people on street corners or sat on pavements, their hands held out. Liliane, though, still felt compelled to keep her scars hidden. She had not bared them in court, but rather, it was the wounds inside that she had shown them, hour after hour, which had fuelled the revulsion and the decision against Malabanda.

Soon, they were back up in the hills that ringed Kigali, and it was nearly time for her appointment at the clinic. It was Anna who had discovered her first. A doctor friend had invited Anna to the clinic when he heard she was coming for the trial, and she had recognised her from Kitabuye. But now, as they got closer, Liliane wished that Anna had kept it from her.

"Stop the car, Augustin." They were not yet at their destination, but she needed a few minutes to compose herself. The main city sprawled in the bowl below them, and the heat and smoke now shimmered above the buildings. She knew this view and if she turned around, she knew what she would see.

It was where Father had brought her on that last day in Kigali. The house was still there. Like all the top ministers, Akayesu had built a house with a commanding view, master of what he could see. The high wall around the property was now broken down and blackened, and the once-pink walls of the house were scorched around the doors and windows. Only the roof seemed to be undamaged. A tangle of brush and scrub had invaded the garden where Father waited while Liliane was inside with the minister.

"Miss?" The driver was anxious they would be late, and she was glad to break the memory and return to the car. It was never about his work with Gatsinzi. It was always about her. It had started with Akayesu. Then it was Malabanda. Father had sacrificed her childhood, sold her innocence as the price for his family's safety. He had, she realised, been as scared of death and the way it would come, as Patrick. The driver continued to stare at her in the mirror, and she realised she was crying.

"This place, it brought some memories back," she said as the car moved away. He gave a nod in acknowledgement. He understood. They all had too many memories. She closed her eyes and tried to think about the fear and weakness that had ruled her father's life and led him to betray his own daughter. Soon the car stopped again. They had arrived. This was her last task before she left Kigali. She had to see Alice.

TWENTY-SEVEN

The white metal and glass building stood incongruous in the devastation around it, as if an alien craft had landed in a primitive landscape. It was a scene of order and efficiency, in stark contrast to the hopelessness in the streets. More of the guilt money was in evidence around the city, salving the conscience of the first world while trying to piece together the shattered lives of people with so many fragments missing.

The sun was higher now and its light radiated off the white metal. One of the doors at the top of the steps was pulled inwards, and a large man in a too-tight suit filled the gap. He was taller than Liliane and seemed twice as broad, but his grip was surprisingly light as he reached out to welcome her.

"Miss Iwo, Doctor Nahimana." His suit creased as he raised his arm and guided her through the door, and she shivered in the air-conditioned atmosphere.

"I apologise, Miss Iwo. It was built by Americans, and the temperature seems to be set for their tastes." His smile was warm, but his eyes were as cold as the lobby.

"It's Liliane, please. I don't mind. I'm still adjusting to the heat after England."

The reception area was all white, which seemed to accentuate the cool temperature. Even the receptionist was clad in a white dress, her skin the only concession to the existence of other colours. Doctor Nahimana's hand was firm on her back as he guided her through some swing doors and into a small room that contained four comfortable chairs arranged around a low table. A glass coffee pot and cups were already waiting for them, but the acrid smell of the thick, dark liquid seemed out of place in the antiseptic atmosphere of the building.

He beckoned Liliane to a chair as if anxious to get on with things. "We don't get many visitors here. Most of our patients don't have any relatives or friends left." Liliane opened her mouth to speak, but he had a message to deliver. "The people we have here are very fragile. We try to regulate their environment and the outside influences on them. Progress is slow. They can be set back very easily." He sat back and savoured the coffee. He had spoken on the phone about ground rules and protocols if she was to visit, and she could tell she was there under sufferance.

As they drank in silence, she was aware of Nahimana studying her. He would have read about the trial. He would know what she had suffered and how she had testified against

Malabanda. She knew what it was like to be raped; maybe it was that, above everything else, that had swayed his judgement.

"You lost your whole family, I believe. You didn't need to come back. This country owes you nothing."

Liliane shifted uncomfortably. "I couldn't live with myself if I didn't come back." It felt like she was in the witness box again.

"This won't be easy for you. You knew Miss Ndayisaba as a friend in school. You were close." She nodded.

The door opened behind her. It was time, and she felt a dull ache behind the scar on her head. She stood and waited for the doctor to lead the way down a long corridor with doors leading off on either side. The silence was oppressive.

"We shall be next door. We can see and hear everything," he said as he ushered her into the room. It sounded more like a warning than reassurance. Liliane looked but saw only a large mirror. The nurse pushed past her and left the room by a door on the opposite wall.

"Please, sit. She will be brought to you soon. Don't be concerned if she doesn't recognise you. Miss Ndayisaba, Alice, is in permanent mental shock," he continued. "If she talks, and I am not sure that she will for she has been silent for so long now, you might hear things that you don't want to hear. You must contain your own emotions at all times. Don't cause her any distress by revealing your own suffering." She felt guilty under his gaze but wasn't sure why. There was so much she wanted to know about her parents and Bernard. And Patrick. Surely Alice could reveal something to her, tell her something of what she had seen down in the town while Liliane was up on the hill.

"I shall do my best." But her words seemed to lack conviction as she felt her nerves unravel. She tried again. "I know what is required." He gave her a curt nod, turned and left her alone.

The room was designed to be comfortable and safe. There were two casual chairs separated by a small table for drinks and a bed with blankets in the corner. Two large, golden teddy bears sat on a rug. Liliane settled herself and tried to show she was composed for the benefit of the watching doctor, but inside she was a cauldron of conflicting emotions. She recalled their last embrace and how, on that day, she had been scared for Alice, who was too beautiful, too desired.

She forced herself to think about their happy times together, how they would gossip about boys in Liliane's bedroom or help out with the babies in the hospital. And then, just a few days before the Interahamwe came, Alice had told her she had slept with Bernard. She had been nervous, as if Liliane would not want to share him with her, yet felt the need to confess or receive her blessing before it was too late. She was still focused on the emotions of that day when the door opened, and a nurse guided Alice into the room and helped her to a chair opposite where she sat, rocking backwards and forwards. The loose, white gown couldn't disguise the thin arms and legs or the emaciated chest that made her look shrunken, as if her body was turning in on itself. Gone was the figure envied by the girls, lusted at by the boys and abused by the men of Kitabuye.

Liliane sat rigid, her fists balled as revulsion, then pity, but most of all, unremitting anger washed through her. Alice's worst fear had destroyed her. The nurse settled a blanket around her and told her in a low, steady voice that her friend, Liliane, had come to see her, but Alice's head stayed down, her eyes on the floor, her movement rhythmic, unceasing.

"You must not touch your friend or try to embrace her," Nahimana had told her, but as she stared at the shadow of a girl before her, she remembered how touching, embracing, and kissing had defined their friendship. Without them, she felt mute, and whatever she said would be inadequate. Would Alice even hear her when she showed no sign of recognition?

In a thin, nervous voice, she said, "Alice, it's Liliane. I've come back." She felt helpless; everything she had rehearsed in the last few days since she had known seemed futile. Alice was a shrunken, empty shell; the life drained from her. She tried again. "I've been in England with Anna. You remember Anna." The rocking faltered at the mention of their teacher, a small glimmer of recognition; then she drew her arms tighter around her shoulders and hugged herself, but at least the rocking had stopped. Her hair, once so thick and wavy, was thin and straggly, and Liliane could see patches of mottled skin. It was hopeless. Whatever she had expected, she could see she would learn nothing about what had happened to her family.

Alice was broken, insubstantial somehow, as if she was melting into the air around her, but Liliane continued her attempts to communicate. She told her about life in England and the café and the friends she had made, but none of it caused even a flicker in Alice's eyes—her face remained featureless. The other girls used to laugh at Alice and say that she spoke with her eyes and face, but now it was as if she was struck dumb.

She wanted to tell Alice about Malabanda and what he had done to her. It might, she thought, just be the connection to unlock her mind, a shared experience to reveal something of what had happened, but she knew Doctor Nahimana would rush through the door if she ventured there. The silence lengthened, and she noticed for the first time how laboured Alice's breathing was.

"I'm going back to Kitabuye." She had said it before she realised it, and Alice looked up, her eyes wide, no longer blank. Liliane saw the same fear in them that she had seen on that last day outside Uncle OK's shop.

Alice shook her head from side to side, the movement pronounced as if to emphasise her objection. "Just for a day…" Liliane began to protest, to justify, but she wasn't sure why she felt the need.

"No." It was barely a whisper. But then Alice repeated it, louder, and again, her eyes fastened on Liliane's. Her features, so impassive before, so devoid of feeling, were now twisted with anguish. "You mustn't." Her agitation caused her to shake. Her hands went to her face, and she scratched at her skin. "No. No. You mustn't."

The door opened, and the nurse hurried to Alice, pulled her to her feet and pushed her to the other door where another nurse waited. Liliane could still hear her shouting that one word as the door closed. "No!"

Doctor Nahimana had followed the nurse and sat with Liliane, silent, while she regained her composure. Alice's distress had been so sudden, but it was the spark that had caused it which unsettled Liliane—the mention of her return to Kitabuye.

"I should have warned you. The place where it all happened…" He held his arms out expansively, as if the gesture settled the matter.

"She was telling me something. I know her."

"You knew her, Liliane." His voice was low but devoid of the anger she had expected. "She's no longer who she was. But then you know that. You saw it for yourself."

Liliane shook her head. The fear she had seen in Alice's distressed features and eyes and heard in her voice seemed to have transmitted itself to her. A sense of dread took hold deep inside her, like an old acquaintance.

"You can see why we don't encourage visitors. Don't blame yourself. There's very little any of us can say or do." Liliane tried to remember Alice as the vibrant, beautiful girl who had brought so much joy into her life, not the troubled shadow that now lay sedated on the other side of the door. "That is the first time she has spoken, Liliane." His tone told her it wasn't progress he welcomed. "Why are you going back? What good can come of it? It's a bad place, you know that."

Liliane stared at him. "There was a massacre there. Three thousand. It's no secret." She paused. "Yes, it has become a bad place. But it's not the only one. And it wasn't always. None of them were." She felt defensive but was unsure why. "Can I… Should I…come back to see her?" The chill was back in his eyes.

"I don't think that would be a good idea, Miss Iwo." The familiarity had gone. This was business.

"Well, when she gets out—"

"She will never get out."

"I would care for her." But the doctor just shook his head as if humouring her, and they sat in silence for a while.

"Why did you come back then, leave Switzerland, for this?" she said eventually, her voice laced with bitterness and his face softened.

"It's my country. It's where I belong. I couldn't have lived with myself if I hadn't." His words caused emotion to stir within her. "I have the skills that are needed." He sat forward and his eyes glistened. Liliane could see the burden he carried, the traumas that he experienced every day etched on his face.

"Liliane, men caused this. Men planned the genocide. Men did the killing. Women are the future of Rwanda. They are the future of Africa, if it is to have one." He stood and held his hand out. "Please remember that. You have done what you came to do regarding the priest. But there is much more to do." The nurse came in after he had left and escorted Liliane back to the reception where Augustin waited, but the doctor's words had unsettled her. Uncle OK had given her a calling. She was in no mood to have another one thrust on her so soon, not before she had fulfilled the one she had set for herself, at least.

TWENTY-EIGHT

The city was spread out below them again as the car crested the brow of another hill, the last before they turned away and took the road across country towards Kitabuye. Liliane turned and took a final glance at the sprawl of buildings and greenery spread out across the dips and contours.

"Stop!" she ordered Augustin. He turned to her, his face a mix of alarm and hope. He had enjoyed the status of driving her around Kigali while the trial was on, and Liliane's celebrity status had grown, but since she had announced her intention to go to Kitabuye, the driver's mood had darkened. She ignored his inquisitive look and walked to the edge of the road. There had been another journey like this long ago. This was where it had all begun. She could see that now—their flight from Kigali, the start of the slow slide to the inevitable outcome. It had been a morning such as this, the clouds gone, the shadows yet to come, a kaleidoscope of greens and reds and blues shining in the valleys below. She could see now that was the moment her heart began to harden, when she first felt the grip of Hutu mastery and her father's subservience to it.

Her thoughts turned to the friends she was leaving behind. She had left the three envelopes with the girl on reception and wondered if, against her instructions, she had called Nick or Geraldine and if, even now, they were on the road behind them, anxious and angry.

"Is everything all right, madam? After yesterday?" the girl had asked, her professionalism and training restraining her from asking the questions that were written large in her eyes.

"Please ensure they get these when they come down. Not before." There had been nothing more to say, but at the door, Liliane turned to look at the girl. She smiled and nodded in return while one of her hands fluttered a farewell. She felt sure the girl would play her part.

She had brought no luggage and didn't know when she would be back or what she would find in Kitabuye or whether he was even still alive. She had to know; she had no choice. If he was alive, he was a killer. She had accepted that when he had turned and walked away from her with the metal in his hand. There was just that one question left, the one thing she needed to know. It had burned into her consciousness as she lay in the field, and it had been there ever since. It had nagged at her even as she struggled to recover her past and fit it in with her new life in The Equator. Only when she saw him, asked him, watched him as he answered her, could she rest in peace and start her new life over again.

She would hear the answer from his own lips, if he was still alive, that day or the next. As she took a last look at the panorama below her, she felt vindicated for deceiving her friends. What could frighten her now? What could be worse than the injuries, the privations and grief she had suffered? But rather than feeling calm, her sense of unease grew stronger. She still didn't know what she would do with it if she did learn the truth about her family, about Patrick. As she settled into the seat and watched the countryside slip by, she tried to balance the implications of what she was doing. She felt sad and angry as she saw the burnt-out, blackened remains of buildings, once homes to families, or the little garages, cabarets and workshops that were being reclaimed by the vegetation. The grass and bushes were thriving in the warm, rainy season, and the machetes that would normally be used on them had been put away long since.

The roadside was dotted with groups of wooden crosses and small stone memorials. Each monument could tell a story, reminders of people who had lived and died there in the same, brutal manner. She saw people sitting by the road, often on their own, looking at the tarmac with the empty, dull stare that she had seen in so many in the last few weeks. They were pitiful, without hope, without life, victims just as much as those for whom they mourned. A girl, much like Liliane, rocked gently on her haunches next to a pile of stones and a small wooden cross sticking out at an angle. Liliane signalled to Augustin to slow down, but the girl, unaware of their presence, continued to stare at the ground, so they carried on. She was aware of the driver's eyes on her in the mirror, but she composed herself. He needed to see her strength, her resolve to go through with this.

She woke to find he had pulled in at a small wood and straw bar at the roadside and parked behind a line of lorries, their ropes pulled tight against the tarpaulins that bulged with cargoes on each of them. The drivers sat around plastic tables and watched. Their conversation stilled as Liliane walked to the counter. She ignored their stares and ordered goat brochettes and bottles of water for them both. The air was still, and smoke from the fire drifted lazily across the front of the bar. She was suddenly very hungry, and her mouth watered as the meat sizzled and spat.

It was served in a warm flatbread, and they ate at a table that Augustin had pulled away from the others, upset by the crude suggestions from the drivers. Liliane laughed as hot fat from the meat dribbled down his chin, and without thinking, she took a napkin off the bar and wiped it clean, oblivious to his embarrassment. He was her father's age, and she saw the pain in his eyes as she had in her father's. She knew the look, a father's concern for a headstrong daughter. She smiled and the moment passed.

They left just as the heavy, overloaded lorries struggled up the bank and back onto the road. Augustin overtook them, but the black, acrid smoke that belched from their exhausts stayed with them for a long time. It stung their eyes and lined the backs of their throats, but eventually, Liliane sat back and fell into a fitful sleep.

The sun was past its high point as the car pulled into another roadside bar; she had been asleep for most of the journey. She knew where they were; this was the point where they left the highway and headed into the forests on the long, broken road to Kitabuye. She arched her back and eased her shoulders, slack and listless after the long, troubled sleep then waited at a small metal table for Augustin, who brought bread, eggs and chicken from the wooden shack. Her dread of seeing Patrick was heightened now they were so close, and it dulled her appetite. She held a cold can to her face and stared at the track to Kitabuye, her eyes unfocused. The main road was busy with a constant thrum of traffic, but the dirt road was empty; there was little reason for anyone to go to Kitabuye.

When they arrived at Kigali Airport, the immigration officer had been curt. "Where are you going?" His head was down while he scanned her papers.

"Here, Kigali. Then Kitabuye, maybe." She had felt the sweat prickle her back.

He looked up slowly and stared at her. "No one goes to Kitabuye," he said, then averted his gaze and began stamping the papers before him. As he pushed them at Liliane, he said, "Stay away from there. It's an evil place." Then he turned and beckoned to the next in line. His words were stuck in her mind as she stared at the dirt road.

There was still time to turn around and go back. She could tell them she had thought better of it, got it out of her system. They would be relieved. But she didn't. She couldn't. There never had been a choice.

The next part of the journey was painful. The frequent rains and wide-tracked tyres of military vehicles had churned and gouged the earth, and Augustin wrestled with the wheel as the car slid into the ruts, the underside scraping and groaning against the earth. Dense foliage strayed across the track and scoured the paintwork. The sun was unable to penetrate onto the track, and Liliane peered forward into the green twilight, anxious for Augustin to persist. She could see the tension in him, and sweat ran down his face, which was fixed in a grimace as he concentrated.

She had heard the stories of the attacks at night and scanned the road ahead, willing them to finish the journey before the sun departed. Her body ached from the constant jolting, but when this torture was over, she would be at her journey's end. They came to a clearing that served as a passing place, which Liliane recognised, and Augustin braked and pulled into the side when she tapped his shoulder. Her joints were stiff as she clambered out of the car and massaged the bunched muscles in her neck. Down in the valley, she could see Kitabuye. This was the road the UN had come down, carrying all their hopes. This was the spot where they had disappeared from sight as they fled with their white cargo…and their hope. And it was the road the Interahamwe had come down, bringing their consignment of hatred.

As she looked across the valley, she felt the shades of the past crowd around her, silent and accusing. She had lived, but her redemption had been fulfilled in Kigali. This was her time now; she had earned it. It was what had driven her to survive. Her eyes were drawn to the church, but it was not as she had seen it that first time as a young girl. The early colonists had cleared the land for the church when they established the tea plantation in the rolling valley beyond. Now the field was knotted with scrub and thorn bushes, and it seemed that the woods would soon reclaim even the church. It still cast a shadow across the land, and Liliane remembered how she had been glad when it reached out to her and the fire on her skin had lessened.

The town looked diminished. The forest had eaten away at

the edges, roofs had collapsed, and there were gaps in all the streets where houses and shacks had once stood. Smoke hung over some homes in the still air. That, and the few people and animals that were visible, were the only signs that the town hadn't been abandoned.

Augustin stood beside her, his face set, his brow furrowed, fingers twisting and untwisting. She didn't know what he had expected to see, but the brooding desolation of Kitabuye seemed to infect his mood even further. "There's still time to turn back, madam. We could reach the highway by sunset. It would be safe there. I know a place we could stay, some family." There was a faint glimmer of hope in his eyes as he waited for her response.

"It will only take until tomorrow. Don't worry. We'll go back then. Go home. Both of us." She laid a hand on his arm, and he let it rest there, as if her touch would protect him from the ghosts. She wondered if it was true. Could she go back to England after everything that had happened and take her place at university like a normal student? This place had been her home, and she felt the stirring of the past, and yet it was no longer the place she knew. There were only Hutus left in Kitabuye. She would be alone, unless he was there. But what had he done? And could she forgive him?

Augustin turned his gaze back to the town, and they stood in silence, each with their own fears. The town is full of evil spirits, he had said while they had eaten in the last roadside bar. But it's me who's the ghost, she thought. I'm the one who's dead. The people down in the valley would think she was an evil spirit come to haunt them. She would be alone and vulnerable. For the first time, she felt afraid, but she had already come too far. Turning back was no longer an option. It never had been.

TWENTY-NINE

Liliane felt Augustin's unease increase as the shadows lengthened in the valley and the light faded. It was too late to go anywhere other than to descend into the darkness that seemed to billow up from the town below them. She was trapped now by her own recklessness, not wanting to go down into Kitabuye yet unable to go back. Her driver's fear was irrational but palpable; this wasn't the only town where slaughter had happened at the church, but his mood was infectious, and her own courage ebbed away the longer she stared at the town. She could feel the restless spirits of her family crowd around her, censorious, accusing, her parent's fingers clutching at her, pulling her home, claiming her as their own once more. They had waited for her, and now, at last, she was home.

She turned to the car as the last of the light faded, and the flames from the fire pits in the cabarets flickered across the valley. She shivered, but this time, it was only the chill of the evening falling on her. But it was Patrick's presence she felt most; he was down there, she was sure. He had whispered his promises to her that he would never leave her. He would protect her, but each time she closed her eyes, she saw him walking away from her into the crowd. She wondered again, as she had so often in the last year, if he ever meant it, any of it. She still didn't know what she would say to him if she found him. She could still hear his father's words that last afternoon on the hill.

"What do you want him to do, Liliane Iwo? Save you? Or die with you?"

The grinding of an engine that sounded like it was lurching into ruts and heaving itself out again broke the silence. An arc of light shone from further around the bend, stabbing up into the darkening sky then pitching down into the blackness of the valley. She waited for the lights to appear, fearful that it might be her friends coming to take her back, yet she knew part of her would be relieved if it was. Augustin came to stand by her, and as the vehicle rounded the corner, Liliane could see that the headlamps were high off the ground. She shielded her eyes and waited until it drew level with them. The lorry was a big, reassuring presence in the loneliness and gloom of the hillside. The driver killed the engine, but the headlamps still bathed the lower track in light.

"Need any help?" He was white and spoke in halting French.

"We're fine," she replied in English. "Just stopped for a while. To look at the town," she added and realised how foolish that sounded.

"You don't want to be out here in the dark. It's still a dangerous country, particularly this place." He seemed pleased to revert to English. "You're headed to Kitabuye." It wasn't a question; there was nowhere else to go. "Want a lift? Or is the car okay?"

"No, it's fine. We're fine," she said. "Thanks."

She could feel him studying her, inquisitive, from the darkness of his cab.

"Look, the track gets pretty bad down at the bottom, especially now it's dark. Follow me down."

"Where are you going?"

"There's a tea plantation here."

"I know," she paused. "I used to work in it."

"Must have been before the…." He paused. No one ever seemed to know what to call it.

"Yes, it was."

He ducked back in the cab, and the roar of the engine echoed back and forth across the valley. She remembered a time, long ago, when she had heard an engine roaring on this track, standing outside Uncle OK's shop, his hands firm, reassuring on her shoulders while Alice cried, her body wracked with fear. If only they had stayed a few days.

"I'll wait for you on the bend," he shouted, and the lorry rolled past, brakes straining, as he struggled against the ruts and contours of the track. As the lights from the vehicle faded downhill, the night draped itself around them again. Liliane was relieved when Augustin started the car and flicked on the headlamps. A few faint lights had joined the kitchen fires, the only evidence that there was a town down in the valley. The car bounced and slid down the hill at an angle. Liliane was shocked at how much of the track had fallen away as she braced herself in the corner of the seat.

Augustin stayed on the tail of the lorry all the way into town and flashed his lights in thanks as it pulled into the town hall. Liliane had peered into the blackness that enveloped the car, trying to see what Kitabuye looked like, but the headlights had been too close to the back of the lorry for enough light to spill out and illuminate the houses and shops on either side. It was only when the lorry rounded the bend that Liliane caught a glimpse of the buildings at the bottom of the main street. She saw the charred remains of the shop where Mother bought her oil and flour. Mr Andama was a Tutsi, and she remembered seeing him at the church, his head bleeding, one of his children cradled in his arms.

Augustin stopped the car, and in the headlights, she could see that they were in the yard in front of the building. The once-white walls were blackened and scorched, and a new roof must have been recently put on because bare timbers jutted out unevenly, corrugated sheets nailed roughly over them. A lamp fixed to the roof suddenly activated and bathed them in a harsh glare. Liliane looked around the once familiar yard, now disfigured. Jagged holes were splayed haphazardly over the front of the building, small craters pock-marked the earth floor, and on one of the walls, about head height, brown stains were spattered across the grey concrete. The door to the building opened, and a young man in a light suit and open shirt jogged across and pulled Liliane's door open.

"Miss Iwo? You are later than you said. I was worried." Lights flickered in the building behind him then settled. "You are lucky; we get two hours a night now."

"The roads are worse than I remembered them." She was standing in front of him now and saw the concern in his eyes despite the broad smile and flash of teeth.

"Everything is worse than you remember." He, too, looked around the yard, as if seeing it for the first time. "Especially here," he added, holding out his hand. "Samuel Bossoso. We have spoken on the phone a few times. Welcome…back to Kitabuye." His voice was flat, lacking in warmth. She felt that she was anything but welcome.

"Thank you, Mr Bossoso."

"Sam, please." He ushered them inside the building. The corridor was dimly lit, but even in the dark, she would have known where she was. Sam turned towards the corridor on the left, Augustin following him. Liliane hesitated then turned in the opposite direction. She could almost smell his cigarettes, the French ones that he had sent from Kigali—third door down, on the left, it was.

"Miss, Iwo? This way, please," he called after her. But Liliane was outside the office. Grief welled in her chest, and she steadied herself against the doorframe. "I've come back, Father," she whispered.

"Miss Iwo, those offices are no longer in use." His voice had the petulance of someone who had been kept waiting, but she had already pushed the door open. It was as she remembered it. The desk was still by the window, facing into the room, his chair neatly pushed in against it, but the papers that used to cover it were long gone. The small table and chair that he would sit her at while she added up columns of figures for him were no longer there, but the metal filing cabinets that he would always lock whenever he left the room were still against the wall. Her chest tightened and her eyes filled. When she closed them, she could see him again, the smoke of his bitter cigarettes making her eyes water.

"Why do you work so hard for them when they hate us so much?" she had asked him once.

He looked up from his papers. "It's best to show them that you're loyal. Keep them happy," he added, his gaze holding hers, a warning or an admission. She never knew.

"Is that what I'm doing with Malabanda, keeping him happy?" He looked down again as if checking something, but he seemed taken aback by the bitterness in her voice. "And Akayesu? Was that the same?" He had never replied, but she knew now anyway.

"You fool," she said to the empty desk. "You sold me, but in the end, what difference did it make?" Her pity for him heightened her sense of loss, and she clung to the doorframe until she felt steadier. Sam was behind her but made no attempt to interrupt until she turned away from the room.

"Please, Miss Iwo. It is late." He ushered her down the corridor and out into the lobby. The walls were scarred by bullet holes, and the green paint was faded and peeling. Neglect was everywhere. It seemed that Sam was the sole occupant of the building now, and he had occupied the office that had been Gatsinzi's.

Liliane followed him into the dimly lit room while Augustin remained in the lobby. The walls had been covered in the old days with photographs of Gatsinzi with ministers and African politicians, his desk with those of his wife and children. The office had been a celebration of his importance, but now the walls were bare, and the plush, thick carpet had gone. The Burgomaster's large, teak desk remained, but it was badly defaced with the graffiti of war. The only light in the room shone from a small lamp in the corner of it. Sam leaned against the desk, his face in shadow. There was a spare hard chair, but he didn't invite Liliane to sit.

"I shall take you to your accommodation for the night, Miss Iwo. It is close by. There are plenty of empty buildings these days. They're used by the few aid workers who come this far and the engineers working on the plantation. You'll only need one night." It wasn't a question.

She hesitated, thrown by his hostility to her. "I…I don't know, I may need longer."

"I warned you. You have come a long way to find out about your family, yet there is little I can tell you. We can go through the records in the morning. The RPF recorded the names of those who died as best they could. And where they died," he added.

"But there are people I might wish to see, to speak to, afterwards." She didn't want to elaborate.

"I don't think there is anyone in this town who would welcome seeing you, Miss Iwo. They are all Hutus. I can't guarantee your safety. Even now, things—bad things—can still happen."

The stress of leaving Kigali, the long, difficult journey and the creeping dread of what the next day held for her had taken their toll on Liliane. She felt unhinged to be back in this place which held all her memories. The awkward conversation and the unexpected coolness of Bossoso's reception had sapped her energy, and she signified that going to their lodgings would suit her.

Sam's teeth flashed in the gloom. The little victory seemed to soften his attitude, and he was suddenly helpful, telling her there was food in the accommodation for her. It was unusual to get visits from relatives of victims, he told her, but he hoped it wouldn't be too upsetting to come back to her old town. He guided them to some of the larger houses that used to be occupied by managers of the plantation. The lorry they had followed down the track was parked outside one of them, but the house was in darkness.

Liliane was glad when the two men left her alone, resentful of how quickly Augustin had recognised an ally in Sam Bossoso; neither of them wanted her in Kitabuye, but it was the administrator's motives that lingered and grew stronger within her as she sat on the hard mattress and stained coverlet.

"You shouldn't have come back. Nothing is as it was. You will only find sorrow and more pain. Haven't you had enough of those?" His last words had stayed with her, and her scars throbbed with the stress. She knew she would find Patrick. She could feel his presence somewhere inside her, in the place only he had ever touched. But there was more waiting for her. She saw again the fear in Alice's eyes and heard the doctor's own warning. "It wasn't her own experiences that frightened and upset her, it was the prospect of you going back to Kitabuye. Your news seemed to trigger some deep, uncontrollable fear that we hadn't seen in her before. Whatever it is she saw or knows, she doesn't want you to find out."

Feeling small and alone, she lay on the bed, her chest tight, as if the ghosts of Kitabuye were suffocating her.

THIRTY

The darkness was oppressive, like a heavy blanket draped over Liliane. She lay still, her breathing shallow, and listened. Outside, grass rustled, and twigs snapped. Shrill calls went up in the trees nearby and were answered from further away. It's only monkeys and pigs, she told herself, but still she strained to hear and imagined there were footsteps on the hard earth below her window.

"No one knows you are here," Sam had said as they parted. "Don't forget, Miss Iwo, you were killed at the church. Your sudden appearance will frighten them. And people react badly when they are frightened."

Her hands gripped the thin edges of the mattress as she imagined the Hutus coming for her. It was as if she had never been away, as if she was back in her own room again, and tomorrow was the day the Interahamwe would come. The familiar knot in her stomach was back. It would have been so much easier to do this if her friends were with her. With a shock, she realised they may no longer be her friends. Her sense of loneliness increased as she imagined their anger and sense of betrayal when each of them opened their letter. She had deceived them and doubted if they would ever forgive her. Her headstrong nature, her unyielding certainty in her own judgement had brought her triumph over Malabanda. But now, in this quest for answers, it felt like she had gone too far, and her fear of what she would find out grew the closer it got to dawn.

Patrick had killed. But nearly every Hutu male had killed. Had it been just once or had he got used to it, become sanitised to the slashing and stabbing? And what choice had he had? He was no worse than the rest of them.

"You make a heavy burden for him, Lili," Uncle OK had said, and she blamed herself again for expecting more from Patrick, as if he was different, stronger than the rest of the Hutu men. Yet he was different; he promised her again and again. And even if there was a twisted, warped justification for what he had done, could she still love him? And so the argument raged within her.

As the night advanced and morning approached, Liliane's resolve weakened. She could be back in Kigali by midday. They would understand; their relief that she was safe would overcome their anger. She would leave after seeing Sam, take whatever he told her and go, quickly. But as soon as she committed to one course of action, other questions pushed forward, and she knew she wouldn't leave so easily. She had to see him, to look him in the eye and watch his reaction when she asked him. He had never been able to lie to her.

The plaintive cry of a turaco jarred Liliane out of an uneasy sleep and announced the dawn. She turned her head to the grey rectangle of thin cloth strung over the window. On the edge of her bed, her hands twisting in her lap, she thought she might pray, but too much had happened and nothing would come. God didn't seem to have come back to Kitabuye, and the magic spells didn't work anymore. She felt unwell; the pressure in her head had grown through the night and was unrelenting. She vomited into a basket in the corner and wiped her damp eyes.

Augustin was waiting in the road when she came out of the bungalow. From the heaviness in his eyes and the slump of his shoulders, she could see that sleep had passed him by as well.

"Mr Sam will be waiting for you," he said, his voice sullen and got into the car. Liliane flushed in anger but picked up her bag and walked to the car, her reproach unsaid. She slammed the door harder than she had meant and his head jolted up. Their eyes met in the mirror, and Liliane glared at him.

The sun had yet to appear, but in the grey light, she could see how derelict Kitabuye now was. Grass grew across the road in places, and many of the shacks appeared to be empty. An abandoned bar was over the road, overgrown by thorn scrub, rusty poles now the only evidence of where the yard had been.

Smoke seeped from a few straw roofs and hung in the still air, as if affected by the lethargy that seemed to hang over everything.

Liliane could see that they were on the edge of town as the car moved off, and the road they had driven down last night stretched away behind them. The lorry that they had followed down the hill was still parked nearby, and a young girl crept out of the driver's lodging, pushing money into her dress. She looked away quickly when she saw Liliane watching her. Already she had seen enough; this wasn't her town anymore but a grotesque shadow of what she knew, a place where darkness lingered even after the sun had risen, and she was glad when they turned into the yard. Sam's car was already there, and he stood in the doorway, his face set.

"Miss Iwo," he said and turned away to his office. There were no formalities, no pretence at pleasantries. He was already behind his desk, his fingers flicking through a thick file when she entered. His eyes avoided Liliane, and he continued to stare at it even though she felt sure he knew exactly what he would find and had read it many times over. She had fought so hard for this chance to know, but the man's mood infected her, and she felt panic in the pit of her stomach when he finally looked up, as if he had just remembered she was there. Neither his eyes nor his face gave anything away, as if he was inured to the suffering evidenced in the thick file, and she wondered how often he had done this. He cleared his throat.

"When the RPF arrived, the dead had not been moved. They still lay where they had been killed."

"I know," she replied. "I was brought back here by the journalists. They filmed it all. I had to suffer it all again." His reaction told her he hadn't known. It gave her a small sense of satisfaction.

"The soldiers tried to identify as many people as they could from whatever they had on them or, if they weren't at the church, where they were found. They had the lists of where all the Tutsis lived, of course. Gatsinzi left them when he fled." He paused and looked down again while his fingers flicked in the file and rested on a page.

"Your family was not at the church when they died, Miss Iwo." Liliane nodded. She had expected that. Father's faith in Malabanda was unshakeable to the end, but the now familiar cocktail of grief and guilt washed over her.

"Your parents were found in the yard. Your brother, Bernard, was in the house, in the main room. They had the usual wounds, and there was no sign of flight." He flipped the binder closed and placed his hands on top of it, his movements accentuated to signify the sheer pointlessness of travelling so far for such inconsequential information. Why did it matter where they died, his demeanour seemed to say. It was still a shocking and painful way to die.

Liliane stared at him, her mouth working, unable to form the questions jostling to be asked. It had all been too quick, too brief. There had to be more. "But why weren't they all together? Why separate them if they weren't trying to get away?"

"There is no more information, I'm afraid. They weren't gathering evidence for a murder enquiry, Miss Iwo. They were just identifying and recording the bodies they were able to. Does it matter?"

"Father wouldn't have let Bernard die on his own. And Bernard would have fought to protect them. Of course, they would have died together." Her voice rose and Bossoso flinched. She bit her lip and sat in silence, her eyes on the file as she tried to focus on what could have happened. The silence became unbearable. "There must be more you can tell me."

"You were there. A few thousand people killed in a day. What more do you want?" He pushed his chair back. If he knew more, he wasn't about to tell her. He wanted her gone. She was a disruptive influence.

"I want to see my old home." Her voice shook, but she wasn't sure if it resonated with grief or anger.

The administrator lowered himself down again and made a pretence of tidying the papers in the folder while he avoided looking at her. "I would advise you not to do that. It is not safe for you here, on your own."

"The war is over, Mr Bossoso."

"You've been away too long. Do you think that jailing or executing a few murderers like your priest will solve everything? You know how long this has been with us. It's in our blood. Revenge still happens, including here. They're afraid, Miss Iwo. Afraid of what the government will do to them, afraid of the killers who live among them. And they're afraid of the ghosts that haunt them. Everyone knows you died. They all knew about you and the priest." He stopped abruptly, and Liliane saw his annoyance; he hadn't meant to give so much away. Then he stared at her, defiant again. "You died, Miss Iwo. You are an evil spirit." She wasn't sure if he was interpreting the mood of the Hutus or if that was his personal opinion. "When they're afraid, they lash out, they kill. It holds no terror for them now."

She felt intimidated by his authority, his knowledge and self-assurance, but her fight for survival, then for justice and, with it, her memory had made her a different woman to the ones Bossoso was used to bullying.

"I've come this far. I can make better use of my time in Kitabuye than sit here."

"Just go home, Miss Iwo." There was no attempt to cajole her now. She refused to meet his gaze, fearful she would wilt under his scrutiny, accede to his demand. "There has been enough trouble here. We're all just trying to move on."

"Move on?" she shouted. "How can we just move on from all this." She gestured out of the window to the town beyond the walls. "I'm not here to cause trouble." Her voice sounded calmer than the emotion that swirled inside her.

"Miss Iwo, I have a feeling that trouble finds you." He sighed, pushed his chair back and stood. "I can't protect you if anything happens. I have no resources."

"My driver…" Liliane stood to face him.

"Is terrified of the ghosts in this place. And so should you be. He would drive off, with or without you, at the first sign of trouble."

He held the door for her. As she passed him, Liliane stopped. "I also need to know where Patrick Biha lives now."

"You will find him." He laughed, and she saw in his eyes that he knew what she would find. "Let the dead be and let the living rebuild their shattered lives without your meddling." He turned his back on her and closed the door. She stared at the flaking paint, unnerved by the abrupt termination of their meeting, and realised that she had forgotten to ask if her old home was inhabited. While she had been with Bossoso, the sun had risen, and the corridor was warm. She dabbed at her forehead, unsure if it was the heat or the stress of the meeting. The building was silent where once it had been noisy. Gatsinzi would bellow from his office, and his staff would scurry to placate his temper while people loitered in the lobby, waiting to flatter him or pay for his support.

More signs of war and neglect were evident all around her than in the gloom of the previous night. Green paint, long faded, lay in flakes on the once polished floorboards, now disfigured by large, uneven stains. She passed through it quickly and out into the yard. Augustin pushed himself upright on the car, his hand moving towards her door, but she shook her head and carried on past him.

"Madam?" he shouted after her, but Liliane had had her fill of the two men, of Bossoso's domineering bullying and the driver's surly expectation that she should plan her trip around his fears. "I hired you. I don't need to explain," she shouted, and the man backed away against the car, his mouth open. "If you're too afraid, go. I'm staying until my business is done."

Bossoso had come out of his office now and stood in the doorway watching. The two men exchanged glances, and Liliane's anger boiled over within her. "I am not a ghost," she shouted at the administrator from the gateway of the compound. "I am a survivor. I survived through my own strength. I have a right to know." She turned, breathless from the emotion that had burst from her. The exchange with Bossoso had unsettled her, and she went over his words again as she walked, aware that something he had said was gnawing away at her. Patrick. He had said she would find him. Where? In his old home? Bossoso had hinted at the violence that lay just beneath the surface. Kitabuye was a long way from the new society that was being built in Kigali. She knew what his family would do if she reappeared in their lives.

Already, she was halfway up the high street before she realised that she was at the turning to her lane and had passed by the rubble-strewn side streets and abandoned houses without a glance. At Alphonse's cabaret, she finally paused and looked around. There were gaps on each side of the road, which itself was narrower as grass and bushes swarmed over it. She looked for Uncle OK's shop, but where it had stood was just a pile of blackened timbers where the front and roof had collapsed, its dereliction complete, a symbol of the decay of the whole town.

It was too sad a sight, and her gaze traversed further up the street to the church. Its brooding presence still dominated the town, unmoved by the deeds that had taken place in its name and in its shadow. The cross still hung over the doors; only the wall in front was gone, crushed under the weight of the bodies. They should have burned the church, not Uncle OK's, she thought. It seemed to cast such a malign presence over the town, a constant reminder of the atrocity, a hindrance to any progress.

She heard the earth behind her scuff and turned to find a

small girl staring at her. Her dress was little more than a torn rag and her feet were bare. When she saw Liliane was looking at her, she turned and ran to her mother who shuffled along the street, a baby slung across her chest, her eyes on the earth in front of her. Liliane looked down at her own clothing and realised the mistake she had made in not dressing differently before starting her journey. The colourful silk around her head and the bright, tailored clothes that had given her authority and presence in the courtroom were stark against the drab, tattered garments of the few people who stopped to look at her. She was too obvious, too different against the brown and grey of the town, but she stared back at the people, defiant. They knew what she was, and she recognised the same hatred that had grown in the town in the months before the war.

A man took a few paces towards Liliane, and she backed away, closer to the cabaret wall until she was at the top of the lane. He watched her edge down the side of the bar, and his eyes were still on her as she turned and hurried down the familiar path, now shabby, redolent with faeces and smoke. She felt no nostalgia for what it had been, just sorrow for the desolation. Halfway down, she stopped to lean against a crumbling earth wall while she gagged on the stench of animal and human filth and batted away the flies that hovered over the carcass of a goat. Soon she would turn and see the house.

Although she was weak from hunger, it was her grief that became more debilitating the closer she got.

She pushed herself off the wall and picked her way through the rubbish strewn across the lane until she got to the turn, where she hesitated. Images of Bernard kicking a ball against a wall and of Father waiting for her at the gate before he locked up for the night flooded her thoughts. They were so vivid that she almost expected to see them. But when she felt strong enough to look, the yard was silent and empty, and she felt an irrational sense of disappointment. They were gone for good. Even their ghosts seemed absent from the emptiness.

Scrub and creepers had grown across the wall, and beneath the vegetation, it was grey and stained by mud. The gates had gone, and the small patch of yard she could see was cluttered with rubbish through which long strands of grass and thistle grew. A thin trail of smoke rose from the building. It was occupied. A sense of outrage flushed her face and neck that someone was living in her home even though she had told herself it would be occupied. It was over four years ago now, and anyway, her home was The Equator, and she didn't belong here anymore. It had been wrong to come. She didn't know what she had expected to find or to feel, but the emptiness inside her told her to go back to the living and not seek answers among the dead. She turned to go; she didn't need to know, and anyway, the place looked too sad. She wanted to remember it as it had been, how Father had kept it.

A shout came from the yard, a woman's. Something in the voice made Liliane check her step. She held her breath and moved closer to the wall, straining to listen, but the woman's muttered words were too indistinct. She edged closer to the gap, her curiosity too strong, the urge to know too powerful. The voice too familiar but still unplaceable.

Feet shuffled across the yard until they were just the other side of the wall, a few steps from the gate. As Liliane stepped to the edge of the nearest pillar, her feet kicked a loose stone, and it clattered against the wall. The woman appeared in the gap where the gates had stood. She was a similar age to Liliane, untidy in a stained, patterned dress that was too tight on her. A goat tethered to a metal stake, its udders bloated, butted her legs. She aimed a bare foot at it and then brushed her long, unkempt hair out of her eyes as she returned her gaze to Liliane. She stood, legs wide apart, hands on her hips and studied Liliane with a perplexed look.

Liliane recognised her. Her legs buckled, and she staggered back against the pillar. Her worst fears had not prepared her for this.

THIRTY-ONE

The woman stared at Liliane then her eyes widened, and a strangled cry died behind her hands. “It can’t be. Not you.” Her words were barely audible. “You’re dead.”

It was Delphine.

Liliane gripped the pillar tighter. She wanted to run, but her legs were too weak. Delphine stepped forward, still peering intently, but Liliane could see the hatred and loathing reignite in her eyes.

“It is you.”

They stared in silence at each other as they each struggled to understand and accept who was in front of them.

“This is my home.” The words rasped in Liliane’s parched throat.

Delphine took a step back as if shocked that a ghost could speak, but soon, the familiar gloating was back on her face, and her mouth twisted in a malicious grin.

“It’s mine now.” The slyness that Liliane remembered slid over Delphine’s features. “And so is he. He's forgotten about you. You're nothing to him. None of your sort are left here."

Liliane's breath got stuck in her chest, and she thought she would fall if she let go of the pillar. The kitchen door opened behind Delphine, and he stepped into the yard, blinked and rubbed his hands over his face as if he had just woken. He was bare-chested and wore only dirty shorts. He looked as he always had but different, thinner, less substantial.

"What's the fuss? That bloody animal needs milking, lazy bitch." He seemed barely awake. The sun was behind Liliane, and he squinted across the yard. "Who's that?" He came closer, his eyes on Liliane, uncomprehending.

"No one. Go back inside." She hurried her reply and stepped in front of him to block his view while she tried to push him back to the house. "Patrick, it's nothing. Don't. She's going." But he shoved her aside and stared at Liliane.

"Come away from her." Delphine pulled his arm, but he twisted it free.

"Liliane?"

Delphine came at him again, to turn him, push him away. "Don't talk to her," she pleaded, but Patrick grabbed her wrists and shoved her against the wall. Liliane stared at him but didn't recognise the aggression of his actions and the malevolence in his face, yet inside she felt an unwelcome surge of feeling for him. The war had changed him; he was bent, and his limbs, once strong from work in the fields, were thin, almost emaciated.

"Go inside." His eyes were still on Liliane, but his clenched fist was pointed at Delphine.

"Patrick, don't," she said as she watched Liliane and Patrick stare at each other. "Don't. Don't." He turned and shoved her towards the house. "Tell her, Patrick. Tell her, or I will." Her hands clawed his face as Liliane once had in her own desperation. He shoved her inside and followed her. Her shrieking stopped, and in the silence that fell on the yard, an awful feeling overcame Liliane. She was afraid. Not of Kitabuye, nor of Delphine but of Patrick. He reappeared at the door and walked across the yard. She backed through the gateposts out into the lane and felt the need to keep her distance from him. He was a killer.

The goat bleated and stones rattled across the yard as he approached. Liliane turned away, her arms wrapped tight around her body, confused by the dread that his proximity aroused in her. His smell, still recognizable, even with the stale mix of tobacco and beer, was suddenly in her nostrils and she felt him close behind her. She remembered the thrill that had coursed through her when he had chosen her over Delphine all those years ago. But with the woman's low, desperate sobbing echoing across the yard, Liliane knew this was not how she had wanted to win, then or now.

"Don't touch me." The words she had rehearsed all the way from Kigali were lost in her panic. She felt lonely and afraid, the defiance she had shown to Bossoso gone. Patrick coughed, a low, rasping rattle, and she felt the sharp bursts of his breath on her neck. His voice was hoarse when he finally spoke her name.

"Lili."

"How could you?" she whispered, just loud enough, her throat dry, her lips cracked. It was beyond anything she had ever imagined, too hard to comprehend. She had tortured herself with visions of him lying with Delphine, but not here, not in her parents' bed. Her skin crawled as she thought of them together in there. She turned, a ghost, risen from the stinking, rotting mess of bodies that had dissolved into the hillside to confront him. His mouth worked but no words came. His eyes stared, not with the tenderness that used to melt her, but with sheer terror. His tongue flicked across his lips. "How could you?" she repeated. "Here…my home…with her."

"You were dead. Pancrace said."

"Pancrace lied."

He coughed again—short, shallow hacks that seemed to leave him weakened as if the shock had sapped the energy from him. She turned away. The lane was still empty; the wall opposite had collapsed into a jumble of breezeblocks, nearly hidden now by the weeds and scrub. In the window behind where the wall had once stood, a woman stared at them.

"How did they die?" They had died here. She needed answers, but only his laboured breathing broke the silence. "Tell me. How did they die?"

Drops of sweat flicked off his face as he shook his head. "They just did." It was his turn to lean against the concrete. "Same as everyone else that day." His weakness seemed to give her strength, the resolve to press on against him.

"They didn't just die. People like you hacked them, cut them down to die in the dirt."

"They were at the church. Everyone was." He wouldn't look at her. She watched the lump in his throat jump up and down. She had always been able to tell when he was lying.

"Liar. They were here. The administrator told me. I saw him today." The lie had come easily to him and too quickly, as if there was something to be hidden.

"Tell her," Delphine had shouted to him.

"Why won't you tell me what happened to them. You know, don't you?"

"It won't bring them back. You were dead." He shrugged. "I made a new life."

"With her." She bit her lip as she felt the old jealousy consume her. This is about my family and him, she told herself, shocked at how petty she sounded amidst the wreckage of her old life.

When he finally looked up and met her stare, he was defiant and angry. "We had to move on afterwards. All of us," he said, but his voice lacked conviction.

"Move on?" Those words again. They stirred her anger, and she was shouting now. "Into here?" She pointed at the house, the yard. "I've spent years living with my guilt. Guilt for living. Guilt for leaving them. But you've just 'moved on'." She took a step closer. "And moved in."

"I didn't want it. The war, the killing. None of us did. You know that. You were here. We were all frightened." He moved his face closer to hers. Her taunts had goaded him, and spittle flecked his lips and face as the words tumbled out of him. His eyes bulged, and Liliane stepped back, afraid he was going to lash out at her.

"You're not the victim, Patrick. You got the house and Delphine in your bed." Her rage emboldened her again, and she grabbed his shirt. "In my parents' bed." Over his shoulder, she saw Delphine at the door. Patrick turned to follow her gaze and made an angry gesture at Delphine, but she stood defiant, watching.

"Why are you here?"

She stared at him. "I had to know."

"Know what?"

"What happened to them. How they died."

"Why?" He seemed alarmed that she would persist with finding out. "Why does it matter now? They all died the same way."

"And how many did you kill?" She tensed as he raised his arm, fist clenched, but he seemed to deflate as quickly as he had reacted and slumped back against the wall. It was in his eyes that she saw the punishment he bore for the things he had done, and she felt her heart pound with love, or pity, for him but steeled herself again to resist his hold over her.

"Is that why you came back? To make me feel guilty?" They were close now, and she smelled the staleness of his body. Neither of them would relent. "I did what everyone else did. What did you expect?"

The hurt and betrayal locked inside her for so long flared uncontrollably, and Liliane flung herself at him. Her fists beat his chest again and again until he crumpled into the dust on his knees while his chest heaved in a spasm of coughing. "You promised me. Then you left me to die." The vehemence of her words made her head throb beneath the scar. As she bent over to get her breath back, her face was close to his, and she was shocked to see how weak he was. She had seen men in Kigali reduced almost to shadows by their imprisonment after the war and she wondered if Patrick had been locked away also.

"I couldn't compete with Malabanda, could I? He was always there, wasn't he?" His voice was weak, the words laced with bitterness. "You killed your parents when you could have saved them." He turned his face up to meet her eyes. There was a terrible vindictiveness in them. "That's how they died."

Liliane straightened slowly and looked away, afraid he would see the emotions that were telling her to run. Delphine had come closer; she had heard it all, and her look showed how much she was enjoying Liliane's discomfort. His words were like ice in her veins. He knew. He always had. She saw it now. Her humiliation was complete. She had to get away from him and her, so she turned and ran. At the bend in the lane, she leaned against the wall and retched. When she looked around, Delphine was at his side.

"Did he tell you what he did?" she shouted. "What he really did that day?" The downtrodden woman was suddenly victorious. Patrick pushed her back into the yard and stepped into the lane.

"Go back to wherever you've been."

Liliane pushed herself off the wall. At Alphonse's, she stopped and bent over, snatching for breath.

"You okay, lady?"

She recognised the man. He was still the same, but different in a way she couldn't place, like they all were. "Adalbert?"

He covered his eyes and then peered through his fingers, as if he would see a different face that way. "Liliane? Liliane Iwo?" He shook his head. "But…you're dead." His eyes were round and sweat pricked his brow. "Does Patrick know?" She nodded. "Fuck. Did he tell you?" That same question again.

She shook her head. "Tell me what?" He backed away from her, his hands up as if in surrender. "Tell me what, Adalbert?"

"You shouldn't have come back." As he ran, he turned and shouted back at her. "You should have stayed dead, Liliane."

THIRTY-TWO

Liliane watched Adalbert disappear down one of the side streets, confused and disconcerted by the suddenness of his disappearance. He had been frightened at first, she knew. The appearance of someone he thought of as long dead must have been a shock for him. But his next reaction troubled her most. It was a different kind of fear. It wasn't for himself but for her. It was her reappearance that had disturbed a ghost that had long been laid to rest. He had always been a quiet, intense child, content to be in Patrick's shadow but not wanting to be outside of it. When the Iwos had first come to live in Kitabuye, Adalbert would do anything for Liliane, before Patrick had claimed her. She would often find him waiting in the main street before school. He spoke little but liked to walk with her, as if being seen with her gave him some inner strength or credibility. It was only later that she realised he had been in love with her. As she stared at the empty lane, she wondered if he would have stood by her and kept his promise. From the look on his face just now and his panicked concern for her, she felt as if she knew the answer.

You should have stayed dead, he had said, when he realised she had seen Patrick. A chair scraped on the concrete behind her. A young girl swept the floor of the bar with slow, lethargic movements. This was where Bernard and Patrick met before a match, and when they were older, it was where they came to drink and watch football—always football—until the rules had changed. She turned her back on the bar and walked out into the main street. An air of decay hung over the town that not even the brightness of the morning could dispel. The houses looked drab and uncared for. A few people stood around, listless and aimless. The town was dead, another victim of the genocide. When she reached the school, she looked around the earth yard. The low wall at the front had crumbled, but the little stone bench where she and Alice used to sit and gossip was still there. Despair dragged her morale lower at the thought of the happy girl who now lay in the clinic, a faded husk of what she had been.

The school building had suffered badly. The RPF had thrown grenades in to drive out the Interahamwe, Sam had told her the previous night, and the holes in walls and the roof had not been repaired. Brightly coloured drawings pinned to the walls, incongruous among the decay and devastation, showed through one of the jagged gaps. The field behind the school was different as well. The goalposts had gone, and there were small craters and concrete debris everywhere, and the grass was now a tangle of scrub and thorns.

She walked around the edge of the field to the small ridge they all used to sit on after school. It was here that he first held her hand once the others had gone. Despite his size and confidence, he had been shy and hesitant. She lowered herself to the ground and closed her eyes, but when she tried to remember him as he was, a kind, honest boy, a gentle giant, all she could see was the man he had become: brutish and aggressive. Yet there was still a vulnerability within him, beneath the hardness that now coated him like an outer skin. She had mourned for her family for so long, but at that moment, she only had space within her to grieve for the man she had loved, whose kind nature had been crushed by the fear and the killings, leaving behind another shadow.

He had done what every Hutu had. There had been no choice, but still, she felt uneasy. It all seemed too simple. They could have fought back, refused to kill. Surely death would have been better than the half-life the people of the town seemed to inhabit. She had fought back against Malabanda. Death would have been easy. It was the living that was killing them now.

She continued to sit where they always had and confronted the uncomfortable truth that she still loved him. Yet something else nagged at her frayed nerves. She had seen it in Adele's gloating and in Adalbert's terror-stricken features. It was something to do with Patrick, something Adele wanted her to know, and Adalbert didn't. Whatever it was, she had to see him again, if only to look him in the eye and watch his reaction as she asked him what she had come all this way for. It had been, she now knew, the one thing that had burned inside her that night on the hillside. Then, as if she could feel her sanity unravel, she wondered how much it mattered anyway. She was alone in a town of Hutus. His parents, or Delphine's, would finish her this time. There would be no witnesses. Even if he lived, Augustin would keep quiet. She would disappear, and no one would know. She was dead, after all, to the people of Kitabuye. Maybe she was meant to die here, after all. She had done what Uncle OK had asked of her. She had brought them the justice they wanted.

The scraping of rubble close by brought her back to the present. It was Delphine. Liliane scrambled to her feet. She was alone—there would be no Uncle OK to rescue her this time.

"Bitch!" She came at Liliane quickly, and her fist caught her unprepared. She toppled backwards and lay still, unable to get breath into her lungs. Delphine leaned over and pulled the cloth off her head. "That's what you're hiding." There was triumph in her voice. "I wish it had been me." She struck Liliane again. Her fist landed fully on the scar on her head.

Liliane's vision blurred, and blistering pain radiated from the cavity as Delphine thumped the scar again. "Glad you came back?" She grunted from the effort of striking Liliane. "He's not what you remember. You won't want him when you know."

Liliane crawled out of her reach and sat back on her knees. They stared at each other, both breathing heavily. Uncle OK had once said that Delphine had a touch of evil about her, and Liliane recognised it in her now. It was the same hatred she had seen in Malabanda as he attacked her, but there was something else. It was fear. There was a bruise around Delphine's eye and blood on her dress, but it wasn't fear of Patrick. Liliane could see Delphine was afraid of her and what her presence in Kitabuye meant.

"You think you know him, don't you. It's not just my blood on his hands." A nasty smirk passed over her face. "You'll wish you'd never come." Liliane stood and backed away, but Delphine seemed to have lost interest in attacking her. She had a different way to hurt her.

"You always thought you were better than the rest of us." Delphine took a step forward, but Liliane kept her distance. "How much could you forgive him? He killed with them, and he raped with them." She was closer, but Liliane was not frightened by the violence within this woman. It was what she would tell her that would hurt her most. "Are you afraid of me,

Liliane?" Her face was beside Liliane's, her fetid breath in Liliane's nostrils. "Don't you want to know what he did?" Delphine's fingers were on the scar on her neck. "What a lovely scar." Liliane was mesmerised by the woman's voice, her eyes. She was like a snake slowly wrapping itself around her while Liliane stood frozen. The fingers tightened on the puckered flesh, and Liliane's legs weakened with the pain that coursed up her neck into her head. She couldn't move.

"He was there when they died in your house." Her eyes were wild, her nostrils flared. "He watched your parents die. Your mother shit herself."

Hatred and rage surged through Liliane. She used her height and strength to knock Delphine's hands off her and struggled out of her reach again, trying to break the spell.

"You won't run. You want to know what I know. It's why you came, isn't it?"

THIRTY-THREE

Liliane's head seemed to be burning from within, and the scar that traversed her neck and chest felt as if it had been ripped apart. Delphine was right; she wouldn't run, but it wasn't because her legs were too weak or her vision too blurred that she stood still. The disturbing truth was that Delphine had a different hold over her than the one that had clamped on her neck. It was a grip that had been strengthened over the years by jealousy and nurtured by the historic hatred that had driven Hutus and Tutsis to murder each other.

Their eyes were locked together in a bitter stare where neither wanted to look away, each seeing their own fear, the anger and betrayal mirrored in the other. In the lengthening silence, Liliane's senses returned, and as her pain subsided, she saw that Delphine was hesitant, desperate to hurt Liliane with what she knew, yet seemingly scared of the consequences and of Patrick, of what he had become. She had won the prize but found that it was tarnished, corrupted by the brutality of the genocide. Liliane felt her own sense of triumph to see how uncertain Delphine was, but it soon seeped out of her and left a hollow feeling of pity that shocked her.

"Tell me." The absence of emotion in her voice seemed to surprise Delphine, and the lack of aggression rendered her mute for a moment.

"He killed your brother. He killed Bernard. He did it to save himself. He's a coward. But you knew that, didn't you? Deep down." Delphine covered her mouth with her hands as if to stop more from coming out.

"Liar," Liliane whispered through clenched teeth, but even as she said the word, she could see that Delphine had spoken the truth, and she staggered back as if the words had hammered into her chest. The woman lifted a hand to the fresh bruise on her eye. Liliane wondered if it was the mark of a threat to keep her silent or the sign of what she could expect if she revealed his secret to Liliane. "Why?"

"Ask him," she shouted over her shoulder as she walked away through the weeds and rubble. "I'm sure you'll see him."

The revelation was beyond anything Liliane had ever imagined, even when the fever had ravaged her mind with all manner of delusions. She slumped to the ground and covered her face, but the truth was already inside her, eating away at her strength and resilience like a virus. They had been almost brothers, their love and devotion to each other apparent, unwavering even when Patrick's parents censured him for breaking their blood boundaries. How could he? Even in the most depraved depths of the genocide, what could have driven Patrick to hack Bernard to death? There was no sense in it. Patrick could never kill Bernard, united as they were by a bond that few would ever know or understand.

She remembered again that day by the lake when the boys' love for each other had deepened. "You saved his life," she said as she bent over Bernard in the weeds on the lakeshore, holding his head while he coughed and tried to get the air in his lungs. Patrick had saved Bernard's life. How, then, could he take it?

"Madam?" The concerned face of Augustin stared at her. She took the outstretched handkerchief from his hand and dabbed at her eyes, the grit and dirt on her face scratching her skin. "The ghosts of Kitabuye." There was no malice in his words.

She nodded and favoured him with a weak smile. "There's just one place I want to see, then we can go."

He showed no impatience now, just shock at her condition. "Take your time, madam. Do what you need. You won't come back here." He seemed so certain, and she saw now that Bossoso had known what she would find. Allowing him to lead her past the holes in the ground and piles of rubble, glad to feel his strong arm around her, she smiled her thanks when they reached the road. He seemed to have taken on the role of a father figure, picking up the pieces after a rebellious daughter.

"Wait by the car," she said, but gently, then turned towards the church and braced herself. Just one last time, she told herself, even though she knew it would torture her. But it was her last hope to try to reach out to the past to find an answer to the appalling truth that she had uncovered.

Patrick had killed Bernard.

The words filled her mind as she walked. She didn't stop at the church but skirted the remnants of the low wall and carried on up the hill, barely noticing the crumbling brickwork or the knots of weed and scrub in the once-even grassland. But at the top, she turned and looked back at the church. The sun was high, yet a large black shadow seemed to spread out across the grass. Her head was still bare, and her fingers felt the contours of the wound, then slipped along the length of the scar on her neck. She felt surprised to feel no blood and hear no buzz of the flies as they feasted on her wounds. And even though she screwed her eyes tight, Uncle OK wouldn't come to comfort her this time. He had gone back to the shades to live among the other million who had died. She had brought them the justice demanded of her, but as the pain of Patrick's betrayal, of her and of Bernard, pounded in her head, she knew that the price for delivering what Uncle OK had asked was too heavy to bear.

The little hollow was still there, free of weeds, the grass

freshly trampled, and she wondered if some other youngsters still came here to make love and lie on their backs to gaze at the stars and make plans for a future that would never come. So often had they laid there, too many memories to count, all now jostling for her attention. Her misery was complete, her future swallowed by a past she had been drawn inexorably to discover.

Patrick had killed Bernard, his best friend, his soul mate. "Why?" It was a whisper, just to herself, her whole body exhausted by the trauma. She could feel Patrick's presence all around her, but no answers because there was no sense in any of it. She understood now Bossoso's antagonism to her. She could see how Kitabuye existed on the edge of survival, scarred by poverty and hunger and haunted by the empty homes of the Tutsis and the relic of the church where no goodness was left. Her arrival had broken the delicate balance that existed between violence and peace, between vengeance and reconciliation. Patrick had killed, and she had seen the violence that seemed to be only a small provocation away from erupting from within him.

A twig snapped behind her. She knew it was him.

THIRTY-FOUR

He was behind her, close enough to hear his breathing, to smell him, to feel his eyes on her. His silence and stillness unnerved her even more than the anticipation that he would kill her. Death didn't frighten her anymore. It had lost its hold over her in this grassy hollow four years before.

"Why?" She turned to face him, and he took a step away from her. "Why, Patrick?" His fists were bunched, and the muscles in his neck and back were tensed. Then, the struggle within him seemed to be over; his shoulders slumped, and his head dropped. His face was damp when he finally lifted it, but he made no attempt to wipe away the tears. His gaze was on the ground, but even when Liliane stepped closer, he would not look up to meet her eyes. She fought the urge to pull him towards her and console him. Her heart had hardened towards him now; his tears were self-pity, not grief or remorse, and she had to stay strong. In killing her twin, he had killed part of her. She wouldn't allow Patrick into that void.

"Why Bernard?" Her persistence seemed to drain the last of his confidence. He had always been the strong one in their relationship, his dominance just the way things were, unquestioned. But Liliane had changed. She had survived through her own strength. Her new life, her business, her studies had given her the confidence to stand tall. Patrick seemed to sense this change in roles. The violence that was his normal answer now would be no help to him.

"I'm not leaving until I know—only then."

His eyes had the look of a trapped animal when he looked up. She couldn't remember how he used to look anymore, before the days when the killing had spread along the valley. She saw only the panic in him as his father and brothers dragged him away and that final look on his face as he disappeared into the crowd with his blade swinging by his side. Nothing else was left. She could see now how thin he was, how gaunt his face, the curve in his spine as if the weight of his guilt was crushing him. A fit of coughing seized him, and he seemed weaker after it had passed. His chin was streaked with saliva, but his hands stayed by his side as if the effort would be too much.

"This is a bad place. You don't belong here." She stepped closer to hear him.

"Is that why you killed us all?" He raised his hands as if he wanted to push her away and hear none of it then dropped them to his side again.

"I think about him every day. He's in my dreams. I smell his blood on me still."

"You should have died with him. He was like a brother to you."

"You weren't there. You don't know…"

"No, I wasn't there." She felt the blood pooling in the wound in her head. "I was being raped and butchered by Malabanda while you murdered my brother." Patrick blinked, his mouth open, but no words came. "Just tell me the truth." He seemed to be in a trance for a long time then started to speak, slowly at first, as if struggling to remember.

He began to tell her they had drunk beer early in the morning, and then the Interahamwe had brought khat and more beer. They were high when they got to the football ground, further intoxicated by the occasion, the camaraderie. It was when the soldier thrust the steel into his hand and slapped him that it had become real. That was when the truth of what they had to do hit them. The knife the soldier held at his throat told them what to expect if they didn't.

"We thought it would never happen." There was still an air of bewilderment about him, as if he expected to wake and find it had all been a dream. "I didn't want to be there, but they shot someone who tried to leave. After all the threats to my family…" He looked at Liliane, helpless. "I was scared. We all were." His face crumpled, and she could hardly hear his words between the sobs. "I just wanted to be with you, up in the hills, like we used to."

He had got caught up in the mob and was carried along by the throng moving to the town. It was when they got to the main street that he was able to get to the edge and slow his pace.

"I saw Bernard. He was in the shadow of one of the lanes. Everyone was looking at the church, so no one else saw him." He had watched Bernard work his way up the street in the shadows. Then the mob surged, and Patrick tripped and got left behind in the frenzy. "I ran after him, caught him by your wall. I still had my blade. He thought I'd come for him." He looked at Liliane. "He'd been looking for you."

She could see the scene: Father behind Mother, his hands on her shoulders while he told Bernard to bring his sister home, as if fetching her for the evening meal. She felt again her mother's anguish, her daughter missing, maybe already dead. She didn't think she had the capacity for more grief or guilt but still both engulfed her again, just like when she lay on the ground through the night.

"He told me to go back, that I'd be in trouble, but I couldn't leave him. Even then, he thought of me first." His misery seemed to deepen as he remembered. "We went into the kitchen. Your mother was on her knees, praying for you. Just your name, over and over." He had helped Bernard pick her up, but there was no comforting her. "She thought you were dead already." He stopped as if he was also back in that little room again. "Your father told me to go. He didn't want me to get caught with Tutsis. But I was sure you would come, even then. There was so much I wanted to say."

Liliane turned away. She refused to let him see the emotion that was overwhelming her as she heard about her family's last moments, nor the confusion he aroused in her.

"We stood in the yard, me and Bernard, arms round each other's shoulders and watched the gate and listened to the mayhem in the town. "I don't know who was more scared." Patrick had refused to leave. A gang of Interahamwe came, drawn by the sign on the wall and bundled the boys into the room while her parents were taken outside. The boys struggled and shouted, but there were too many of them. They heard screams in the yard and some thuds, then silence. "It happened so quick. Then they came back."

The leader of the gang grabbed Patrick's blade and held it up to the others. "Clean." He turned, and his face was a few inches away from Patrick's. "You know what happens to Tutsi lovers." The others came closer, their faces streaked with blood. They had tasted it. They wanted more. He thrust the blade at Patrick. "Show us your loyalty. Save yourself. Kill him." He nodded at Bernard. "If he doesn't, kill them both," he had said to the others.

"There were four of them. They gathered round me, pushed and shoved me towards Bernard. I cried, and they laughed at me, but Bernard was calm. He was concerned for me, Lili." She heard him cry again, but she was too overcome to turn and look or comfort him.

"Bernard screamed at me, "You saved me once. I owe you. Do it.""

Patrick had tried to run, but they were all around him, shoving him. Their blades were raised.

"Bernard screamed at me like I'd never heard him do before. "Just fucking hit me, man," he shouted over and over. The Interahamwe were in a frenzy."

The small room was filled with screams and shouts. "They pushed me at Bernard. One of them put a blade to my throat, and I felt blood on my neck." His voice broke. "He said he forgave me even as I—"

"Don't!" She didn't want to hear. He had told the truth. It was in his voice, and when she turned, it was in his face, his eyes haunted by a ghost that would never leave him.

Their shadows had lengthened, and the heat lay over them like a heavy blanket. The effort of telling her had sapped his strength, and she thought he would fall. His clothes were darkened with sweat. Bernard had been strong at the last, even as death snatched at him. The confession seemed to have broken Patrick. He had chosen to live but had found it was worse than anything he could have faced in death. So many questions filled her mind, but there was really only one. There always had been since she had lain here. It had driven her to survive, to live again. It was why she had come back.

"And what about me?" His eyes widened. He was frightened. He knew what she meant. "What if I'd been there?" His hands were in front of his face as if he could hide from the question. "Would you have killed me as well?"

He collapsed to his knees, his face hidden from her.

"Don't," he whispered over and over, but Liliane turned and walked down the hill.

She had broken him but felt no triumph nor any anger towards him. There was no point anymore. Something Anna had said to her one evening came back to her. They had been talking about how the genocide had started, how it had spread so fast and so deep into the country. "I don't know what I would do if my country went mad like yours did. If the knife was at my throat. If it was kill or be killed. I hope I would choose death. I feel sure I would." But then she stared out of the window, and Liliane could tell her friend was back in Kitabuye. "But I guess I'd only know when I felt the cold steel on my skin."

Patrick had promised her so much, but when the blades were raised, he had been too afraid to die. She stopped halfway to the church and looked back. He was still kneeling, his face turned to hers, watching her go. She never knew how long she stood there staring at him while her whole life in Kitabuye, all they had shared, filled her thoughts. When she finally turned, she felt consumed by anger at the government and the Church for fostering the hatred and forcing people to choose and at the UN and the West for ignoring their plight. In the end, they were all victims. No one survived genocide, least of all those who lived.

At the hospital, she stopped and clutched the handrail at the bottom of the steps, light-headed from hunger and drained by the emotions that had roiled within her all day. The door kicked off its hinges by the UN soldier was patched up with bits of plywood, but Liliane doubted from the hospital's appearance whether anyone would come out any healthier than they went in. It seemed to have suffered more than the shops and dwellings in the years since she had seen it. She felt her anger rekindle as she thought of how the small UN convoy had sentenced them to death.

She turned back to the church, planks nailed across its doors, its windows boarded up. "God just left in that truck," Uncle OK had said, and it looked like he had no plans to come back to Kitabuye any time soon. How could anyone ever pray in that place again? she wondered and wished the RPF had pulled the place down once the bodies, or mainly the bones, had been removed. The noise of a vehicle disturbed her mood, and she turned to the bottom of the street where a large, shiny 4x4 had stopped, its bright paintwork and shiny chrome incongruous against the drab backcloth of the town.

Its doors opened as the engine died, and two large, uniformed men jumped out, handguns drawn, just like the UN once had. Sam Bossoso hurried out of the yard, and Liliane could see he seemed rattled by an unexpected arrival in his town. His precious equilibrium was about to be further unsettled as Liliane saw Nick step out of the back, his arms reaching up in the air, then behind him to massage his back.

THIRTY-FIVE

Even with the length of the street between them, Liliane could see the tension in Nick, the sudden, nervous movements as he turned his head to look at the town, smoothing his hair or rubbing his stiff joints while he listened to Bossoso. Liliane had slipped into the shadow of the hospital, and when the two men turned towards her as the administrator pointed towards the church, she knew she was invisible to them.

Her thoughts raced in conflicting directions. She was relieved that Nick was here, the solid presence of the car and the soldiers comforting, yet fearful that he would try to control her life once more when finally her destiny was her own to decide. He turned and walked towards the church, alone, and when the sun hit his face, she saw in him the younger man who had spoken into the camera, surrounded by death, scared and hesitant.

He's as nervous as me, she realised and wondered if it was Kitabuye or the prospect of meeting her and explaining his presence. His stride was slow and measured, and he seemed to be storing the details of the wrecked buildings and overgrown sidewalks away in his mind for an article or to describe in another documentary. At the hospital, he stopped as if he sensed her presence and turned to her.

"Liliane?" He squinted into the sun and then stepped into the shadow and stared at her. "Liliane, is it you?" His eyes were fastened on her head and neck—she remembered he hadn't seen her wounds since the day he had rescued her. The confidence she had instilled in herself as she watched him approach ebbed away. She felt naked without her hijab and embarrassed. Her clothes were torn and dirty, and she could feel the grime and tear stains on her face.

"What's happened to you? Has someone…?" He didn't seem to know what to ask her first as the words tumbled out of him.

"You shouldn't have come. This is my business." She stepped away from him as he held out a hand. "It's for me to sort out." In the time it had taken for him to walk the street, the relief of being safe had quickly turned into bitterness at his intervention.

"We were worried sick, Mother, Anna, all of us. It's dangerous. You could have been—"

"But I wasn't. I survived worse than this." She pushed at the stains on her blouse and pulled at the holes in the delicate fabric. "It's nothing. A fall." She could see how his eyes were drawn back to her scars and remembered seeing her scarf in the long grass behind the school.

"I've come all this way for you." He sounded petulant, like the spoiled young man she first knew. "You must come. We're flying home tomorrow."

"This is my home." Her words seemed to shock, then deflate him. He turned and stared around the town, as if his derisive survey of the hovels, the rutted road, and the listless inhabitants was enough to dismiss the notion that anyone would claim this as home over the comforts that his family's money had given her in England. When Liliane had left Patrick kneeling in the field, her only desire had been to find Augustin and leave, but Nick's scorn for the notion that anyone would choose this town as home inflamed her loyalty anew for Kitabuye. His sense of superiority and condescension reminded her of all the years she had suffered the abuse and dominance of the Hutus. She had once been happy here before Malabanda had exerted his hold over her. It was where her family had lived and died, and the pull of the town grew inside her. But could she forgive these people and live among them again?

Her face must have betrayed the conflict within her, and Nick's attitude changed. He stepped close, his hands spread in supplication. "I'm sorry, Liliane. I guess you've been through it, coming back here, the memories…and everything." He looked to the church as he spoke. "It's just we were so worried. We all love you." He looked at her. "I love you. I guess I didn't think beyond your safety to what you might find here. Or that it might still have a hold over you." She saw the anguish in his eyes now. "You never said about coming here. I thought you'd moved on from all this."

Those words again. She had come here for unfinished business. Until she knew and her questions were answered, no new life was possible. But starting anew with her studies, relationships, facing the future with hope and excitement seemed impossible. She had shed one burden but, in its place, had assumed the weight of history, the jealousy and hatred, the violence and death. All this was fuelled by the betrayal of those she loved: her father, who had traded her innocence and freedom for his own safety; and her lover, whose protestations of enduring love had wilted in the fight to save his own life, even to the point of killing his best friend.

Nick was right; why would she stay? How could she stay when forgiveness and healing would be impossible?

Behind Nick, she saw the shuttered, neglected streetside bar where Father would meet his friends to play cards and talk politics. She closed her eyes and saw The Equator as she would always remember it, filled with lively and happy people, Adele and Zee laughing as they served, their new lives before them, gradually sloughing off the nightmares of their past. Why would she choose anything else? And when she opened her eyes, there was only the wreck of a café, a symbol of the town, broken and lifeless, full of ghosts and bad memories.

She was glad of Nick's silence and his good sense to let her be alone with the past. In his face, she saw real concern for her, and affection. She wondered what he would do if faced with the same dilemma that had been forced on Patrick. But there was no future in thinking like that. He had risked his life to find the truth and tell it. He could have died in the bush, and Liliane knew how the grief of losing their only child would have swept Geraldine and Charles away.

She nodded to him and smiled, then turned away from the church towards the car, allowing Nick to take her arm, his grip strong and substantial amidst the fragility that was endemic in Kitabuye. They walked in silence, she for fear of waking the ghosts that lay among the streets and lanes and Nick lest he broke the spell that was propelling Liliane back to England.

At the place where Uncle OK's Emporium had stood, she paused as if there was something that needed to be said, some mark of respect paid, but it would serve no purpose now, she knew. He would always be within her as he had been since the day she lay in the field. He was part of her past but he could be in her future also; his wisdom and love were ingrained within her. She would live a life worthy of him, she vowed as she kept walking.

When Nick squeezed her arm, she edged closer to him and saw his smile broaden as he glanced at her. As they approached the car, his pace quickened as if he wanted to get her away from Kitabuye as quickly as he could. Her bag lay by the large vehicle, and over the bonnet, she saw Augustin's car leave the Burgomaster's yard and turn towards the hills.

A movement in the corner of her eye distracted her, and she turned. It was Patrick. He had come out of one of the lanes and stood just a few feet away. Liliane stopped so suddenly that Nick stumbled and fell to his knees.

"Liliane, don't," she heard him shout as he scrambled up.

Liliane and Patrick stared at each other. His face was covered in a sheen of sweat, his shirt was damp and his breathing laboured, and even when a bout of coughing shook his body, his gaze never wavered from Liliane's face.

"I'm sorry, Lili." There was no strength in his words, but she felt them and shivered as the emotion they carried seeped into her. "Don't go." He spoke louder this time, as if her silence had given him confidence. She held a hand up beside her as she felt Nick come closer.

"I'm dying, Lili. I'm frightened." His voice broke, and tears mingled with his sweat. "Stay with me."

THIRTY-SIX

Patrick's breathing was shallower and more irregular in the early light of dawn, and Liliane had to bend close to his face to hear it. She had fallen into a light sleep after the coughing that had shaken his emaciated body had subsided, but it was the silence that jolted her awake. There was a barely perceptible movement in his chest where the ribs protruded through the thin skin, and she felt the slight warmth of his breath on her cheek.

"It's only a matter of days now, Miss Iwo," the new doctor at the hospital told her the day before. "Perhaps hours," he added. It was his way of warning her not to stray too far from Patrick's bed, the one her parents had once shared.

"He's got AIDS, Liliane. You can't stay with him. It's not safe," Nick had pleaded with her, a last desperate attempt to change her mind.

"I'm hardly going to sleep with him, Nick." They still spent what felt like hours arguing about her decision to stay until neither of them had anything left to say. Nick had recognised the intransigence in her and fallen silent while he stared into the hills, like Patrick once had, his mind far away.

"But he's a killer, Liliane. He butchered your own brother, for God's sake," he had said, but his attempts to shock her out of her decision only made it more entrenched in her mind.

"God had nothing to do with it. He wasn't here. That's why it happened," she told him, and the argument was over. But as she drew the curtain aside and saw the tidy yard and whitewashed walls, she felt a surge of affection for Nick yet still tinged with a residue of resentment. He had accepted the futility of arguing, and she had recognised a new purpose about him when he had turned to face her; he had thought of a different way to organise her life.

We're both too stubborn for each other, she thought as she opened the window and felt a rush of hibiscus bloom waft over her into the fetid air of the room. "It'll only be for a few months," she told him as he got into the vehicle, surprised at how calm he was. But he still left one of the soldiers behind to watch over her, and within days, a small convoy of trucks had bounced down the track into town with food, medicine and labourers who, under Bossoso's guidance, began to clear the debris of the war and bring order to the town. Her life felt choreographed once more, but her irritation had lessened when a British doctor arrived soon after, and she had been able to give Patrick the care she had stayed for. Charles's money came at a price, she knew, but she would face that challenge when this was all over.

At the sound of the door, she turned back into the room and watched Delphine kneel beside the bed. A bowl of water was in her hands, and she wiped Patrick's face. Most mornings, he would wake at the touch of the cold cloth, but today, barely a muscle twitched. Liliane could see that the hours the doctor had predicted had started to run out. The two women had moved beyond an uneasy truce to quiet acceptance of each other's right to minister to Patrick in his final months. Sam Bossoso had urged forgiveness and reconciliation on Liliane. She was the intruder, after all, and Patrick had made his choice, Sam had argued in the strongest of terms. Liliane had realised that her continued presence in Kitabuye depended on his patronage.

She smiled and nodded at Delphine when she turned for her approval; she had shown Delphine how to bathe Patrick's body without disturbing him or causing him more pain than his weakened state could bear. So many men and women were now dying from the disease in Kitabuye that the doctor needed every healthy person to learn the nursing skills to help him.

"It's another genocide," Bossoso told her one evening as they drank whisky in his office, "but this one doesn't care about blood or history."

"It's in our blood," Uncle OK had said near the end. Maybe

it is, Liliane thought, but this seemed worse in some ways. The painful, lingering death was in their blood as well. There was no escape from that either. Patrick had followed where others led. Drunk and high, he joined the frenzy of rape and shared in the toxic pit of germs that spread through the town and back down the valley where it had come from. As she stared at him, a broken shell of the strong man she would have liked to remember, she wondered again when her country would ever be able to free itself from the shackles of the genocide. It was in those last few days and weeks that her mind hardened and her ideas crystallised. She forced herself to be reconciled with Delphine, to apologise for the way she had behaved over the years and felt humbled by the tears and grief that the other woman displayed.

But forgiveness for Patrick was harder to find within herself. There could be no future for the country without it, but neither could there be without remorse. She stared at Patrick as the life ebbed out of him and felt again his tears on her face as he begged her forgiveness. She felt the rebuke in Delphine's eyes for the hardness in her heart. But it was the grief she felt for her own family, for Bernard felled by Patrick's hand, that haunted her thoughts and blocked her emotions. Uncle OK had urged her to bring them justice, but the Hutus had brought justice on themselves, and it lay on the bed in front of her.

Delphine left the room, and Liliane knew she would once more make a broth for Patrick, which her simple faith thought would revive him. But every day, it would trickle out of his lips and down his chin, and the woman would cry in frustration until Liliane pulled her close. They would each mourn in their own way for the man they had loved.

Patrick stirred, and Liliane realised his eyes were open as he tried to focus on her. She sat on the bed, careful not to touch his fragile body that hurt so easily. She lowered her head so he could see it was her and felt glad when he smiled in recognition. His skin felt cold as she stroked his face with the tips of her fingers and then wiped away the tears that welled up and filled his eyes.

His lips formed soundless words, but she knew them anyway. "I'm sorry, Lili." She closed her eyes and remembered him as he had been, the biggest boy, the strongest, now laid low. His hand gripped hers, and when she looked again, there was pain in his eyes, not from the disease but remorse for his actions. She lowered her face to his to be sure he could hear.

"I love you, Patrick." Behind her, the door opened. "I forgive you. I forgive you for everything." She felt Delphine's hand on her shoulder. Together, they watched him smile up at them. He had what he craved from her. Liliane was glad she had told him. It was the only way she could face the future.

THIRTY-SEVEN

Liliane took the box from Kwizera. He had made it that morning as soon as he had heard what she wanted to do. The wood was rough against her fingers, and she had to hold the ill-fitting lid in place. No matter. It would be empty soon enough. She would do what she had to do today, and then she would leave this place.

He held the door open for her, and she stepped past him into the high street. The box wasn't heavy, but she used both hands to hold it out in front of her. It seemed more respectful that way. The church was ahead of her, and she kept her eyes on it to avoid the stares of the few people who were around.

She paused where Uncle OK's shop had been. The charred remains had been cleared, and a small, inscribed stone stood where the door would have been.

'Olivier Kayyali. The last good man in Kitabuye.'

There were no dates because no one had ever known how old he was. He had always been there. But today was for other memories, and she continued up the road. As she passed the hospital, the people waiting outside lowered their heads. They knew what she was doing, but no one spoke. They did not want her here now. She was a reminder of what they had done.

From the outside, the church looked the same. The cross still hung over the doors but the low wall around the grounds had been rebuilt now. She hesitated on the steps. The paint on the doors was fresh, and there was a new sign on the wall for visitors. Even though it was no longer used as a church, she didn't want to go in, but she knew she had to say goodbye.

It was so different inside now. Some of the old benches were left. They had been moved to the middle for the visitors to use, and a few people sat on them. They looked as if they were praying, and Liliane wondered if prayers would still work in here. The red earth floor that she remembered was now covered with patterned tiles. In one corner, an old lady dressed in black was on her knees polishing them. When she saw Liliane, she pushed herself up and left through a side door.

The walls had been covered in plaster and painted white, and glass cabinets lined both sides of the church. The skulls were packed into them in neat rows, staring back at the visitors who peered in. Many had been bleached white by the sun, while others were grey. Most were damaged in some way. There was also one cabinet on its own against the front wall, where the altar had been. It was larger than the others, but the skulls were all smaller. Above the cabinets, on the walls, were wooden boards with the names of everyone who had been identified and who had been brought here to rest.

Information displays had been set up in each corner, telling visitors what had happened on that day and how reconciliation was so important for the town. Except there are no Tutsis left to be reconciled with, she thought. She sat on the bench at the back, the box on her knees. It was cool in here after the heat of the afternoon, and she waited until the last people had left. She didn't know which cabinet her parents and Bernard were in or even if they were together, but their names were on one of the boards, and that was good enough for her. The loneliness that had been such a part of her life since that day lifted as she sat there with them.

"I'm sorry I left you that morning. I should have been there with you. I should be here with you." Her voice seemed loud in the emptiness of the building. It was what she had come to say. She fingered the box and looked at the cabinet at the front. There was nothing left to be said. The door opened, and more visitors came in. It was time to go. She took one last look around, then left.

The sun hurt her eyes when she came out, and she stood in the shade of the door for a while before walking up the slope towards the trees. The land had been levelled in places and replanted with new grass, and she walked past some benches and tables that had been set up for visitors. When she was near the edge of the savannah grass, she stopped, set the box on the ground, and then looked back down the slope to the church for the last time. She knelt in the little hollow and pulled the lid off the box. A tear ran down her cheek and made a dark patch in the grey dust inside, and she drew her head back. Her forgiveness of Patrick had made her love for him so much stronger, but it meant that saying goodbye was even more painful.

She forced herself to stand. The box seemed heavier now. The sun was lower, and her shadow had lengthened. It was time to leave here. She lifted a handful of the ash and allowed it to trickle through her fingers onto the ground. A breeze was blowing from the lake, and it caught a few specks of dust. As they brushed against her skin, each one brought with it a memory.

She remembered Patrick's words when he had confessed to her and told her how Bernard had screamed at him, telling Patrick to kill him because he owed him his life. Now he could take it back and save his own. Liliane knew that Bernard would have done that for his friend.

As the shadow of the church lengthened, she let the last of the ashes slip from her fingers, and with them went the memories that had been with her for too long. There was movement in the grass behind her, and another shadow moved near to hers. She knew whose it was, but she didn't turn round.

"They're together now. Patrick and Bernard. They're probably playing football up there, best friends again, just like they were here."

She nodded at the thought. He stepped forward, and their shadows merged until they became one. "I loved him despite what he did."

"You've done what you came here to do. What you always had to do. You found the truth. You forgave him, and he knew it."

She set the box down in the hollow and then, undoing her hijab, let it fall through her fingers until it covered the box and the ashes that were spread on the grass around it. As a last few traces of dust swirled in the air then fell to rest on the ground, she turned and walked up the slope, away from the church.

Nick hesitated, looking down the slope to the church and the town. But Liliane never looked back.

Rome

2017

THIRTY-EIGHT

Neither of us spoke for a while after she finished. Liliane was lost in her memories, and I tried to give her the space she needed. A waiter slipped the bill in front of me, and as I turned to him, I realised that we were the only diners left. I walked to the reception with him, paid and pressed a large tip into his hand for the inconvenience.

When I sat with her again, she had regained her composure. I took her hand, and when she looked across at me, I saw the beautiful girl who Patrick had fallen in love with.

"It was all a long time ago." It sounded inadequate, but it seemed to fit her mood. "None of us were the same again." She squeezed my hand. I took strength from that and tried again. "It wasn't your story I came here for, Lili. Or the apology." I looked into her eyes, trying to tell her all the things that I had rehearsed but suddenly wouldn't come.

"I'm sorry, Nick. It was a long time ago. And you're right, we have all changed. There will never be anyone else. But I have my work. It's what I was spared for. I saw that after he died." There was a finality in her words. There was nothing more to say.

We walked to the street, and she kissed my cheek as her driver held the door for her. "I couldn't have done what I have for my people without you. Thank you, Nick."

Then she was gone, and I turned to walk to my hotel. Despite my sadness, I was so proud of her that night, for all she had achieved after so many setbacks, but also for the example she had been to the women of Rwanda and the rest of Africa. Women were beginning to shine, to achieve, to declare their equality and their ability to run things better.

I didn't know then that it would be the last time I would see Liliane. A year later, something went bad in her head, as she had always feared it would. The coroner blamed the trauma to her brain, and no one could argue with that. Her funeral was over too quickly for us to attend, but given that we were the only people who were like family to her, we were allowed to have her ashes as long as they stayed in Rwanda.

Mum, Dad, and I took them to Kitabuye a month later. We sat in the church for a long time so that Liliane could be close to her mother, father and Bernard, and then I scattered her ashes where she had scattered Patrick's. It was late in the day by then, and as the sun dipped in the sky, the shadow of the church lengthened and covered the spot where her ashes lay, as if her family were reaching out from within it to embrace her and welcome her home.

AFTERWORD & REFERENCES

The genocide in Rwanda in 1994 claimed the lives of nearly a million people, mainly Tutsis but also many brave Hutus, in just a few months.

This book is a work of fiction but is based on real events and stories I heard from my travels in Rwanda. It started as a story about three friends separated by blood lines and historical hatred, but it was always going to be more than a Romeo and Juliet-type story of forbidden love and friendship. It was the terrible choices that people, particularly Hutus, had to make about whether to join the killing or be killed, that stayed with me and influenced much of the story. A Time For Machetes by Jean Hatzfeld was an excellent description of life for ordinary people in the towns and villages as the genocide rolled towards them.

However, the more I researched about the genocide the more I read about the failings of the international community and the politics behind the inability to protect the people of Rwanda on both sides. Shake Hands With the Devil by Lt Gen Romeo Dallaire, force commander of the UN mission to

Rwanda, is the best account of the Rwandan genocide and how the UN was unable to stop the killing.

I remember watching Fergal Keane's BBC Panorama documentary in June 1994, towards the end of the mayhem, and being appalled by what was happening. He has spoken recently about the trauma that he experienced from what he witnessed. The idea of Liliane being rescued by journalists was inspired by the bravery of Fergal Keane and his team but there the resemblance ends. Nick is a purely fictional character whose strengths and weaknesses were imagined to fit the storyline.

The BBC has been a great source of information for many of the other sub plots within the story. The Panorama documentary When Good Men Do Nothing from 1998 investigated why the West stood by and did nothing. In addition, many articles on the BBC News website helped me to understand how priests, accused of complicity in the genocide, later reappeared in Europe. The main ones were:

- Church hides Rwandan priest in Italy- 16/7/2001
- Rwandan priest fights extradition- 19/7/2001
- Nuns jailed for genocide role- 8/6/2001
- Rwandan priest to be tried in France for genocide- 7/1/1998

I also found the Guardian's investigative journalism extremely helpful in unravelling the story of how priests were helped to evade justice. Particularly useful were:

- Hiding in plain sight in France: the priests accused in Rwandan genocide by Chris McGreal - 7/4/2014
- Rwanda genocide: the fight to bring the perpetrators to justice by Owen Boycott- 2/4/2014
- Rwanda genocide 20 years on by Chris McGreal- 12/5/2013
- Rwanda genocide: Catholic Church sorry for role of priests and nuns in killings, Associated press- 21/11/2016

All the characters are fictitious, apart from the Pope and President Kagame in Chapter One. The apology did happen although I have imagined the actual event, apart from the quote. I thought it was appropriate to start the book with that event as much has been done over the years by many organisations, especially the many different denominations, to redress the failings that led to the genocide.

There is much more information available on the internet but it was as I was bringing all the strands of research together that I came up with the novel that appears here. Essentially though, it is the story of a brave girl who survived and fought back. It was only at the end of one of the many rewrites that this story has been through that I realised that it was Liliane's fight against male domination and abuse that was the real undercurrent of the whole novel. I feel humbled, as a white male, to be telling the story of a Rwandan girl, but it's not a story that has been told before and I thought it was time for it to be told. After witnessing the aftermath of the genocide, about which I rarely speak, I hope that I have done it justice.

ACKNOWLEDGEMENTS

This book has been eight years in the making and has mostly been a labour of love. However, it wouldn't have made it into print without a lot of support and inspiration from a number of people.

Firstly, I'd like to thank the teacher in my junior school, whose name I can't remember now, who encouraged me to write my stories and told my mother she was sure she would see my books in the library one day. If you're reading this, I hope you enjoyed it.

It was a Tearfund trip that first introduced me to Rwanda ten years after the genocide. This charity does amazing work and deserves all our support. It was on this and subsequent trips that I heard about the dreadful experiences that no one should have to suffer. Much of what I heard is in this story.

I owe a huge debt of gratitude to Shelley Weiner at The Faber Academy, who took a risk on me and gave me a place on her course. Shelley is a wonderful tutor, and this book wouldn't exist without her guidance and encouragement. I hope this book makes her proud of me.

And, of course, I owe so much to the Faberites, my wonderful friends from the course. They have been on this journey with me from the start and have truly inspired, encouraged and taught me in equal measure. Thank you, dear friends, for life. You'll recognise some of the chapters. I think they read a bit better than my early attempts.

A special thank you to Kirsty Rouse, a local artist, for the amazing cover. Kirsty is so talented, and it brought a tear to my eye when she showed me the painting on canvas for the first time. I hope this book makes us both famous.

Thank you also to Estelle Maher, my editor and publisher from TAUK Publishing. Thank you for giving me the final push over the line. You're a great editor, and your enthusiasm for my story meant so much to me.

To our son, Dave, and my daughter, Kate, this is what all those hours locked away in my study were all about. I hope you'll be proud of me.

And finally, nothing I've achieved in the last forty years would have been possible without the love, support and inspiration of my dear wife, Fiona, who believed in this book when I was struggling with it. Thank you for encouraging me to keep going. The story is finally told—as it always had to be.

ABOUT THE AUTHOR

Colin Short had a long career in insurance, during which he travelled extensively, including a four-year posting to Toronto. When he returned from Canada, he left insurance and decided to achieve a lifelong ambition to be a published author. He then completed a six-month writing course at The Faber Academy in London.

Colin has been on numerous visits to Africa for charitable work, and it was the time he spent in Rwanda that inspired him to tell this story. He lives in Haslemere with his wife, Fiona.

Printed in Great Britain
by Amazon

40468229R00235